BRUCE ROBERTS (U.K.) LTD.
73 HIGH STREET, BEXLEY, KENT, ENGLAND
Telephone: CRAYFORD (STD 0322) 522694
Registered in England No. 1183622   VAT Reg. No. 206 8966 36

BOATBUILDING WITH STEEL

BOATBUILDING WITH STEEL

by Gilbert C. Klingel

including
BOATBUILDING WITH ALUMINUM
by Thomas Colvin

INTERNATIONAL MARINE PUBLISHING COMPANY
CAMDEN, MAINE

For Virginia, my wife, fellow sailor, constant companion, and enthusiast about ships and the sea, this volume is affectionately dedicated.

Contents

Publisher's Preface

International Marine Publishing Company, located in the heart of Maine boatbuilding country, publishes a comprehensive list of books on boatbuilding and design. We have books on basic and advanced design, and on boatbuilding in wood, ferro-cement, and fiberglass (both the molded and foam sandwich methods). Until now, our shelves have been empty of books on building metal boats. For that matter, the shelves of all American book publishers have been so empty, despite the fairly large metal boatbuilding industry in this country.

We decided to rectify the situation and went to work with two of the foremost practitioners of the art: Gilbert Klingel and Thomas Colvin. Both men speak with the authority of experience: Klingel has been a boatbuilder for over twenty years and, at his Gwynn Island Boat Yard, has built countless custom steel craft of the first order; Colvin has been building and designing boats since 1947 and, at his Miles, Virginia yard, has built scores of high-quality custom aluminum and steel boats. Both men are expert sailors, which gives them the opportunity to test their theories at sea.

We originally intended this book to be on steel alone, but mention the word steel to a boatman and he will want to know how it compares to aluminum. The last chapter, then, is on aluminum construction, not because it was an afterthought but because the chapters on steel lay the groundwork for an understanding of aluminum. For that reason, if you are reading this book because of an interest in aluminum craft only, it would serve you best to begin reading at chapter one, rather than at chapter thirteen.

If you think high quality boat construction is dead because of the preponderance of mass-produced plastic craft seen today, read on.

Peter H. Spectre
International Marine Publishing Company

BOATBUILDING WITH STEEL

INTRODUCTION

This book came to be written because of an acquired preference for steel boats created by many years of experience, and also because there exists in the collective mind of the so-called boating public a long list of prejudices against them which should be discussed and, if possible, laid decently to rest. A few of these prejudices are specific and have a reasonable basis; most are ill-defined; others are without any basis whatsoever.

Almost everyone who is interested in small boats, that is to say any boat from a six-foot dinghy to a hundred-foot schooner, whether for pleasure or for commercial use, is full of prejudices and equally stocked with a number of preferences. Sailboat men look down on powerboats; powerboat people view with pity the poor sailing craft becalmed or idling in a near-dead sea; the racing skipper considers the cruising yacht with disdain; the owner of a ketch wouldn't trade for a cutter twice the size; and Cleopatra's barge wouldn't interest the owner of a Chinese junk, even with the Queen of the Nile aboard.

The list of preferences and prejudices is endless. It applies to rigs and rigging, to modern design versus the traditional, to every facet of boating. But most of all, strong preferences and prejudices are expressed about the materials of boat construction. In the past, there was a strong preference for wood and an equally potent prejudice against any other structural material. Boatmen were exceedingly conservative people; successful boats had been made of wood for a couple of thousand years, and the use of any other substance was looked upon with extreme caution or outright scepticism and even hositility. Only in the last twenty or thirty years has much of this ingrained conservatism been lessened and new materials been readily accepted. The mere idea of a ferro-cement boat, for example, as recently as 1950 would have given most boatowners and builders the shudders, and an old, dyed-in-the-wool, wood boat man would consider the very idea a desecration.

The change in public attitude to construction materials came about largely by the advent of plastics, particularly fiberglass, and by virtue of mass production coupled with intense advertising campaigns. Some of the same people who once so avidly championed wood have now reversed their preferences and prejudices and wouldn't take a wood boat as a gift. This has happened despite the fact that wood still remains a fine material of construction with many advantages when used and cared for properly.

Curiously, while a considerable number of books have been published over the years about wood construction and a smaller number about other boat materials, such as fiberglass, almost none are available for the small boatbuilder, either professional or amateur, about a much neglected but versatile material—steel. It is true that many hundreds of fine steel craft have been produced both in this country and abroad. It is equally true that many hundreds of very inadequate steel boats have been made, and that these have, unfortunately, given steel a bad name as a construction material for boats. This is not warranted by the facts.

Shortly after World War II, large numbers of poorly made, poorly designed, and inadequately finished steel-hulled pleasure craft were mass produced and sold to an uneducated and naive public. The troubles caused by these improperly fabricated craft created an unfortunate image, which has taken years to erase. This image obscured in the public mind the fact that steel, when properly used and properly treated, is not only an adequate material, but in many respects a superior one. In this book, I would like to correct the misconceptions so fostered and to change a general and uninformed prejudice to an informed preference.

I have owned and sailed a variety of boats over a span of forty years. Included are boats of steel, fiberglass, wood, and aluminum. I have also been building boats for over twenty years, and in so doing, have acquired a distinct preference for steel. This does not infer an opposite prejudice against other materials; indeed, there is no one material that is the answer for all problems, nor is there likely to be one. But on balance, after many factors are weighed, steel has much to offer. It is my hope that this book will help others, particularly those contemplating a new boat or those not fully satisfied with other materials, to take full advantage of the benefits of steel, to make the most of its unique and special properties, and to avoid the mistakes and pitfalls of the past.

It is strange that an age which accepts without question the undeniable success of large ships of steel (how many wood or plastic ocean-going cargo vessels exist?) should have any doubt about steel for small vessels or for pleasure craft. This has come about by a combination of circumstances, including the lack of readily available references—the conditions prevailing during the transition of preference from wood to plastics—the ill-starred early attempts at mass production where cheapness for profit was a goal in itself, by inadequate training of designers in steel construction for small-boat work, by misconception about weight and corrosion, and by the inability of small boatyards to adapt to steel from wood, thus making it difficult to secure a good steel craft even if no prejudice existed. Even today, the number of yards in the United States specializing in small boat construction in steel is small.

Also, curiously, the tradition of craftsmanship which characterized many of the old-time builders of wooden vessels, a craftsmanship in which there was an inherent pride of workmanship, has not necessarily been carried over to the new materials. This failure is not common to boatbuilding alone, but is evident in many fields of endeavor. Mass production has limited the feeling of personal accomplishment, which should be part of the boatbuilder's stock in trade. The use of repetitive production techniques by unskilled help, and the division of labor in which the laborer contributes only a small segment of the whole, has often diminished the value of the product and inhibited the pride in making it. There are today literally thousands of sleazily built boats on the market, built hurriedly, though not necessarily cheaply, to fulfill production requirements and advertising campaigns. Many boats are sold by virtue of a catchy trade name and the artificial creation of a snob class appeal. It is a common malaise.

Another malaise is the careless use of inherently good materials to save labor, or to do a job quickly because craftsmanship is too much trouble. A typical instance is the current popular craze for ferro-cement by some amateurs on the mistaken theory that some iron rods, chickenwire, and a few days with the help of the neighbors in the backyard will produce a cheap and seaworthy boat. This is a delusion, but please do not infer that a carefully done ferro-cement boat may not be a good one.

This book is not directed to the commercial firm with mass production in its schedule; nor to the amateur who is, oppositely, intrigued with the idea of quickly slapping together a hull with some metal plates and a few quick hours of welding; nor, indeed, to the professional who is interested only in the making of a fast buck because steel may be amenable to considerable construction abuse with unskilled or semi-skilled help. Rather, it is directed to the prospective boatowner who wishes a superior boat and who wishes to know if this can be expected of the

5

medium; to the builder who, above all, has a pride in his product and who, beyond being a steel worker, is also a craftsman and an artist of sorts; and to the architect or designer who may already be an artist but who is not sufficiently versed in steel to take full advantage of its potentialities. Each year I have drawings submitted for quotation by otherwise quite competent designers who are still designing or thinking in terms of wood, or who simply do not know steel or the problems of construction associated with it. These drawings, as a result, are frequently inadequate, not conducive to either beauty of finish, permanence, strength, or maximum benefit.

Few objects, in this mechanized modern world, instill in their owners as much concern and love as their boats. I am not referring here to those benighted people, becoming increasingly common, who own a boat because it is fashionable to do so, or who require a floating cocktail lounge to take them from marina to marina or between the nearest electric outlets. I am referring to those men who love boats for their own sake, who find in their vessels an expression of their personalities, who want a boat which is a thing alive, strong, seaworthy, and also an object of beauty unlike any other creation of man, and who will not knowingly tolerate cheapness, ugliness, gross imperfection, or poor quality in the subjects of their attachment.

It is assumed, then, that the philosophy of excellence, that the best is only good enough, that only the superior will do, will prevail in our discussions which follow. No attention will be given to shortcuts or half-way measures, to economies that are ultimately expensive, to techniques that are not inherently sound, or to methods that detract from finish or permanence. We should believe that when we build, we build forever, and that what we build should be as lovely or as graceful in after years as it was when it was produced. There is no real reason, given reasonable care and attention, why a steel boat should not be as beautiful and as sound after five decades as it was in its conception, assuming, of course, that it met those standards to start with. Indeed, popular and uninformed opinion to the contrary, a vessel of steel stands a better chance of surviving the attrition of the years than boats of any other common contemporary material. The price of permanence is attention to detail, pride of production, a preference for nothing less than the best, and a prejudice against the poorly done, the cheap substitute, the inadequate.

1 STEEL

It is only reasonable to begin a discussion of steel boats with some definitions of steel itself. Steel in one form or another has been in use for hundreds of years and is today one of the most common structural materials. Indeed, our civilization is almost totally dependent on it. It is the basis of almost all our large buildings. Without it, transportation could not function, agriculture would revert to primitive forms, industry would grind to a quick halt, and many of the amenities of modern life would simply disappear. Life has advanced by the refinement of metals; the progression from the stone age to the bronze age was a real achievement; the step from bronze to iron and then to steel marked the beginning of technical civilization as we know it today.

Steel is ubiquitous. It holds our houses together and is an integral part of most of our machinery. It carries our power—our electricity in towers, our fuel in pipes—conveys our water, processes our food, paper, shoes, and clothing, prints the news, and does a million other tasks. Yet, for all its frequency, its constant and daily use, and its automatic acceptance, surprisingly few know precisely what it is, what its properties are, and what it can and cannot do. Even people in the metal fabricating business are often not fully aware of what they are handling or why. There is many a mechanic who can adjust a valve with precision, or machine an intricate part, or grind a complex gear to within a few thousandths of an inch, but who has no real understanding that while the valve, the part, and the gear may all be steel, they are for their separate purposes quite different kinds of steel, possibly in quite different conditions, made in quite different ways, under quite divergent methods. Steel is not just one simple material, but a whole family of materials, some with relatively simple characteristics, some capable of almost bewildering variations.

Basically, steel is an alloy of iron and carbon, in which carbon can be up to about 1.7 percent of the whole as an essential ingredient. This is a little like saying that a man is a two-legged mammal with opposable thumbs, a good enough designation except that it does not go far enough.

The categories of steel, all within the designated limitation of carbon content, are numerous. There are steels that are soft and malleable, which may be readily formed, bent, twisted, spun, or stamped; others are hard and almost as brittle as glass; some are resistant to heat and retain much of their strength under red-hot conditions. There is a whole legion of steels for tool purposes, to cut, shape, and machine other steels and other metals; there are special steels for electrical requirements, for transformer cores, for magnetic purposes. Still others are made to be easily cut and machined; some are designed to provide corrosion resistance to various chemicals and other active media; some provide toughness to abrasion and rough usage, some are highly elastic and springlike. There are steels that are little affected by extreme cold and, conversely, others that become quite fragile when frozen. Often a single machine may contain several dozens of types. The common automobile, for example, possesses many varieties of steel in one unit.

To provide this assortment of properties and attributes, besides the main and magic ingredient carbon, many elements may be added in a wide assortment of proportions. Most common are manganese, silicon, sulphur, nickel, chromium, tungsten, vanadium, copper, cobalt, columbium, and molybdenum. The possible combinations are legion. Thus, there are steels of almost any composition, to perform almost any conceivable role, to fit almost any mechanical or structural need.

Fortunately for the boatbuilder and designer, unless they are contemplating some very unusual or bizarre craft, the choice of steel is not complicated at all; their requirements are relatively simple and there is little necessity to go in for the special or more exotic alloys. The plain, low-carbon steels containing from about 0.10 to 0.20 percent carbon are more than adequate for most boat construction, and possess without complication a sum of desirable properties. These simple steels are the most common and generally the most useful of the whole family of steels, and are useful to boatbuilders for the same reasons they are valuable to a whole host of other fabricators. Also important, they are readily available all over the world in a diversity of shapes and sizes. Any steel suppliers worthy of the name can furnish these steels from stock. Availability is an important consideration. There is no point in designing around some special steel because its apparent properties may seem desirable only to find that almost no one carries it in stock, or that it is available in only a limited number of sizes and shapes, or that it has to be specially processed by some individual or distant mill.

What is needed by the builder of boat hulls is a steel that is strong, that is stable in properties, that does not lose its toughness with extreme changes in temperature, that is resistant to fatigue and alternating stresses, that is ductile enough to be readily shaped but still stiff enough to withstand the forces of the sea without failure, that is amenable to easy welding, that can be readily drilled, tapped, ground, or machined, that does not harden or become brittle locally when cut with a torch, or that does not alter its properties when subjected to red heat for shaping. The plain carbon steels fulfill these requirements very nicely.

However, as versatile as these ordinary steels are, designers in recent years have been specifying other steel alloys for their extra stiffness and strength in an effort to use lighter metal for weight advantages, particularly in sailing vessels and boats of relatively small size. These steels are marketed under a variety of trade names such as "Cor-Ten," "Jal-Ten," "Mayari," etc., depending on the producer, but in essence are relatively low carbon steels (about .12 percent maximum) containing small but specific amounts of manganese, copper, chromium, and nickel. This combination provides a material of greater strength than mild steel, coupled with resistance to abrasion and impact, and relatively better resistance to atmospheric corrosion. Recently, these steels have become popular for buildings in which the steel work is deliberately allowed to rust; once rusted, further rusting is slowed naturally and painting is not required. This property, while perhaps adequate for inland buildings, bridges, electrical towers, and the like, should not, advertising to the contrary, be considered as a solution, or partial solution, to the problem of corrosion in boats. In salt water, these high-tensile steels, if not protected, will deteriorate nearly as rapidly as ordinary steel. Nevertheless, this group of steels has proven useful where a favorable strength-weight ratio is of importance, and where welding distortion is a problem in light gauges, as it usually is. It should be borne in mind, however, that while there is a gain in strength, there is also a loss in ease of forming. The material is more difficult to bend and shape; it is also more expensive than mild steel.

The designer or builder looking for lighter, stronger, more corrosion-resistant steels should ask some searching questions before committing himself to any specific alloy, no matter how attractive the apparent mechanical properties may be. There are a host of steels available with remarkable tensile properties, far in excess of those of mild steel, but careful evaluation will usually indicate some drawback making them undesirable for boat work, although, of course, they may be nearly perfect for the use for which they were originally intended.

An understanding of the general nature of steel is helpful. As a general rule, although there are numerous exceptions, as the carbon content of steel increases, the hardness and tensile values increase also. But at the same time, ductility decreases until a point may be reached when the steel will have little or no "give" and may become brittle and fragile. The various alloying elements can suppress or enhance strength or ductility, or provide other attributes.

Steel should be envisioned as a more or less elastic material which, to some degree, great or negligible, can be stretched, bent, twisted, or compressed and which will return, like a rubber band, to its original position when the stress is released. This, in essence, is what a steel spring does; it bends and returns to the place it occupied originally. However, when stretched beyond a certain point, it no longer will do this; it will begin to stretch like a wad of taffy or gum, and as it stretches still further it will begin to diminish in cross-section until it can stretch no more and it abruptly fails. Ductility in steel and other metals is measured by the amount of plastic stretch expressed by the percent of elongation and by the percent in reduction of area of the cross section as stretching occurs.

Many factors affect ductility besides chemical content, and a few of these should be considered here. Ductility in boat steel is of prime importance; a nonductile boat segment could lead to just as disastrous results as a cracked plank in a wood boat or a void in a fiberglass craft. Ductility and strength are opposite sides of the same coin and of equal import.

Chief among the factors which affect ductility are what are known as stress-raisers, generally highly local, sometimes quite small, sharp-contoured notches where loads or stresses of some sort are highly concentrated. While the general area of the stress-raiser may be carrying loads well within the ability of the metal to support, the effect of the notch is to focus many times the actual load on a small, sometimes almost microscopic, area. The ductile limit of the metal is then locally exceeded, and a crack develops which then further concentrates the stress. Such a crack, once formed, is usually self-propagating, and will progress until the load causing it is released or complete failure of the metal occurs.

Everyone has read of wartime Liberty ships and other large vessels that have broken apart at sea. In about every known case, this has been caused by the presence of stress-raisers, such as the sharp corners of deck hatches, which were usually aggravated by other stress raisers in the

10

form of improper welds and by the use of steels which, while most adequate at normal temperatures, undergo a ductile-to-brittle transformation at freezing or below-freezing conditions. Most of the early failures took place in the winter or in the Arctic area. They were caused by poor design, lack of knowledge of, or selection of, the metals involved, improper workmanship, or a combination of all three. This type of failure, it should be noted, is not peculiar to steel or other metals, but is equally common to almost all structural materials, including ferro-cement, wood, and fiberglass. I mention this because, when steel ships are discussed, someone inevitably brings up the subject.

While such catastrophic failure of small vessels is quite rare, indeed almost unknown, it is worthwhile to remember that ductility-damaging stress-raisers should be eliminated by good design and proper workmanship, particularly in welded zones, and by the selection of proper steels for the job to be done. This applies to every segment of a boat, from the propeller shaft to the chain plates.

It should be understood also that steel, like all metals, is crystalline in its basic nature. Steel is formed of many thousands, or millions, of cubic or hexagonal crystals, depending on the condition or composition of the alloy. These crystals, depending on the conditions of manufacture, group together to form grains of various sizes. Often, during examination of a broken piece of steel, the grainy fracture of the break is clearly evident and the uninitiated say the metal has "crystallized." This is incorrect because metals are always crystalline, except when they are molten, when they are true liquids. Thus, a weld when first laid down is a liquid, then, as it cools, it is a semi-liquid in which newly-formed crystals float, and finally it is a group of grains created as the crystals grow rapidly in all directions until they meet and form distinct boundaries between grains. Sometimes these boundaries contain substances, such as carbides, that are weaker than the grains themselves, or which are not as resistant to corrosion as the steel itself. This is a condition sometimes found in some of the stainless steels and, when it occurs, corrosive attack can proceed in the grain boundaries. This is controlled by proper quenching procedures and other methods which insure that the grain boundaries are homogeneous with the rest of the metal.

Very often, I am approached by someone who wants to know if stainless steel would not be ideal for a boat and who is surprised when I advise that it would not. The stainless steels, of course, have many excellent boat uses. For rigging and fittings, they are most useful. They are also useful for fastenings, rails, decorative trim, and propeller shafts, as well as a number of other applications. But many of the stainless steels are not at all suitable for boats, and for hull fabrication pose more problems than warranted by their possible advantages. Before making any sweeping statements about the stainless steels, it should be pointed out that there are over a hundred varieties, many for very special purposes, and that any discussion should be qualified by what type is under consideration.

In general, stainless steels fall into three main categories: (1) the straight chromium martensitic steels hardenable by heat treatment, (2) the straight chromium ferritic types, which are not, and (3) the chromium-nickel steels, which are hardenable only by cold work. It is this last group that is most useful for boat work. These steels are very strong, tough, and most corrosion-resistant. However, it should be noted that the stainless steels are not always at their best in salt water or salty atmospheres, and under certain corrosive conditions, particularly where there is oxygen starvation, may pit, bleed rust, or undergo grain-boundary deterioration. Best in salt water exposure is Type 316, an alloy of chromium, nickel, and molybdenum. However, for most trim work, rails, and the like, the ordinary chromium-nickel stainless steels, such as Type 304, are satisfactory. To these stainless steels should be added the precipitation-hardening types, such as 17-4 PH, which are generally good in salt water and which may be obtained in very high tensile strengths. In recent years, this alloy has proved excellent for propeller shafts. It is superior to bronze and monel on a strength/weight/cost basis.

For hull fabrication, the stainless steels are difficult to form and shape, they transmit heat poorly, and they are prone to severe warping during welding. They do not cut readily with a cutting torch, except when special, rather expensive cutting equipment is used with special fluxes or powders; they are not easy to machine or cut cold and they pose special corrosion problems in welded segments due to carbide precipitation. In addition, stainless steels are very expensive. There is some careless use of stainless steel in boats, and a thorough knowledge of the many types with their limitations and advantages should be acquired before their application. It is beyond the scope of this book to treat them in detail, but further attention will be given in the chapter on welding and elsewhere. Detailed descriptive literature is readily available from any stainless steel supplier.

With all steels, consideration must be given to its condition. Steel may be "as-cast," as in a foundry-poured fitting; or it may be hot-rolled, hot-rolled and leveled, hot-rolled and pickled, cold-rolled, cold drawn or otherwise cold worked, annealed, hardened, hardened and stress-relieved, hardened and tempered, or some combination of these conditions. For most boat hull work using the low-carbon mild steels, the hot-rolled condition is usually supplied and usually is satisfactory from the viewpoints of smoothness and levelness. Generally, where flatness is not adequate, the fault will lie with the supplier or the mill from which the steel was rolled. Sometimes hot-rolled steel sheets will have a slightly wavy configuration, and such sheets should not be accepted. A very small out-of-flatness in the original sheet can be very troublesome to eliminate or may be unsightly when the finished boat is painted. Some of the high tensile steels are prone to this fault due to inadequate or uneven cooling at the mill, particularly in the light gauges, which are the most useful. The builder should inspect incoming hot-rolled steel for this possible defect.

The annealed condition is not often used but may occasionally be helpful when severe cold bending or forming is necessary. Annealed sheets are about as free of locked-up stresses as any condition and sometimes are less prone to warping after welding. Annealed steels are generally quite ductile but become less so as they are cold-worked.

There is not much use for hardened, or hardened, tempered, or stress-relieved steels but they may be used for special purposes, as for high-strength fittings and members carrying heavy loads. Fully hardened steel, it should be remembered, may be very strong but also very brittle; it is also subject to a phenomenon called stress-corrosion, which will be discussed later. Stress-relieved or tempered steel is more ductile and less prone to failure.

The cold-worked steels are generally used on boats only where dimensional tolerances are of importance, as in rudder shafts that turn in close-fitting tubing or bearings, or similar situations.

Also to be remembered is the possibility that fabrication may change the condition of the steel being worked. The heat of welding may alter the strength of the steel in the heat-affected weld zone; a welded high-strength fitting conceivably becomes annealed, or partially so, if heated to annealing temperatures if torch cut, or conversely, fully hardened and possibly made brittle.

It is not my intention in this book to pose a large series of possible hazards for the potential steel boatbuilder, but rather, instead, to avoid these same hazards by imparting a little knowledge of the basic metallurgy of steel.

Steel is a remarkable boat material with many advantages if used intelligently and with attention to some basic details. Know your steel and its properties; be cognizant of its condition and of the effects of use or fabrication on that condition. Be wary of odd lots of steel that may be cheaply available in somebody's storage shed or junkyard, or of steel purported to have unusual or unique attributes. There is no value in a metal that is exceedingly strong but becomes brittle adjacent to a weld or, conversely, dead soft in the same area. A ship of steel, like a chain, is as strong as her weakest section.

Some experience should be acquired about discovering possible metal defects. Steel, like wood or any other manufactured material, can possess faults that may adversely affect surface finish or strength. Most mills have fairly rigid quality controls but sometimes, in spite of these, defects will slip through. Most common are: "pipe," a center segregation or porosity in the ingot that will cause the center of a bar or plate to be weak; gassiness, an entrapment of gas during pouring that causes voids or laminations; scabs and slivers, created during hot-rolling; and mechanical tears, caused by improper handling. Stock that contains these defects in an appreciable degree should not be used either from the viewpoint of strength or surface finish. Deep slivers and surface laminations can be most troublesome as they will, in time, "bleed" rust over a nice, painted surface. The bleeding will persist until the defect is completely ground out. Any steel that reveals laminations should be rejected or the laminated areas removed. Fortunately, this is not a frequent problem and most suppliers willingly replace such faulty stock.

Steel is readily available in a wide variety of shapes and sizes. Bar stock comes in rounds, squares, hexagons, flats, ovals, tees, and rectangles, as well as a number of special configurations. There are a host of angle sizes and a wide selection of structural beams, channels, and zee shapes. For hull plating, decking, tanks, and the like, there is a considerable range of sheets and plates, of almost any thickness, width, and length that can be transported or handled. In addition, pipes and tubing can be obtained in rounds, squares, and rectangles in a number of weights and wall thicknesses. Also, treads, gratings, and perforated items are stocked in an assortment of patterns and designs.

Further, nearly all steel warehouses are equipped to cut, shear, or otherwise produce special shapes from patterns or drawings. Large, heavy, curved stem pieces, for example, can be precision torch cut by the steel warehouse with less waste than can the boatbuilder working from plate; similarly, cambered deck beams can be accurately and repetitively curved by warehouse-connected fabricators at a fraction of the cost of the yard and with much greater accuracy. Steel distributors often perform many services beyond simply supplying listed steel sizes and shapes.

With steel, the boatbuilder has at his beck and call a variety of useful shapes, a material of remarkable strength that does not inherently deteriorate with age, and a versatile metal capable of many duties readily performed by no other inexpensive structural substance. Steel lends itself to precision work and, properly used, will give predictable and dependable results. With imagination and some sense of the artistic, boats of pleasing form and beauty can be created which possess, in addition to appearance, greater resistance to the stresses of the sea than vessels of any other type. Because of misinformation, persistent myth, unfamiliarity with metal working and metal-working tools, steel has not become the amateur builder's province in the sense that wood has. Yet steel fabrication is actually no harder than wood or fiberglass fabrication, or ferro-cement for that matter. In many cases it is easier. The methods and procedures are different but not beyond the scope of anyone with a reasonable mechanical aptitude.

2 ADVANTAGES AND DISADVANTAGES OF STEEL

Obviously, no material, including steel, is the answer to all boatbuilding problems and no pretense is made here that it is. All boat structural substances have their drawbacks and limitations, though one might not think so after reading some of the advertising literature in the boating magazines. The advertisements are, in fact, often grossly misleading and are a poor source of information about true or even relative merit, nor do they provide any objective evaluation to go by.

Actually, all the normal boat materials are good when used in the proper context and when worked with care. Wood is a fine structural material; so is aluminum and fiberglass. The fabricators of mass fiberglass boats have been most guilty of exaggeration about their product, but, nevertheless, innumerable fine fiberglass boats have been produced and the substance today commands a large share of the boat market. Very recently, some lyrical prose has been written about ferro-cement, but some time will elapse before a real evaluation of the material is possible.

The sensible boatbuilder and prospective owner will take the best of all forms for his individual purpose, or the limitations of his pocketbook, and perhaps combine several materials in one boat. So, trying to be as objective as possible, and as free of preference and prejudice as human nature allows, I have listed the advantages and disadvantages of steel versus the other materials as follows:

Strength
Without much question, steel is the strongest of all boat materials, and in a strength-weight basis is superior to wood, fiberglass, or aluminum. Ferro-cement construction would not be possible without the steel core

to hold it together. Cement, itself is excellent in compression but very poor in tension and shear. It has no ductility worth mentioning.

Ordinary mild steels have typical tensile strengths of 50,000 to 60,000 pounds per square inch and typical yield strengths of 30,000 to 40,000 pounds per square inch, which is to say they will sustain loads in that order before beginning to stretch or yield without returning to their original positions. At the same time, they are very ductile and will elongate 30 to 40 percent (as measured between two marks two inches apart on a tensile test specimen) before failure. Thus, a steel boat in a collision or cast ashore on rocks may sustain repeated loads or blows that would irretrievably shatter wood, fiberglass, or ferro-cement boats, and yet still be in floating condition when hauled off, though possibly have some bad dents. One of my boats, built in 1947, a 31-foot sloop, went aground in the Bahamas and survived a night's pounding on a coral reef. It was hauled off and is still sailing today more than twenty-five years later. Another was deposited 300 feet from the normal shoreline by hurricane Hazel and was dragged off bodily by a Navy tug (the owner was an admiral) with no hull damage whatsoever.

The high-tensile steels are even stronger with typical yield points of 50,000 psi (pounds per square inch) or more, and ultimate tensile strengths of 70,000 psi or better. Ductility, of course, is less, but still greater than other materials. I know of one producer of steel-hulled boats who took great glee in demonstrating the strength of his hulls by running them through an old, abandoned wood pier, usually to the consternation of his prospective clients.

In comparison, the yield strength of the aluminum alloys of the 5000 series, commonly selected for their higher corrosion resistance over ordinary aluminum, is only in the order of 13,000 to 35,000 psi, depending upon temper. As strength increases with temper, ductility drops rapidly, until at the higher yield strengths it becomes almost negligible, typically only about four to eight percent elongation in two inches. Plain aluminum has very low properties, with typical yield strength of barely 4,000 psi and ultimate tensile strength of but about 12,000 psi.

The strength of wood, in itself, has little bearing on the strength of a hull built of it. While many woods have excellent tensile properties, their transverse values are usually quite low. The strength of a wood boat cannot readily be compared with one of metal because (1) wood is not an homogeneous material, and (2) it is only as strong as the fastenings and the friction that hold it together. This is not to infer that a wood boat cannot be immensely strong when new; many are, but by mere virtue of having less transverse strength and by being made, ordinarily, of many hundreds of relatively small pieces, a wood boat is inherently or incipiently weaker than the monocoque hulls of welded steel, aluminum, or fiberglass.

Fiberglass, properly laid up with a minimum of resin in proportion to glass fiber, can be a very tough material, but strength is predicated on more than this alone. In assessing the strength of any fiberglass hull, or of any fiberglass segment, the method of layup is of considerable importance. The presence, or lack, of bubbles, voids, or dry areas, and the orientation and number of layers of fiber all have an appreciable effect. It is difficult to assess the strength of any fiberglass hull with accuracy because so many variables may exist. Interestingly, the load-carrying ability of the individual, exceedingly thin, glass fibers expressed as ultimate tensile strength in pounds per square inch of cross section is very high — 300,000 to 400,000 pounds or more, equal to that of high-tensile steel wires of the same small diameter (0.00020/0.00100 inches).

But this is a deceptive measure of the strength of a boat hull made of these same fibers woven into cloth or randomly oriented and held together with a resin inherently weak in comparison to the fibers themselves. Nevertheless, in the small boat sizes, fiberglass is more than adequate; its strength-weight value begins to fade in comparison to steel as size and length of the hull increases. I have been on a number of fiberglass sailboats, seemingly well built and of seemingly adequate hull thickness, which twisted under sail or sea load so much that doors and drawers could not be opened or shut until the boat went about on another tack.

While there is information available to show that carefully laid up fiberglass laminates with a very high percentage of glass possess ultimate tensile strengths approaching that of steel, the data also reveal that the yield point and the ultimate failure point of fiberglass are almost identical. This means that there is no ductility left to absorb blows or impact damage. Both steel and aluminum may increase in strength after the yield point is reached; thus, while the vessel may be dented, disastrous failure need not occur. Fiberglass advocates can claim that boats of their material can be designed to the "ultimate," that is to the point where it fails or breaks, but note should be made that the "ultimate" is also the point of no return.

There are other measures of strength besides tensile strength or load-carrying ability. They are: (1) resistance to impact, (2) stiffness, (3) resistance to abrasion, which may be a reflection of hardness, and (4) fatigue. In all of these categories, steel is in the first rank. As already noted, a steel hull will survive grinding or collisions that would be fatal to other materials. Because a steel hull is one integral unit, with the strength of all its joints essentially equal to the plating of the hull, there is no "give" or deflection as in a wood hull, and its inherently greater stiffness causes it to be more rigid than the hulls of softer metal or of fiberglass. Neither aluminum, plastic, nor wood will last very long if abraded severely against pilings or against sand or rocks. The fatigue strength of most materials is usually in direct proportion to their ultimate tensile strength. Any vessel that is subject to the repetitive flexions of the sea, or the constant vibrations of a power plant, is subject to fatigue. Fatigue failure generally starts as a small crack, which can then progress rapidly. While wood isn't particularly prone to fatigue, its fastenings are. Fiberglass is, but the symptoms are often not recognized. Some of the disastrous cracks and splits which occur in fiberglass hulls are really fatigue failures.

Strength is the first and greatest attribute of a steel vessel.

Weight

Weight in a boat material should be considered as half of a dual entity. Comparing the weights of wood, fiberglass, aluminum, cement, etc. as the measure of their volumetric displacement is meaningless as far as boats are concerned. What must be considered is the strength-weight ratio; that is, the weight of a given boat member to achieve its functional strength. On the basis of weight alone, steel would be at a considerable disadvantage; it is heavier per cubic inch than wood, aluminum, cement, or fiberglass. But when considered as the quantity necessary to attain the desired strength, steel is usually ahead. This is why, today, the manufacturers of modern high-speed aircraft use high-tensile stainless-type steels in place of the aluminum alloys once so universal. There is, however, a joker in the pack. While steel usually has the best strength-weight ratio, and boats of quite thin stock are theoretically feasible, the welding of very thin sheet without unseemly distortion is difficult. This applies equally to thin-gauge aluminum.

At least one sailboat up to 60 feet long has been fabricated with steel plating as thin as 1/8 inch and has been successful from a strength viewpoint. I have used 1/16-inch steel for the cabin trunk on a thirty-one-foot sloop that was stronger and lighter than the combination mahogany, plywood, and fiberglass trunk it replaced. For welding reasons, then, the advantage of steel for boats under about 28 feet is questionable, although I designed and built a series of thin-gauge 16-foot workboats that were successful and very rigid. One was accidentally dropped 20 feet from a crane and survived the fall with only a dent.

On a strictly strength-weight-cost basis, steel becomes more and more advantageous as hull size and severe service requirements increase, until there is no other practical substitute.

Life

There are a number of myths about the durability of steel boats. It is a common belief that the life of a steel ship is only about twenty or so years due to corrosion problems. It is, of course, true that some steel boats have rusted through in very short order, just as some wood boats have dry-rotted in less than a year. In every instance where destructive rusting has occurred, the fault has been directly due to one of two causes — gross neglect or improper techniques in finishing, building, or design. Today, all the means are at hand to insure that with any reasonable care, such as a once-a-year painting and inspection, the life of a steel boat will be indefinite. Except for corrosion, when it is permitted to progress, steel does not deteriorate with age; its properties remain constant. Corrosive decay is inexcusable in most cases, because it gives plenty of warning and correction is simple and easy. Assuming proper design to allow easy access to every part of a boat, it is not unreasonable to believe that a steel boat should survive intact for over a century. My first steel boat was built nearly thirty years ago and today is as sound as the day it was launched; its entire life has been spent in salt water.

In contrast, the life of a wood boat is always a touchy affair, a constant battle against rot, worms, disintegration of fastenings, cracks, expansion, and contraction. The long-term life of plastic boats has yet to be proved; all resins break down with age and sunlight, by fatigue and micro-crazing. Aluminum, too, will survive long periods if given care but must be constantly protected and maintained.

Maintenance

For the short haul, fiberglass requires less maintenance than steel or aluminum. Except for the usual crazing of the exterior gel coat and discoloration of the surface from the sun, fiberglass requires a minimum of maintenance effort. However, the exterior of steel hulls properly finished to start (and this is important) is a matter of a once-a-year paint job, usually less tedious than for wood. Above the waterline, only a light smoothing with sandpaper followed by a finish coat is all that is required; below the waterline, replacement of any loose barrier coat and an application of anti-fouling paint is all that is needed. The interior, except in the bilges, which may require local touch-up with barrier coat once a year, may go a number of years without repainting. Inside painting is often more a matter of aesthetics than necessity. Thus, maintenance is less than that of a wood boat but more than that of a fiberglass one; it is roughly the same as an aluminum boat.

Noise

An often-expressed opinion is that steel boats are more noisy than comparable boats of other materials. This is simply not true. Of course, there may be individual boats that may be noisy, but they are the exception. Steel sailing craft are remarkably quiet and do not creak and groan like their wooden counterparts. There are sounds peculiar to steel hulls which are different than those of wood or fiberglass but they are minor; water sounds may at times be more distinct and sometimes the "talking" of marine creatures is transmitted. Motor noises are no more annoying than those in a wood or glass boat and, in some instances, due to the more solid character of the hull, less. Where motor noise is a problem, it is more likely a matter of engine mounting or loose fittings than the character of the hull itself.

Condensation

Another belief that is frequently aired is that steel boats are unduly subject to condensation of moisture in cold weather. Condensation can occur, but it is no worse under equal conditions than with wood, aluminum, and fiberglass boats and probably less than with ferro-cement. Any material that may be temporarily or permanently colder than the surrounding air will condense some moisture or "sweat" to some degree. While wood appears to be less subject to this, it has the alternate fault of retaining condensed moisture longer than the other materials. Thus the appearance and growth of mildew, which is an index of retained moisture, is much more common on wood than the metals and the plastics. Good ventilation, a desirable feature in any boat, whether heated or not, readily controls condensation. After thirty years of owning and living intermittently aboard a steel vessel, during all seasons of the year, I have encountered no undue problems due to excess condensation.

Fire Resistance

Obviously steel, together with aluminum, is more fire resistant than either wood or the plastics. Contrary to popular opinion, the fiberglass laminates can burn quite readily once enough heat is built up to ignite them. A steel hull can survive a fire that would be catastrophic to hulls of other materials and probably would be still in floating condition after fire has been subdued.

Space

Because of the relatively small frames and other structural steel members, and the wider spacing possible, coupled with the feasibility of building water and fuel tanks integral within a steel hull, a considerable gain in living or working space is available in steel hulls compared with those of wood. Of course, similar advantage can be claimed for aluminum and, in some cases, fiberglass.

Limitations of Shape and Design

Probably one of the main disadvantages of steel, and this applies equally well to any of the metals, is the limitation of shape. Now it is true that steel, like aluminum, can be shaped to just about any configuration a designer can dream up, provided the boatowner has an ample pocketbook to make it possible. The limitation is economic rather than technical. Hulls with severely rounded or compounded sections, wineglass shapes, and the like are quite feasible with time, effort, and equipment but are relatively costly. For this reason most metal-hulled boats are deliberately designed to facilitate fabrication and reduce expenses. This is why most metal vessels are of hard-chine design with modestly compound curvatures, or, preferably made to conform to multiconic sections. To express it another way, the surfaces of most steel boats are "developable." A developable surface is one that is either flat, a segment of a cylinder, or part of the surface of a cone. Metal plates curve readily into cylindrical, oval, or conic shapes but resist deformation, by virtue of their very strength, when forced into shapes of compound configuration. A multiconic hull is fabricated easily with a minimum of equipment.

This does not suggest in any way that "developed" or multiconic hulls are any less efficient than their compound-curved counterparts, or that they are less attractive. Indeed, many conic-sectioned boats may be more efficient under various conditions, and beauty is not limited to any category of shape. The choice of compound or other form is a matter

Forty-two foot steel-hulled ketch D'Vara *designed by Thomas Colvin and built by the author's Gwynn Island Boat Yard. Her chine construction made her ideally suited for steel construction.*

of personal preference rather than of any sound, proven data to show one superior overall to the other. Often the imaginative designer can use any of a variety of devices, such as the use of multiple chines, to give a compound or curved effect, if this is desired, and still save fabrication expense.

Before undertaking the fabrication of any metal vessel, the prospective builder should carefully consider the lines of the boat and try to assess whether the boat's surfaces are amenable to sensible construction. Even some designers, who should know better, become carried away when designing metal boats and provide the builder with drawings that have little relation to the realities of metal working or the prospective owner's purse. Amateur builders, particularly, should scrutinize the lines of their proposed boats carefully before attempting construction.

Ease of Fabrication

A great many boatbuilders, both professional and amateur, shy away from steel because they are afraid it is difficult or beyond their talents. This is a false premise. Assuming a reasonable set of lines, a steel boat is no more difficult to fabricate than a comparable one of wood or fiberglass. In some respects, it may be easier. It should be mentioned that no boatbuilding worthy of the name is "easy." There is always, whatever the medium, a goodly portion of tedious, hard, back-breaking effort with its attendant problems. Once the basic principles of steel handling are grasped, the work is fairly straightforward, though perhaps different. Cutting a piece of steel is easier than sawing a piece of oak, for example; welding steel is far less trying than boring thousands of holes in wood, then driving an equal number of screws, nails, or bolts, and finally plugging the holes. Grinding steel is unpleasant and noisy, but it is no worse than the itching that is companion to working fiberglass, or the discomfort of the sticky, messy, smelly, rash-raising resin that must be used. The uninitiated regard welding as something of a mystery, a rite performed only by distant associates of Vulcan, the God of Fire, but actually anyone with a sense of touch and distance can do it ably within a few days of practice. Steel is heavy, and some of the pieces to be handled may seem, at first thought, to require a large amount of brawn. But, practically, a minimum of brains and equipment solves this problem very nicely. A lever or two, a pair of rollers, a simple jack, and block and tackle or chain fall will place the heaviest steel plate exactly where one wants it with no more effort than that required to position a single plank on a conventional wood boat. With two rollers, a single chain fall, and one light block and tackle, I have easily placed, alone, steel plates twenty feet long by eight feet wide, weighing about 1,600 pounds, on the side of a hull to within 1/8" of accuracy in less than an hour. Compare this, almost one-sixth of an entire hull skin, with the labor and time of planking the same area in wood.

On the opposite side, however, must be mentioned the dirty, unpleasant, gritty necessity to sandblast any steel hull. While the operation is not ordinarily of long duration, nor necessarily physically arduous, it is a distinct deterrent for the fastidious. Even with tight clothing and a proper helmet, gritty sand seems to work its way into every fold of one's apparel. On a hot summer day, it can be a mean, scratchy business.

As in any other boatbuilding program, ease of fabrication is largely a matter of some prior knowledge and experience. Steel lends itself to precision work; it can be troublesome if the builder is not willing to measure, layout, or template carefully. But when handled correctly, it forms up readily. Cut right, shaped precisely, steel can be a pleasure to deal with; conversely, sloppy work creates no end of problems that can multiply endlessly. Mistakes or careless work, particularly in frame-up, can be more difficult to rectify than with wood. At the same time, no steel boat builder has ever been faced with the appalling knowledge that his laboriously formed hull is irretrievably stuck in the mold for all time to come.

Relative Cost

Steel per pound, or by strength-pound ratio, is by far the least costly basic boatbuilding material readily available. In comparison, the cost of wood, aluminum, or fiberglass is relatively high, often five or six times as much. But the per-pound cost cannot serve as a proper basis on which to judge the relative cost of any boat. There are so many variables that must be taken into consideration, even with a single design suitable for all materials. It is no more proper to make sweeping statements about the relative costs of steel versus wood, aluminum, or fiberglass than it is valid to price completed boats on a per-pound basis, a practice which has become common lately and which can be a concealed trap for the unwary. There is no substitute for meticulous evaluation of each and every design, and a dollar calculation of all the known factors involved.

Nevertheless, some general observations are possible. As the years have gone by, as good boatbuilding woods have become more scarce, as the labor of skilled workmen to shape them have become more costly, and because wood boatbuilding is inherently a time-consuming process, the cost of first-class wood boats has progressively increased. Ultimately, wood will be priced out of the market. Also the costs of maintaining wood boats because of susceptibility to rot, worms, decay of fastenings, and other inherent weaknesses, are by and large, greater than steel, aluminum, or fiberglass. The aluminum alloys suitable for boatbuilding are quite expensive; the cost of fabrication, in general is equal to or greater than steel. Maintenance costs, while not necessarily higher than steel, are likely to be, because aluminum, in salt water, will tolerate less neglect and is subject to quicker deterioration unless meticulously maintained.

It is well known that the cost of fiberglass boats, at the present state of the building art is competitive only when the boats are manufactured in a given minimum quantity to amortize the cost of the molds. Custom-built fiberglass boats are not economical, particularly as boat size increases. Fiberglass, all other factors aside, is not the answer for the owner who wants his own, special, individual boat tailored to his specific needs — requirements, perhaps, that no one else has but are his nevertheless. The man who wants a custom fiberglass boat can be compared with the man who wants a motorcar unlike any other in existence. The car can be obtained, but the price is usually inhibitive.

Steel, on balance, within the limitations defined in the preceding pages, is likely to be the least expensive, most durable material available today for boats thirty feet and up, particularly boats produced on a single or custom-made basis, or boats that, because of their ultimate intended use, must be exceedingly strong to carry cargo or passengers safely, or withstand the stresses of ocean sailing, and which must also be manufactured with a minimum of effort and expense.

3   TOOLS AND EQUIPMENT

Contrary to popular and uninformed opinion, the steel boat builder does not need a large assembly of special tools to accomplish his tasks. Probably, the total investment need not be more than that required to set up for wood boat construction for vessels of comparable size. Good welding and cutting equipment, the essential items, are no more costly than powered band or table saws, planers, routers, and the like necessary for a first-grade wood shop, or the expensive molds and resin- or glass-handling tools for plastic construction.

There are, however, certain minimum requirements that must be met for good work and without which the builder cannot function. They are: (1) adequate steel-cutting equipment, (2) a reasonably versatile welding machine, (3) sandblasting and metal-spraying units, and (4) an assortment of small but necessary tools. To these can be added any number of extras that the desires or pocketbook of the builder permit. With the described minimum, however, boats of any size up to 100 feet, or even more, can be fabricated, assuming there is no pressing time limit or need to maintain a rapid production schedule. The essential tools are these:

Metal Cutting Equipment
Steel boatbuilding would be all but impossible without the most useful instrument of all — the gas cutting torch. Because most parts are curved and the cutting of straight lines a minor aspect of the job, and also because most of the steel to be shaped is beyond the practical capacity of saws, slitters, shears, or nibblers, the cutting torch is the only economical way to cut easily steel boat segments. The torch also has a number of uses beyond simple cutting, such as for local heating to facilitate bend-

3-1.   A gas hand torch with a 90° head.

ing, stretching, or compression; for piercing, scarfing, and expanding metal; burning off scale and paint; brazing; soldering; and more rarely for gas welding. There are quite a number of gas torches on the market. Some are simple cutting torches intended for that use alone; most, however, are combination units in which the welding and heating tips can be exchanged at will with a cutting segment, as desired. The cutting segment, which is attached to the same handle that holds the welding tips, has a provision for holding cutting tips. The size of the tip is governed by the thickness of the metal to be cut (see Table 2, Chapter 7). The torch is typically equipped with two valves for stopping or permitting the flow of gas. Another valve for adjusting the shape of the cutting flame for preheating before actual cutting begins is attached, as is a trigger for actuating the flow of oxygen during cutting or shutting the oxygen off when cutting is done.

The cutting torch comes in a variety of designs, with tips at various angles, and in a variety of sizes and weights. For most boat work, a heavy torch is not desired; a light torch is much easier to handle and control, particularly when making precision cuts, which is most of the time. Also, a cutting torch with the tip at 90 degrees to the torch handle is most useful and more generally versatile than the angled tips sometimes provided. Any reputable supplier will gladly furnish detailed information about cutting torches and their attachments. It is suggested that some care be given to the selection of a torch; it is the steel boat builder's most versatile and frequently used piece of equipment.

No cutting torch would be operative without two auxiliary pieces of equipment — the gas control pressure regulators. These regulators, one for oxygen, the other for acetylene (propane and natural gas are sometimes used) assure the uniform flow of gas into the cutting or welding torch and control its pressure. There are two basic types: (1) the single-stage and (2) the two-stage regulators. The single-stage regulators are less expensive but have the fault of requiring constant adjustment as the pressure from the gas cylinders decreases. The two-stage regulators

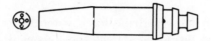

3-2. *A cutting torch tip.*

3-3. *A two-stage gas control pressure regulator.*

3-4. *Metal worker's goggles.*

preserve a uniform flow until the gas cylinders are virtually empty. For boat work, the two-stage regulators are suggested. The regulators measure, by needle and dial, the amount of gas in the cylinders and the actual pressure being delivered.

The remaining components of the total torch cutting system are: (1) the hoses to convey the gases from the regulators to the torch itself, (2) a pair of goggles to protect the eyes and render the flame and steel cutting action properly visible, (3) a flint lighter, (4) a tip cleaner, and (5) welder's gloves to protect the hands.

Sufficient hose should be provided to reach any portion of the boat being built, preferably from the ground. Only hose made specially for this purpose should be used; usually such hoses are molded into a single unit, marked *oxygen* and *acetylene,* and provided with proper fittings to mate with the regulators and the torch without mix-up (by use of right- and left-handed threads). A light hose (about 3/16", inside diameter) is preferable because it is more flexible and subject to less drag during precision cutting.

The cutting gases, oxygen and acetylene, are supplied in steel cylinders of varied capacity, usually 122 or 244 cubic feet of oxygen at about 2,200 psi, and 60, 116, and 250 cubic feet of acetylene at a much lower pressure. The cylinders are available almost anywhere from a large number of dealers and are generally supplied on a contract, which permits 30-day usage with demurrage accruing after that interval. Arrangements are available, also, for the payment of a flat sum for each cylinder on a lease plan, which eliminates demurrage. When construction is to take place intermittently or over an extensive time, this can be worthwhile.

Not absolutely necessary but well worthwhile is a cylinder cart to carry the tanks and cutting equipment from place to place. Gas cylinders are heavy and awkward to handle and, inevitably, will have to be moved frequently. You can weld your own providing you have a set of wheels.

Welding Equipment

The second vital requirement for the steel boat builder is, of course, an adequate welding machine. Some thought should be given to its selection because, to a degree, the quality of the welds that hold the boat together is as much a function of the equipment as the skill of the operator. This does not mean that one must necessarily invest in an expensive electrical tool; quite a few excellent machines are available at moderate prices. Price, however, is not always an index of the efficiency of a welding machine; some very poor "mail order" apparatuses are offered at prices not much lower than those for reputable equipment. "Home workshop" welders should be viewed with caution. While they are, perhaps, suitable for occasional or hobby-type welding, they are often not versatile or rugged enough for proper boat work. At the other extreme, one can easily go overboard if lured by the literature on automatic or semi-automatic machines which, at first glance, may appear very fine but have very little practical use in small-boat work. They are used extensively in large ship construction, where they do an excellent job, particularly where long, straight seams in heavy plates are involved. But in the small boat shop, their value is most limited.

Regardless of what apparatus is contemplated, or what price range

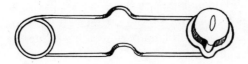

3-5.   A *flint lighter*.

3-6.   A *tip cleaner for the cutting torch*.

3-7.   A *cylinder cart*.

the builder feels he can indulge in, there are certain basic criteria that the machine must meet. They are: (1) the ability to supply a stable, non-fluctuating current to the electrode and weld zone free of pulsation, flare, "arc-blow," or other electrical peculiarities, (2) sufficient amperage, in relation to voltage, to give proper weld penetration for any given weld situation common to boat construction; penetration is of importance in producing proper welds and any machine that is under-equipped in this respect should not be used), (3) versatility in the selection of the current range for control of the character of the welding arc and for electrical efficiency in relation to welding cost, (4) adequate cooling system for the protection of the life of the machine, and (5) safety features to insure no injury to the operator or others.

The specific character of the machine to be selected will depend on the situation prevailing at the scene where the boat is to be built, the type of electricity available, the voltage supplied, whether the current is single or triple phase, or, if there is no electricity at all. Most commercial welding machines are designed to operate on a 230/460-volt, single or three-phase, 50/60-cycle current and, in general, they are the most useful and reliable types. Ordinary 110-volt house current imposes limitations and usually only home workshop welders are geared for this low voltage input.

Welding machines may be roughly classified into two basic groups: (1) motor-generator machines and (2) rectifier welders. The greater part of all steel welding is done by direct current, which, by and large provides a smoother, more controllable arc. Most electric current supplied in the United States at least, is alternating current, and one of the functions of the average welding machine is to convert alternating current into direct current. This is accomplished by (1) use of an alternating-current motor which drives a direct-current generator, or (2) by a selenium or other type rectifier, which does the same task with no revolving parts except for a fan for cooling. In motor-generator sets, a fan is incorporated. Rectifier sets are quieter than motor-generator machines and emit only a low hum plus a fan noise. When no electricity is available, or where the current is inadequate, gasoline or diesel motor-generator units are used. Such units can be set up to provide current for power tools, lights, and the like, as well as provide power for welding.

Some alternating current is used for welding, particularly for gas-shielded welding of aluminum and stainless steel. Machines are available that can be switched from alternating current to direct current at will. Unless the builder proposes to work with aluminum, or other metals requiring inert gas shielding of the welding arc, such machines are not required. Aluminum alloys and some other metals, such as the stainless steels, when molten tend to form thick, refractory oxides from the air. During welding they inhibit the proper flow of metal in the weld pool, making good welding almost impossible. One of the cures is to surround the welding arc and the molten metal with an inert, oxygen-free gas, usually argon. Commonly a tungsten electrode is used to maintain the arc, and aluminum or other metal rod is fed into the oxide-free pool created. The tungsten electrode, because of its extremely high melting point, is not consumed, or is consumed only at a very slow rate. A modification of this technique is to feed a consumable wire of the alloy desired through a gun. The wire, surrounded by inert gas, is melted at a constant rate and is deposited in the weld zone. This technique is excellent for aluminum, magnesium, and stainless steel and is adaptable for ordinary steel, where a cheaper gas than argon, such as carbon dioxide, is often used. The process has the advantage of producing slag-free welds, which is labor saving, but the equipment is expensive and the gas relatively costly. In my opinion the gun also has the disadvantage in boat work of being cumbersome in tight places and has the more serious fault of being more amenable to continuous welding than to the short, scattered, and intermittent welding desirable for distortion-free work.

While the advocates of gas-shielded welding contend there is less heat input than with regular "stick" or flux-coated consumable welding, and thus less likelihood of distortion, the human tendency with this equipment is to take advantage of its favorable continuous features and overweld, a practice which can be disastrous in boat work, at least in the thinner gauges of steel. In general, the most useful and versatile welding equipment for the small boat builder is a conventional direct-current welder using stick-type, flux-coated consumable electrodes.

One of the prime considerations in a welding machine is its ampere rating on the output end. Commonly, welding machines are rated by the maximum ampere output available or by the ranges of ampere output available with different settings of the machine. It is the ampere rating, or rather the ampere output, that primarily controls the *intensity* and nature of the welding arc. It is the intensity of electrical energy that governs the depth of penetration possible with a given electrode and thickness of metal to be welded, as well as the heat of the arc and the force by which the molten droplets of weld metal are directed at the molten weld pool.

As electrode size increases, greater amperage is necessary to melt the electrode and "penetrate" the metal being welded. For example, an 1/8" mild steel electrode would typically require between 80 to 120 amperes, a 3/16" electrode from 140 to 250, a 1/4" electrode from 200 to 400, and larger sizes even more. For all practical purposes, a machine capable of delivering up to 200 amperes is adequate for the small boat builder. Except for heavy keel members and a few other pieces, the bulk of welding will be done with electrodes under 3/16", mostly 1/8" and 5/32". For the relatively few welds necessary with thick metal, a series of multiple passes will accomplish what is needed, often with less chance of distortion than with large diameter electrodes. Of course, if expense is no problem, a 300-ampere machine will give wider latitude.

Before purchase of any welding machine, it would be wise to consult with a reputable company and outline exactly the limitations of electricity available, the conditions prevailing, and the extent of work contemplated. For the once-only builder who does not want to invest in permanent equipment, welding machines can be leased or rented.

Along with the welding machine itself are certain essential extras that must be provided. They are:

Flexible Welding Cables Welding cables differ from ordinary electrical cables in that they are made of many strands of fine wire so woven and braided that the cable is highly flexible and free of the tendency to kink no matter what position the operator is in. Without the cable's special "limpness" and flexibility, welding would be most difficult, particularly in tight corners or overheads. Two cables are necessary, a ground wire and an electrode cable. The size cable will depend upon the maximum amperage to be used and the length of the cable in feet from the welding machine. Typically, a 200-ampere machine will require a No. 2 cable for 50 feet, a No. 1 cable for 75 feet, and larger cable for additional distances. (See Table 1). Use no more cable than comfortable for the job; short cables are electrically more efficient than long ones. Cable connectors are available for conveniently and quickly

Table 1.

CABLE SIZE SELECTION GUIDE

This guide shows current carrying capacity of various sizes of cable recommended for various amperages at various distances from the welding machine. Distances shown here are half the lengths of cable required for a welding installation. For total cable length (welding lead plus ground lead) double the figures.

DISTANCE IN FEET FROM WELDING MACHINE

AMPS.	50	75	100	125	150	175	200	225	250	300	350	CABLE SIZE
100	4	4	2	2	1	1/0	1/0	2/0	2/0	3/0	4/0	4
150	4	2	1	1/0	2/0	3/0	3/0	4/0	4/0			
200	2	1	1/0	2/0	3/0	4/0	4/0					2
250	2	1/0	2/0	3/0	4/0							1
300	1	2/0	3/0	4/0								
350	1/0	3/0	4/0			BASED ON 4 VOLT DROP						1/0
400	1/0	3/0	4/0									
450	2/0	4/0										2/0
500	2/0	4/0										3/0
550	3/0											
600	3/0											4/0

connecting and disconnecting unneeded cable lengths or, conversely, adding to them.

Ground Clamps and Electrode Holders One cable will require a ground clamp for quick attachment to the boat hull or segment being welded. The clamps are usually spring actuated and may be quickly transferred from one spot to another.

The other cable will need an electrode holder which is usually a spring actuated device with a serrated jaw for firmly grasping electrodes in any of several positions. A variety of shapes and sizes are available.

3-8.   *An electrode holder.*

Welding Helmet A helmet is a necessity for shielding the face from the arc glare and heat and to provide a receptacle for the glass welding plates, which give protection from the infra-red and ultra-violet rays from the arc. The plates are deeply tinted and are protected by clear cover plates, either glass or plastic, which prevent breakage and damage from weld splatter. The welding plates are available in a variety of shades and selection is predicated on the intensity of the arc to be viewed and the welder's preference. The style of the helmet is also pretty much a matter of preference; a series of shapes are available. Preferably the lighter and more comfortable they are the better.

3-9.   *A welding helmet.*

Welding Gloves Welder's gloves are distinguished from most work gloves in that they are of soft and pliable leather, with an insulated lining. The stitching of the seams is turned inside to prevent failure of the threads from heat or sparks. Select gloves that are comfortable and do not bind.

3-10. Welding gloves.

Chipping Hammers and Wire Brushes Both chipping hammers and wire brushes are essential to get rid of slag and for the general cleaning of weld areas before welding. For boat work where there are many narrow corners, a long-nosed hammer is preferable (see Figure 3-11). Also valuable is a cup-type wire brush or a disc-type brush for use on a sander-type power tool. A fairly stiff bristle is best, and the twisted style lasts longer. Wire brushes are useful for other work as well.

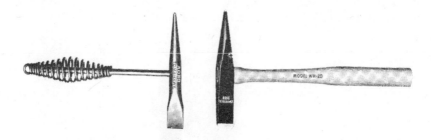

3-11. Two chipping hammers, one with a steel handle (left) and the other with a wooden handle.

Sandblasting and Metallizing Equipment

Most of the problems associated with steel vessels in the past in respect to their resistance to corrosion has been due to the neglect of the finishing process and the unwillingness of many builders to invest in the equipment necessary to do a first-class job. This is illogical; it makes little sense to spend thousands of dollars building a vessel and then not prepare it for a long life for the sake of a few hundred dollars. The cost of the equipment involved can be more than justified by the savings in maintenance in only a year or two. All steel vessels, except perhaps large commercial vessels that carry such heavy plate that progressive corrosion is a relatively minor problem in relation to the expected life of the ship, should be meticulously sandblasted on all surfaces exposed to the sea. This is especially true of yachts and other small craft with thin plating where sometimes only 1/8″ of metal lies between the interior and the salty ocean. Even for fresh-water boats, sandblasting should be a requirement because none of the finishes available today are fully efficient when placed over scaled or dirty metal. In the as-fabricated, as-welded condition, steel hulls are covered with an oxide scale, dirt, grease, and an assortment of other contaminants. These must be removed and a spotlessly clean surface exposed for subsequent finishes. Failure to do this will inevitably result in flaking paint, unsightly rust streaks, unseen pitting, bleeding scale, and ultimately severe local or general deterioration.

Most shipyards are highly averse to sandblasting because it is an unpleasant job and also because fine sand tends to invade their paint shop areas. Many are not willing to invest in the equipment because they do not have a steady use for it. Nevertheless, the steel boat builder who is not willing to undertake this necessary task should be avoided, no matter what rationale might be presented to eliminate it.

The properly sandblasted boat hull will present a silvery-white sheen without streaks or blemishes, and such a surface will be a proper bond for the subsequent metallizing operation, and for whatever paint finishes that follow. Done properly in the beginning, sandblasting makes the difference between a trouble-free boat and one that can be a perpetual headache or an unsightly "rust-bucket."

Sandblasting equipment is not necessarily complicated. In its simplest form, to be used where strict economy is a must, it can consist of a simple air hose attached to a Y-fitting with a shut-off valve, a nozzle, and a short length of "sucker" tube (see Figure 3-12). The sucker tube is inserted in a container of sand and the sand is pulled into the com-

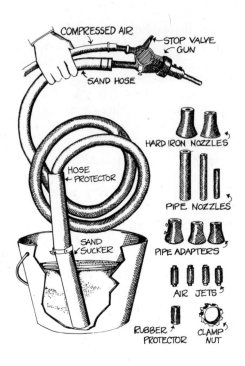

3-12. A simple sandblasting system.

pressed air line by the force of the air stream and then ejected through the nozzle at the surface to be cleaned. It operates somewhat on the principle of a vacuum cleaner, except that the sand, instead of being retained in a bag, is ejected forcibly. While this uncomplicated apparatus does a satisfactory job, it has the fault of being rather slow and the flow of sand is uneven.

A much better arrangement is a conventional sandblasting machine. This consists of a welded cylindrical tank, filled with sand, with appropriate valves for admitting and controlling the entrance and exit of compressed air. It has a mixing valve for maintaining an even flow of sand in the air stream and, usually, a moisture trap for removing condensed water from the air stream. Compressed air is fed into the tank and the exit hoses, is mixed with the sand at the mixing valve, and ejected steadily through a hardened nozzle of specific size at the work. These units are manufactured by a number of companies in a variety of sizes. For most boat work, the small units, holding from two- to three-hundred-pound bags of sand are more than adequate and have the ad-

3-13. A conventional sandblasting machine.

vantage of being readily moved from one part of the boat to another. They come equipped with various lengths of nozzle hose, as specified. Usually about twenty feet is enough for most operations.

Obviously, the sandblasting operation will require an air compressor. Air compressors of the capacity needed are expensive pieces of apparatus, and unless one is contemplating full-scale, continuous production, their cost is rarely justified. Fortunately, they may be easily rented or leased for reasonable fees from a large number of companies all over the country catering to the construction industry. The usual type available is a gasoline- or diesel-driven compressor on wheels for easy towing, they are a common sight wherever building or road repair is going on.

The important thing is to use a compressor of sufficient capacity. The minimum practical requirement would be a delivery of about 100 cubic feet of air per minute at a pressure of no less than 65 psi, preferably more. Delivery of this amount of air, necessary for efficient work, requires the expenditure of considerable horsepower and a suitable engine to supply it. The small air compressors found commonly around garages and small shops are not adequate for this sort of work. Don't skimp on the capacity of the air compressor used.

Between the air compressor and the sandblasting machine, a suitable length of air hose and appropriate couplings will be necessary. It is advisable to keep sand away from the air compressor as much as possible; the length of hose needed will depend on local conditions. The firms that rent air compressors also supply hose. Ordinary hose will not do.

3-14. A sandblaster's helmet

Another accessory that is necessary is a sandblaster's helmet. They are available in several styles but, in essence, consist of a rubber or cloth hood supported by a head band. Visibility is provided by a viewing glass or plastic shield. Some helmets have hose connections for air, and this type is preferable. It is important that the operator breathe clean air or air properly filtered through a dust-removing respirator. An excess of sandblasting dust collected in the lungs could cause silicosis, the quarryman's or miner's disease. If an air-hose type helmet is chosen, the air source should be inspected with care to insure that exhaust fumes or oil vapors are not inhaled.

Clean air will be needed also for the metallizing operation if zinc is used. Zinc fumes can cause a temporary illness, which is most uncomfortable, though not necessarily dangerous like silicosis.

Theoretically, sandblasting followed by a proper finishing system of metal conditioning paints should be all that is necessary to provide a corrosion-free steel boat. Some of the paint manufacturers make claims

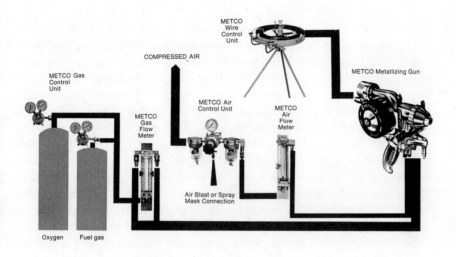

3-15. A complete metallizing system.

to the contrary, but none of the paint systems on the market today are sufficient by themselves, no matter what the advertising literature may say. This does not mean that certain of the metal boat finishes are not good products, for they are, but none are completely effective and all are subject to mechanical or chemical damage from one cause or another. When this occurs, whether from abrasion, scratches, scuffing, the action of barnacles or other marine growth, or whatnot, bare steel is exposed and corrosion begins. The result is local pitting, rusting, unsightly bleeding, or other deterioration. This is why supplemental preparation is of first importance, particularly in yacht work where appearance as well as corrosion-resistance is a necessity.

For complete freedom from this sort of failure, whether for aesthetic or preservation reasons, metallizing is a requirement. Metallizing, at least until someone devises a fool-proof paint system, makes the difference between difficult and easy maintenance, between a rust-free boat and one that is never quite devoid of tell-tale streaks.

Once sandblasting is accomplished, metallizing entails very little effort, no more than a single course of paint spraying. The added cost is negligible compared to the results; the dollars ultimately saved are far in excess of the price of the operation. The life of any steel boat will be increased by many years if metallizing is done in the beginning. It is surprising, when one considers that the process has been readily available for over a quarter of a century, that so few steel boat builders have made use of it. I consider it a vital part of the steel boatbuilding process.

The equipment consists of a metallizing gun, which is a hand-held mechanism powered by a small, high-speed, compressed-air turbine that pulls zinc or aluminum wire through the gun at a constant rate. Acetylene and oxygen are fed into the gun in controlled amounts and, when ignited, melt the wire as it passes through an orifice. Here, the molten metal is blasted by compressed air in exceedingly fine droplets onto the steel to be protected. The metal solidifies in a thin layer and is bonded to the newly roughened sandblasted surface. The gun is an ingenious device and is capable of spraying zinc or aluminum at very rapid rates. Other metallizing guns are made for other types of metals — steel, bronze, stainless steel, etc.—but are not suitable for boat work because they are slow and do not feed the wire as quickly as desirable.

Several accessories are required: a gas-flow meter and two gas pressure regulators. The same regulators used for oxygen and acetylene cutting are suitable here. A reel for conveying wire to the gun is convenient but not a necessity.

Handling Equipment

Unlike boatbuilding in wood or fiberglass, or even ferro-cement, where the individual segments of construction are fairly small and relatively light, the steel boat builder will be required to handle, sometimes with precision, some heavy, rather large, even awkward pieces, some of them weighing hundreds of pounds. A steel sheet, for example, 3/16" by 8 feet by 20 feet, can not be readily maneuvered by ordinary muscle power, or hoisted and held in position, without some sort of equipment, however simple or even primitive. Frequently such heavy segments must be positioned and held to within close welding tolerances until adequate supports are available. Ordinary rope blocks and falls are practical and inexpensive but are not quite as convenient or as capable of precision positioning as a chain fall. Chain falls can be left in any degree of hoist with no danger of the load sagging or falling. They are available in a wide variety of types and capacities. In general, the worm-geared types are best as they are least prone to fouling during use.

Another related and very useful piece of equipment is a device commonly called a "come-along" but which is more properly known as a lever hoist. It is valuable not only for vertical lifting but also for pulling in horizontal or other directions.

Whatever type of hoist is used, chain fall, rope tackle, winch, or other, it is essential that the capacity be equal to the job. Steel plates are often

3-16. *Hoisting equipment — a chain fall (left) and a "come-along" or lever hoist.*

3-17. *A plate clamp or "dog."*

very heavy and the edge of one can be the nearest thing to a guillotine ever devised.

A companion piece to any steel hoisting equipment is a device called a sheet or plate clamp or "dog." It is simply an open-jawed fixed clamp with a movable, hinged, or pivoted serrated jaw, together with a steel ring for engaging a hoist hook. The "dog" is slipped over the edge of the plate and, as the hoist is actuated, the serrated jaw engages and becomes ever tighter as the load increases. It is one of the safest hoisting clamps devised and much more positive than an ordinary C-clamp.

Another necessity will be a crow or pry-bar, preferably two or three.

43

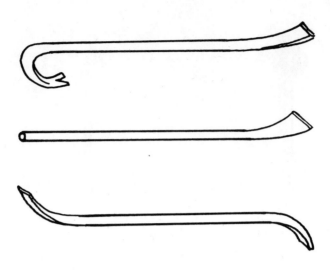

3-18. Typical crow- and pry-bars.

One straight bar about four feet long is desirable; another with a bent end (see Figure 3-18) will be valuable for all sorts of tasks. A small, light, wrecking bar will be handy, too.

It is recommended, also, that at least one screw or hydraulic jack be available. A screw jack is more laborious to use but has the advantage of being more precise when a weight is being lowered and does not tend to "drop" the load by creep or when the fluid is released.

Screw or hydraulic jacks have another valuable use — as a power source for bending pipe, bars, or sheets. A large metal shop will usually possess a power brake for bending or for turning sheet edges, but the expense of one of these for the occasional builder or the small boatyard is seldom warranted. However, with a little ingenuity, some quickly welded fixtures, and one or more screw jacks, innumerable shapes can be achieved at nominal cost.

An assortment of rollers, either solid steel or pipe, will ease the chore of moving steel from place to place. One can push a ton of steel with one hand with a few rollers; the same load without them is almost immovable. Short pipe segments filled with cement will sustain enormous loads and are less expensive than solid rollers. They are very handy when the time comes to move the hull and cradle for launching.

Rope or steel cable slings will be useful, too, and can be quickly fabricated as the situation and need dictates.

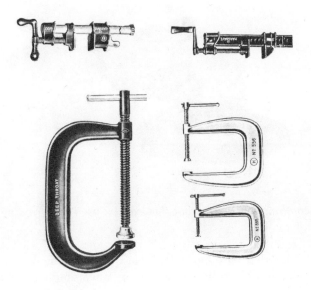

3-19. *Clamps useful for steel work.*

An assortment of clamps will be required. Most useful are the so-called C-clamps; a variety of sizes from four to six inches are indispensable. Preferred are deep-throated clamps of rugged, forged stock; cheap cast-iron clamps are brittle and can be dangerous if failure occurs. The wooden clamps common to wood boat shops are not very suitable for steel work. In addition to the C-clamps, a number of clamps four to six feet long, or more, will be needed. Ordinary pipe clamps can be made as long as desired and are inexpensive and practical.

Another essential item is a hand power tool which, by changing heads, can be used alternately as a grinder, sander, or power brush. It is the most frequently used instrument in the steel boat builder's assortment. It is required for beveling, slotting for weld preparation, removing slag after welding or torch cutting, grinding edges to precision finish, getting rid of weld spatter, smoothing weld beads, preparing plates and bars for priming and painting when sandblasting is not used or not required, and rounding corners or cleaning steel for welding. Because of the constant and rugged work involved, it is suggested that a good industrial type be secured with sturdy bearings to withstand the severe service. A lightweight tool, consistent with ruggedness, is to be desired. Much grinding will be done overhead, and a heavy grinder can tire you out. As accessories to this tool, a coarse-grit cup wheel, a number of abrasive

3-20. A combination power tool that can be used for grinding, sanding, and brushing.

discs, a stiff-bristled wire cup wheel, and a thin, stiff, flat, wire wheel, plus a regular flexible rubber disc for ordinary sanding are all that is essential. Other heads can be added as special situations dictate. Along with this tool should be proper safety glasses or eye shields. No grinding, sanding, or power brushing of metal should ever be attempted without adequate eye protection at all times.

One other power tool is indispensable — a good drill of at least 3/8" capacity. For steel boat work, the slower rpm, high-torque tools are generally best. Also handy is a drill press, but it is not an essential piece of equipment.

During fabrication, quite a bit of template work will be done, and for this some sort of power saw is invaluable. A band saw is most convenient, but not absolutely necessary; where expense is an item to be considered, a small saber saw will accomplish all that is necessary. About 90 percent of all cuts will be curved, so a table saw or radial saw is not of much use, at least until one gets to wood decorative trim, when a full set of woodworking tools is necessary.

With this list of equipment, plus the usual assortment of small hand tools common to almost any shop — screwdrivers, pliers, wrenches, hammers, a plane, and the like — almost any steel boat of reasonable dimensions and design can be built. Where unusual situations are encountered, where unusual forging or forming is necessary, or where machine work must be done, it is usually much more economical to have a specialty shop fabricate the segment involved than to buy or hire the equipment to do it. Commonly there are not many such parts in a hull, and there are not many small steel boats that cannot be produced with the equipment listed, particularly if a little imagination is used and the special properties of steel taken into consideration.

Perhaps, one additional item might be mentioned for emphasis — a good rule and strict reliance on it. There is not much point in possessing a first-class welding machine and not having a proper fit-up of steel to be welded with it. With an accurate measuring tape should be a steel scribe for marking lines to be cut with precision. Incidentally, an ordinary, old-fashioned ice pick makes a first-class scribe.

4 DESIGN AND CONSTRUCTION CONSIDERATIONS

If there are any basic principles that should apply to the design of steel and other metal boats, they should be the rules of reasonableness and simplicity. In almost any given year, I have had prospective clients submit sketches, drawings, photographs, or descriptions of boats for steel construction. Many of them are quite pretty — and quite impractical. This does not mean that almost any design that can be dreamed up by a marine architect, amateur designer, or boat enthusiast cannot be translated into steel. The realm of possibility is endless — and so can be the labor and expense.

It is not within the scope of this book to advise about design; this is the province of the architect, good, bad, or merely indifferent. Nor, is it my purpose to limit the possibilities of architectural imagination, but rather, instead, to enhance design with some realism, to help the prospective owner assess whether his drawings are amenable to steel construction, to make the most of the material.

Probably the first and most important consideration is whether the design has been drawn specifically with steel in mind or whether it is an adaptation from wood construction. A surprising number of drawings are simple conversions from wood to steel, and some are almost slavish in the delineation of construction details. This is particularly true of framing, even to the spacing allowed, as well as jointure, bracketing, and dimensions. The same frequently applies to stem-keel systems and such segments as horn timbers, keelsons, floors, clamps, stringers, knees, and the like. These items may or may not be necessary in a steel hull, because that hull is an integral unit, welded as a unit of great strength, and not a system of multitudinous pieces relying one upon the other to maintain the integrity of the whole. Generally, when the architectural drawing for a steel hull closely resembles that for a wood boat, it is an indication that the architect may not be overly familiar with steel.

Now, of course, if the proposed design is traditional in style — and many of the most attractive steel vessels fall in this category — it may be highly desirable that the boat resemble, as much as possible, its wooden forebears, at least as far as the external appearance is concerned. But it does not mean, necessarily, simply because the boat is traditional, that it should be laden with unnecessary pieces that serve no useful or real function and that may add only needless weight or take up valuable space. Bearing in mind that steel is an exceedingly strong material that does not depend on bolts, screws, nails, or simple friction to hold it together, the individual segments should be. evaluated for their real structural value in terms of steel, not wood and a decision should be made if they are really necessary or desirable. Here, the rule of simplicity comes into effect; complicated segments are rarely necessary in steel construction. The best arrangements are usually simple, straightforward, and uninvolved.

If, as it should be, the design is predicated in the beginning on steel and is not just a wood-to-steel adaptation, the second important premise will be to see if the plating lines are reasonable and within the pocketbook of the owner or the mechanical ability of the builder. In an earlier page, I have already commented on the relative expense of multiconic versus compound-curved surfaces. A quick glance at the lines will readily determine whether the hull is conic, of hard or multiple-chine construction, or mildly or severely compounded. One may be sure that wine-glass cross-sections, severe tumblehome, and double-curved and highly flared bows will be time consuming and expensive to construct. Now, some compound curvature can be desirable and will produce a strong hull and a pleasing appearance, but there is a dividing line between what is readily possible and what is laborious. Here again, the rules of reasonableness and simplicity apply.

Where there is an element of doubt, or where one's purse is not unlimited, there is a simple way of determining whether the proposed boat will be easy to plate or a possible construction nightmare. This is to make a plating model, or half-model, to scale. The model can be made of wood, in the traditional manner of half-models, or of plaster, fiberglass, or plastic, or of any other convenient material so long as it is to scale and proportionately correct. On the model can be tentatively traced in pencil the outlines of probable plate sizes. The reasonableness of the outlines can then be tested by cutting platelets of thin tin, copper, aluminum, or other light, sheet material, and laying them over the outlines. If they will bend easily to the hull and fall into place without buckles or crimps, so will sheets of steel. If not, at least some idea may be had of the amount of forming necessary, whether local heating and slitting will solve the problem, or whether the proposed shape is impossible without pressing, stretching, forming over a mold, or other expensive techniques. A plating model, thoughtfully used, can be well worth the effort of making it, can save much full-scale experimentation, and, of course, ultimately, save quite a few dollars.

After an inspection of the lines and, at least, a determination of the reasonableness of the basic hull shape in respect to plating, the next obvious step is a consideration of the construction plan. Construction drawings delineate in detail all, or almost all, of the segments of the boat, specify the shapes and sizes of the structural members, the thickness of the hull plating, and the dimensions of bulkheads, fuel and water tanks, deck beams, cabin structures, engine beds, rudder, keel, stems, and all other important parts. Here is revealed, more than in any other drawings, the suitability of the plans for steel construction and the familiarity, or lack of it, of the designer with metal, and with steel in particular. I have received many construction drawings based on very attractive exterior designs, which, if meticulously followed as drawings should be, would produce boats most unlovely in appearance because of welding stresses, or hulls subject to hidden corrosion because of built-in traps for condensation, or interiors quite difficult to trim out inside because of use of impractical, though perhaps common, steel shapes, or areas structurally weak because they are almost impossible to weld properly.

First and foremost, the construction plan of any steel vessel within the scope of this book, particularly the thinly plated yachts, sailing craft and powerboats, should specifically be directed toward the production of a smooth hull. The appearance of a yacht and, indeed, of almost any vessel, is of prime importance. It is in this area that so many steel boats have been needlessly deficient in the past. Fortunately, the most useful technique for the creation of a smooth, wrinkle- and distortion-free boat is the same for creating a hull of greatest strength. The method of framing is of the essence and is the most significant construction requirement to this end, except, possibly, welding sequence.

In the past, most steel yachts and other small vessels below 100 feet were framed much like conventional wooden boats, with numerous, rather closely spaced transverse "ribs" or frames. In wood boats, and

50

4-1.   Longitudinal framing on the 62-foot twin-diesel yacht Manteo.

in large commercial steel vessels, steamships and the like, where very heavy plating is used, this makes good sense. But in small steel vessels in which the plating is in the order of only 3/16″ or 1/8″, it most definitely does not. For one thing, closely spaced transverse frames are not necessary in steel boats; they do not serve quite the same function they do in wooden boats — to hold a mass of relatively small planks together — but only add unnecessary weight. Modern steel construction dispenses with a great many transverse frames; those that remain are often widely spaced; they serve mainly to give the boat shape and to provide support for an entirely different sort of stiffening — relatively light longitudinal frames.

Hull plating welded to vertical transverse frames almost inevitably distorts, particularly if there is carelessness in the welding sequence or if there is overwelding. Such "washboarded" steel hulls are an all to common—and unnecessary—sight. The slightest transverse deviation from a smooth surface will inevitably catch the eye, especially if a high-gloss paint is used or if the light strikes the boat along the axis of the hull. The eye is automatically "offended" and the boat loses its inherent attractiveness. The same amount of distortion occurring longitudinally does not have the same effect. The seams in longitudinal wood planking are not at all unpleasing and, in fact, longitudinal lap-seams, for all their inherent discontinuity, are often quite pretty. However, welding distortion does not occur as readily with longitudinal framing as with transverse because the curvature of the plating as it follows the hull seems, usually, to be more resistant to weld deformation. Also, when a boat is framed longitudinally, the hull skin is supported in all directions so that shrinkage deformation and edge puckering, as along butt-welded seams, is resisted and largely prevented. Of course, successful steel boats with no longitudinal framing at all have been built, but production of a smooth hull using this method is much more difficult. Why do it the hard way when there is a simpler and better method?

Steel allows much greater choice in the matter of keel structures, and keels need not be the massive members so common in the past. Surprisingly few designs take full advantage of keels and often neglect them as possible storage units for fuel or as heat-exchange units. Some types do very nicely for both. Box keels, properly compartmented and sealed, are very good fuel tanks and, because of the relatively good heat transfer rate of steel, can serve as efficient heat exchangers. In recent years, many tugboats and other working commercial vessels that cannot afford to have exposed pipes or conventional keel coolers, have converted their keels to this purpose or have incorporated welded-in pipes or channels as part of their built-in cooling systems.

Steel keels commonly fall into three categories: (1) bar keels, which are simple vertical rectangular bar sections, (2) wide-flange beam-keelson systems for interior straight keels, often with a short skeg aft, and (3) hollow or box keels. The first two are most generally useful on power vessels, the latter very adaptable for most sailing craft. Sailboat box keels may have their ballast all or partially welded in as an integral part of the keel, usually as a heavy bar "shoe," or may carry their ballast inside the box in the form of scrap metal, iron or lead pigs, cement, or lead shot. Lead shot has the advantage of being easily removed and re-distributed for trimming fore and aft, as changing cargo or other conditions warrant. Other keel systems are, of course, possible, such as com-

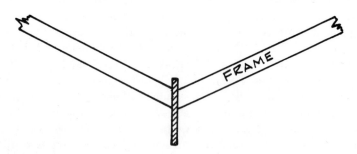

4-2. *Cross-section of a bar keel.*

binations of bar keels and bullet-type castings, as in certain racing hulls, or partial keel-centerboard systems.

A word of caution about keel castings is in order. Do not expect to weld ordinary massive cast iron to an upper steel keel member or to the bottom of the boat. Cast iron does not weld very well and is prone, particularly in massive sections, to cracking from contraction and expansion from weld heat. The welded areas are inherently weak and not

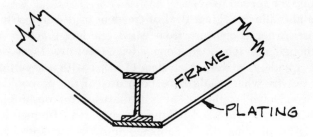

4-3.   *Cross-section of a beam-keelson system.*

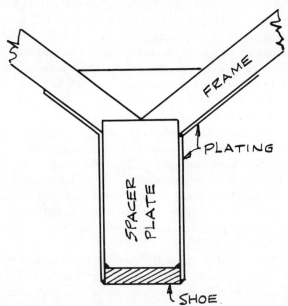

4-4.   *Cross-section of a typical box keel.*

to be depended on. There is no reason not to use a casting if this better serves a purpose or provides a shape not readily fabricated from ordinary steel stock, but be sure it is a *steel* casting and not a cast iron one if you expect to keep the keel as a permanent member of the boat. Many foundries are not equipped to provide steel castings, or do not care to do so; however, steel castings are readily available from the proper sources. This applies also to any other cast structures that may be incorporated into the hull, such as rudder sockets, water screens or inlets, fastenings, or special gadgets.

Steel also allows a great deal of freedom in designing stems, and this is an area where departure from wood building practices is quite possible though not too often done advantageously. Most drawings will require a wide, relatively thick stem together with a knee that duplicates almost exactly what would have been used if the proposed boat was to be of wood. Unless the vessel is to be used for pushing or ramming, there is often no real need for the massive stems frequently designated. There is no planking to be rabbeted into the stem itself, and often a very light bar is all that is necessary. Indeed, where a rounded stem is used, no stem bar at all need be utilized; the very great strength of a semi-cylindrical or segmented cone of such a bow is more than adequate as far as strength is concerned. So, too, a simple strip of flat bar stock bent to the curvature of the stem will give the support that can be used when it is welded to the side plating. Similarly, a bent round (bar of round cross-section) or pipe will serve the same function but is not as easily welded from inside. In this matter of stems, there is a wide latitude for architectural imagination and improvement over old practices.

In practically all cases, except possibly for certain workboats, the steel stem knee is an unnecessary appendage and a relic from the old wood boatbuilding days. A steel stem welded properly to its mating keel is as strong, for all practical purposes, in the welded area as either of the two joined segments. The knee ordinarily adds only weight and takes up space. Steel is a material of great strength; it is pointless not to take advantage of that property. If there is an element of doubt, or the boat's service is to be severe, by all means use whatever strengthening features may be desired, but the question can be asked legitimately whether the stem knee serves a useful function.

The same can be said, also, about the stern or transom knee; it is very desirable in a wooden boat, of questionable worth in a steel one. This applies, too, to much bracketing, such as chine brackets and deck-to-frame brackets.

Because of its strength, steel offers a great deal of versatility in rudder

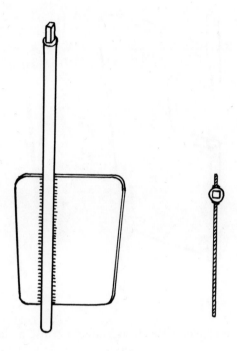

4-5. Single blade rudder.

design. Rudders can be fashioned with a virtual feather edge if desired;
propeller apertures can be readily cut out with no significant loss of
strength. A steel rudder does not depend on an elaborate system of
bolts to hold it together; it is an integral unit. Steel rudders can absorb
a grounding that would destroy any other type. They may be either of
two basic types: (1) blade rudders consisting of a single plate welded to
a rudder post, either conventional or counterbalanced, or (2) hollow-
blade rudders made of two matching plates welded at the forward edge
to the rudder post but tapered aft. While hollow rudders require two
plates instead of one, the plates may be much lighter for a given size
than a single-plate rudder, and may be stronger and more buoyant.
Single-blade rudders are commonly used on power craft, the hollow
types most frequently on sailboats.

The sheer or gunwale area can be profitably scrutinized also for construction details. Here, quite frequently, the design does not take full
advantage of the possibilities. Commonly, the main sheer, as distinguished from the top of the bulwarks, will have a rub rail of some sort

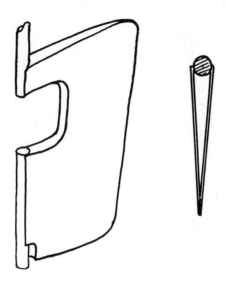

4-6. A hollow-blade rudder.

to provide protection when the boat comes against a dock. Many designers will specify a split pipe welded onto the hull at this point. While this is satisfactory, it is not a particularly strong arrangement, especially in an area where stiffness and strength is desired. It also does not facilitate fabrication when a deck is to be joined at the same level and when a bulwark of lighter metal is to be situated immediately above. An improved arrangement, if a round rub rail is to be used at all, is to use a *full* pipe inset into the transverse framing so that only half of it projects outside the hull plating. This gives the same effect as a split pipe but more than doubles the strength and, in addition, provides a convenient welding area for hull, deck, and bulwark plates. The handling of sheer pipes will be discussed in the chapter on framing.

Another design item that can stand improvement is the indiscriminate use of angles or tees for framing, deck carlings, and stringers. Now, there is nothing basically wrong with an angle or a tee; they are good and strong structural shapes, but once installed in a boat they are almost impossible to clean properly of scale, rust, or dirt prior to painting and they are difficult to maintain. There is just about no way to get a wire brush behind them for painting preparation. Under exposed exterior decking, canopies, or walkways they are particularly objectionable and cannot be properly sandblasted or metallized. Also, in transverse framing, the interior angle faces become increasingly disoriented in respect

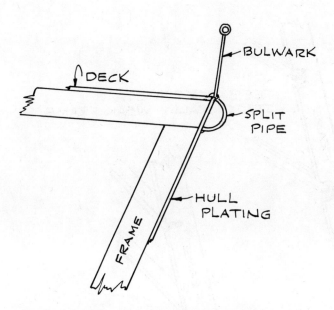

4-7. *A split pipe used as a rub rail at the main sheer.*

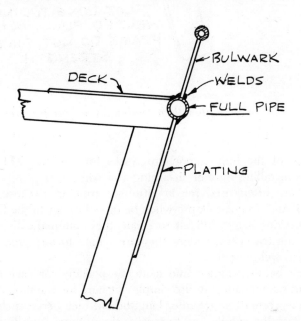

4-8. *A full pipe used as a rub rail at the main sheer.*

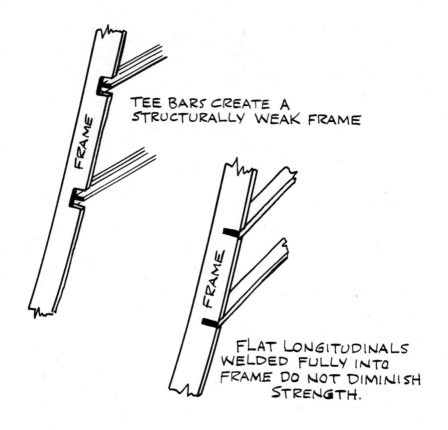

TEE BARS CREATE A STRUCTURALLY WEAK FRAME

FRAME

FRAME

FLAT LONGITUDINALS WELDED FULLY INTO FRAME DO NOT DIMINISH STRENGTH.

4-9. Flat longitudinals, rather than tee-bars, are best for preserving the strength of a frame.

to the curve of the hull as one progresses fore or aft. This presents problems in installing interior sheathing and trim.

Tee-bars are often used for longitudinal framing because they are laterally stiff and do not collapse when being cold bent to the hull shape. However, besides being difficult to clean, they automatically lower the strength of the transverse frames they are joined to and create a notch impractical to weld together.

It is much better, simpler, and neater, especially for easy access for painting and maintenance, to use simple flat bars for framing. There are no impossible corners to get into, longitudinal members can be welded completely into the notches cut to receive them, there is no loss of transverse strength, and there are no built-in traps to collect dirt and moisture.

Flat bars are also easier to reach during welding. In theory, the angle bar or tee-bar would provide greater strength or resistance to side pressures, but, to be practical, the flat bar when welded to the hull or decking becomes, in effect, a tee with all the strength reasonably necessary. It may be argued also that it is difficult to curve flat bars on edge during framing without sideways collapse or distortion, but this is not so. It is a rare boat that has longitudinal curvatures so severe that flat bars cannot be bent smoothly to conform to its shape. The techniques for doing this are discussed also in the chapter on framing.

By one of those peculiar little twists of human behaviour, generated unconsciously, I think, by the erroneous belief that because steel is inherently heavy and that a boat made of it is more prone to sinking if damaged, there is a tendency whenever a design is being discussed, or a boat planned, to start thinking about watertight compartments. There is nothing wrong with watertight compartments per se, but often a little thought will reveal that the disadvantages of overdoing this feature more than cancel out the benefits. Watertight bulkheads in commercial vessels carrying heavy cargoes can be highly desirable, but the advantage of bottling up several segments of a yacht or powerboat is dubious. The prospective owner or builder should ask himself if the proposed bulkheading is really necessary.

First of all, it should be recalled that the steel boat, properly built, is the strongest type of vessel obtainable. The probability of opening a seam or holing it at sea is fairly remote compared with vessels of other materials. The small steel vessel does not depend, ordinarily, on full bulkheading for its integrity, and while bulkheads will, of course, add to strength, they also add a great deal of weight, often, as in the case of sailboats, just where it may not be wanted. A distinction should be made between bulkheading and partitioning. Partitioning can be done with other and much lighter materials. It costs money to push unneeded weight through the water. Sometimes it has been the practice to place bulkheads in the vicinity of masts on the premise that the boat needs stiffening at this point. In steel this need not be true; indeed at the time of this writing, I have just finished building a 51-foot sea-going schooner that does not have bulkheads, and also has masts mounted on deck. In steel, this is quite strong and practical.

Excess bulkheading inevitably inhibits ventilation and also imposes limitations on usable space. The best and most livable yachts are those that are open to fresh air from one end to the other and those in which there is freedom of movement and a feeling of comfortable space. Many otherwise spacious boats have been spoiled by excess compartmentation into a number of boxlike rooms and cubbyholes.

It should also be borne in mind, particularly in very thin-gauge hulls, that a bulkhead to be truly watertight must be welded completely transversely. Great care in welding sequence must be exercised to prevent distortion at this point. Carelessly done, the bulkhead will be readily visible and be a detriment to the aesthetics of the hull. The welding of watertight bulkheads is treated elsewhere in this volume.

Living space can be augmented by taking advantage of the adaptability of the steel hull to tankage, whether water or fuel. There is no point in taking up good space with separate tanks when they can be built into the hull, or the keel, at any location where weight considerations or convenience best indicates. The objection may be raised that the maintenance of such integral tanks could be a problem, but with adequate cleanout openings and proper treatment in the beginning, this is not the case. A possible exception may be made for gasoline tanks; once installed, they cannot be removed or altered with a cutting torch without considerable danger. This is not true of ordinary diesel fuel tanks. Integral tanks add to the structural strength of the hull.

Steel decks and cabin trunks have the advantage of being both strong and watertight, a feature appreciated by wood boat owners who are frequently plagued by persistent dripping at deck and trunk seams. It is a real blessing not to have to worry about the deck opening up in dry weather and spoiling one's carefully stowed equipment when it rains again. Consideration, however, should be given to the weight specified for the deck and cabin trunk components, particularly in sailing vessels, and most particularly in sailing boats under about 35 feet. In small sailboats, it may be advantageous not to use steel at all for the deck and cabin trunk but instead to go to plywood and fiberglass or combinations of other light materials. Whether or not to use steel for decking and trunk will depend not only on the size of the boat but also, to some degree, on the contours of these parts. A well-cambered deck and house top will permit the use of very light-gauge steel which, with judicious use of longitudinal framing, will be very strong. I have built cabin trunks of steel as light as 1/16" in boats only 30 feet long. They were quite successful but care in welding was necessary to prevent distortion. Ordinarily, in yachts from about 35 feet to 55 feet, 1/8" decking is quite practical when supported properly, and is well within reasonable weight limits.

Decking made of diamond-tread plates, or embossed patterns of other design, is sometimes employed, especially in commercial vessels, but

The deck of Manteo. *Note the smooth deck, tapered stanchions with nested pipe top, and louvered air intakes for the engine room.*

usually does not look very well on yachts and pleasure boats. Embossed plates are not too dependable, ironically, for footing, especially when they are wet. They have the additional fault of wearing badly on the sharp corners of the raised embosses where they can become locally rusted. A smooth deck painted and sanded is much less slippery, much more attractive, and easier to maintain and keep clean.

Expanded metal can be very useful for engine-room flooring, provided it is properly coated to begin with. And, when metallized, expanded metal has been used with some success adjacent to bowsprits in lieu of the traditional foot ropes. It makes for excellent footing while stowing head sails, and when used with discretion can be attractive as well as utilitarian.

Centerboards and centerboard wells, no matter how valuable they may be, are usually a source of trouble. In wood boats, particularly, they ultimately leak or alternately become residence for a host of happy teredoes and an equal number of busy barnacles, clustered tunicates, or corrosive, boring sponges. There is no real excuse for this; the fault lies in failure to provide for easy maintenance. The steel centerboard well is, at least, leakproof and no worm can penetrate it. However, it must be

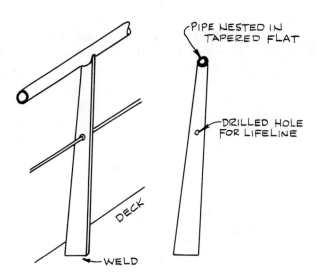

PIPE NESTED IN
TAPERED FLAT

DRILLED HOLE
FOR LIFELINE

DECK

WELD

4-10. Use of a tapered vertical flat to provide a more attractive railing.

cleaned out periodically like any centerboard well and repainted with anti-foulant. For some reason, not very clear, some designers insist on making centerboard wells so narrow that it is almost physically impossible to insert a cleaning tool to remove marine accumulations, let alone introduce a paint swab. Also, most will carefully arrange the centerboard pin so that it may be withdrawn and the centerboard *dropped*, forgetting completely that on most marine railways this just isn't practical and the only recourse toward reconditioning the well, and the board, is to drop the board in the water. Putting it back can be a nice problem, especially in cold weather.

Recently, during construction of a 75-foot centerboard ketch, with a centerboard weighing approximately 5,000 pounds and measuring roughly 13 by 10 feet, the problem was solved by arranging the construction so that the board could be *lifted* intact out of the hull through a slot in the deck. The slot was made wide enough so cylindrical wire brushes could be used for thorough cleaning before repainting the inside. In many wood and fiberglass boats, this is not practical for strength reasons, but a steel deck slot, properly designed, is quite strong and no detriment to deck integrity. The slot can be closed by suitable bolting between seasons.

The steel centerboard well, thoroughly metallized inside before construction and thoroughly coated, will last the lifetime of the boat given

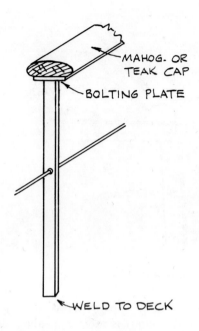

MAHOG. OR TEAK CAP

BOLTING PLATE

WELD TO DECK

4-11. A steel rail with a wooden cap.

care once a year. Friction from the movement of the board can be minimized by providing interior strips of nylon or similar slippery plastic,
bolted in position and bonded and sealed before assembly. Scrutinize
carefully any plans for centerboard construction to determine if the well
can be maintained easily and if the board can be removed without
undergoing a traumatic experience each year. Also be certain that the
well interior is pre-conditioned during initial assembly to assure at least
a chance of indefinite life.

Quite frequently the appearance of an otherwise attractive steel hull
is spoiled by unimaginative bulwark, rail, and stanchion design. The
most common fault is to make too-convenient use of common pipe for
rails or angle capping for bulwarks when other forms and combinations
might be used. Pipe rails are, of course, quite strong, very practical, and
easy to install but sometimes possess a somewhat "tacky" appearance.
Some simple modification often transforms an ordinary pipe rail into a
stylish-looking unit. For example, instead of employing pipe vertical
members in a vertical railing system, the use of a tapered vertical flat
with a horizontal pipe nested into the top measurably improves the appearance of the whole assembly and gives a feeling of stability which

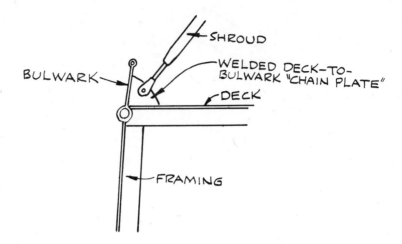

4-12. An alternate to the more conventional chainplate arrangement.

ordinary pipe verticals fail to convey. Also, the use of square or rectangular tubing for rail systems is more appealing than ordinary round pipe. The use of stainless steel tubing will immensely improve the deck area, as will combinations of flat steel rails capped with mahogany or teak. The possible railing combinations are legion and limited only by the imagination of the designer.

Steel offers versatility in chain-plate construction too, but occasionally one still comes across a design showing the old-time strapping down the sides of the vessel. With judgment, conventional chainplates can be eliminated altogether and replaced with other, more simple, ways of doing the job—and with equal or greater strength. One satisfactory method is to incorporate the plates into the bulwarks and decking or make use of the upper end of a transverse frame when its location is suitable. Another is to provide a bar welded to the sheer and drilled at whatever spacing required to receive the shrouds, or alternately, if the hull design permits, simply extend the side plates a few inches above the sheer line for the same purpose. Padeyes welded to the deck are also satisfactory for this purpose, so long as the deck is adequately welded and stiffened locally to take the strain. Even padeyes welded to the tops of bulwarks are, quite often, adequate. A properly welded bulwark, even a very light one, possesses great strength in vertical tension usually far in excess of the shrouds.

The subject of ventilation was mentioned earlier when bulkheads were discussed but, perhaps, can stand a little reiteration here. It is

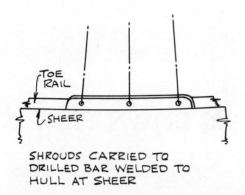

SHROUDS CARRIED TO
DRILLED BAR WELDED TO
HULL AT SHEER

4-13. The chainplate as a welded bar above the hull plating.

highly desirable that all portions of one's boat be easy of access and that air can circulate to every crevice and cranny, particularly when the boat is laid up for protracted periods. Inspect the proposed design to make certain that no area is perpetually sealed off, or is impossible to inspect or reach. In very few cases is it really necessary to close completely a space so that one can never get at it again except by a major operation. Even where insulation is employed, some arrangement should be made so the metal in back of the insulation can be occasionally looked at, and so that the insulation is not acting as a built-in condensing unit for moisture accumulation. I have found that many of the interior failures in steel boats, where accumulations of rust promote accelerated decay, were due to one of three causes, or a combination of them: (1) failure to prepare properly the surface in the very beginning, (2) sealing off the area to all circulation of air, and (3) the omission of provision for drainage of moisture from the bilge, condensation, or other sources. Of these, adequate ventilation is of the utmost importance. It is incredible how frequently unnecessary interior corrosion is encountered, a local area converted to a mass of rust, when by the simple expedient of permitting reasonable access and ventilation there would be no problem at all. This problem is inexcusable, really, but a point so seldom considered by both builders and designers that it is worth special mention here. No one would dream of living in a house in which the cellar was partly filled with water or in which the walls were perpetually wet with accumulated dew; nor should a comparable situation exist in a boat, whatever the material of construction. A steel boat, given half a chance, will be drier and sweeter than a wood one; it is a simple matter to keep it so.

5 LAYING DOWN THE LINES

Having assured ourselves that the proposed boat is suitable for steel, that its construction is going to be practical and will conform to the basic principles of reasonableness and simplicity, and that it isn't going to cost a fortune to translate into reality, it is time to prepare to lay down the lines.

Now, basically the art of laying down the lines of a steel boat is no different than doing the same job for any other boat and, in some cases, may be somewhat simpler. However, it should be borne in mind at all times that steel is less forgiving of error than some other materials and that one doesn't twist it, bend it, sand it off, or add to it, quite as readily to adjust mistakes, and that, also, every segment of the boat must be brought into acceptable spacing for welding. This, practically, means that every joint in the metal, whether of frames, plating, or other parts, must match within narrow fractions of an inch. If they do not, if wide gaps in weld zones must be filled with weld metal, inevitably distortion will occur, the strength of the welds will be in question, or welding may be more time-consuming or laborious. Further, errors in layout seem to have the faculty of compounding themselves, of becoming progressively aggravated until one ends up with a hull that is not fair or in which unsightly wrinkles, puckers, or bulges are common. In a wood boat, a bulge can be easily planed or sanded off, or a hollow can be filled with a glued piece; in a steel boat, a deviation of only 1/8" can be unpleasantly eye-catching.

Therefore, be prepared to lay down the lines as accurately as human frailty will permit and also be prepared to transfer the laid-down lines to the actual members of the boat with the same degree of meticulousness. Failure to do so will cause a lot of agony later on, some of it perhaps irretrievable, or nearly so.

If this sounds frightening to the novice, it need not be. It is actually no more difficult to measure to 1/32" than to 1/16" or to 1/8" or 1/4", for that matter. Practically, however, most layout measurements from the table of offsets provided by designers are to 1/8" tolerances. However, carelessness in fairing out the lines, or in marking the layout floor, can easily translate from 1/8" in the offsets to 1/4" in the lines to any old distance in the fabricated frames or hull. The lines must be correct to start with; the finished hull will only be as good as the lines originally prepared for it.

The first requirement of lofting is a place to lay the lines on. Ideally, a smooth, wooden floor as long as the boat and as high as the profile and as wide as half of the beam is desirable. Practically, except in a yard with a regular mold loft, such a floor is rarely available, or conveniently available close to the scene of actual construction. However, a very practical substitute can be arranged utilizing sheets of ordinary plywood laid down in convenient units to make up the area necessary. The sheets should have sufficient thickness to support thin nails driven into them without bending. One-half-inch plywood does very nicely. The sheets may be used later for bulkheading, partitions, cabin soling, cabinet tops, or any number of uses. The sheets should be laid down so they will not move until the layout work is complete, and a coat of flat, white paint on the layout surface will make the lines readily visible.

Before making up the layout floor, a decision should be made whether the boat is going to be laid out full scale, one-quarter scale, one-half scale, or some other fraction of full scale. This will depend to some degree on the size of the finished boat. A seventy-five-foot boat, for example, laid out full scale will use an inordinate amount of shop space and the use, in this case, of a full-scale layout is not readily necessary. It is necessary, however, to lay out all transverse sections full scale, but the profile of the boat and the half-breadth may be reduced, longitudinally, to whatever floor space is available or convenient. In fact, any errors in fairing the longitudinal lines will become more evident on a partial-scale layout than with a full-scale layout and, hence, can actually be more accurate. Of course, some longitudinal segments such as the stem profile, keel, etc., will have to be laid out full scale for fabrication, but these may be accurately picked off the reduced layout and either transferred directly to the actual members being fabricated or laid out full scale on the layout floor, where they can be superimposed over the original lines. In this case use of a different colored pencil will permit easy visual separation of lines which otherwise might become confusing.

The lines as supplied by the architect on the drawings should next be scrutinized to determine (1) if the measurements provided in the table of offsets are projected from a baseline or from above or below a given design waterline, and (2) if the measurements are to the inside or outside of the plating. If from a baseline, a true, straight baseline must be drawn on the floor, or, if plywood is used, the bottom edge of the joined sheets may become the baseline, provided they are lined up precisely. The simplest and most accurate way of securing a straight baseline is to stretch a straight chalkline, or wire, and using this as a guide mark off suitable distances to be ruled off with a true straightedge, or adjust the plywood edges to conform exactly to the stretched wire. If a waterline is the source of all measurements, it may be achieved similarly with a chalkline or wire. So, also, may the centerline for the half-breadth lines; usually the baseline and the centerline can coincide or be used for either purpose.

When measurements are given to the *outside* of the plating, care must be taken to deduct the thickness of the plating when laying out the frames, or, conversely, the amount must be added when given to the *inside* of the plating to arrive at the outside dimensions of the hull. Noting this properly can be of critical importance later when the lines are "picked up" for frame fabrication.

For some reason, the table of offsets often mystifies the novice, but it need not. The table is only a series of measurements taken as accurately as possible by the architect from his original drawings to give the distances of the essential boat segments, such as the bottom or top of the keel, the chine, sheer, bulwarks, rail, cabin trunk, etc., from the centerline or baseline, or from a waterline as designated. They are usually given in feet, inches, and eighths of an inch; sometimes a metric system is used, though rarely in the United States. The accuracy of offset tables varies a great deal, depending on the care of the architect in scaling his measurements and sometimes how good his eyesight may be. It is not unique to find errors in the offsets; these become readily visible when the lines are laid out. Corrections must be made on the layout floor so that the lines are fair and the curves run smoothly from point to point.

No table of offsets, however, will be of value, nor will the lines be fair, unless the station lines are laid out accurately. Once the centerlines, baselines, and waterlines are laid down, the next procedure is to erect the station lines at exactly ninety degrees to these lines. The station lines are simply imaginary lines or planes that transversely intersect the axis of the boat much as if it was cut into a series of segments like the slices

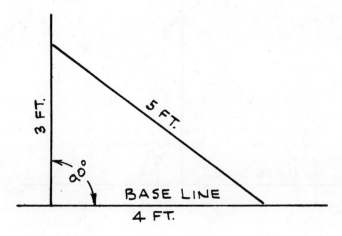

3 FT.

5 FT.

90°

BASE LINE

4 FT.

5-1. The 3-4-5 method of determining a 90° angle to the baseline.

of a loaf of bread. The station lines sometimes coincide with the framing lines; many times they do not. Frequently they are evenly spaced, though not always. But evenly spaced or not, they serve to provide location points for the offset measurements given for each station. Unless the station lines are truly vertical to the centerline, baseline, or waterline, all the offset measurements taken to them will be inaccurate, and the boat will not be in accordance with the drawing.

Erecting a vertical station line is quite simple but so often not done. It is not enough to use an ordinary carpenter's square for this purpose. Unless one has a very large true square, or goes to the trouble of making one, the results are dubious. Station lines may easily be erected correctly (1) by use of the so-called 3-4-5 method or (2) by use of the scribed-arc intersection method. In the 3-4-5 method, a distance from the proposed location of the first station line (on the baseline, centerline, or waterline) is measured in any multiple of four feet. Then a tentative vertical station line is drawn, very lightly if by pencil, or by use of a chalkline, and a similar multiple of three feet is marked on it. If it is truly square, a line drawn diagonally between the two points will measure exactly the same multiple of five feet. If not, adjust the tentative station line until it does. Once a single station line is truly vertical, the others may be struck by simple measurement parallel to the baseline or waterline.

The scribed-arc intersection technique merely uses the old geometric principle of intersecting arcs. Measure any given distance each way on

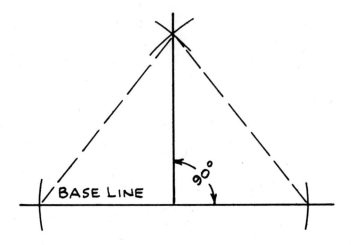

5-2. The scribed-arc intersection method of determining a 90° angle to the baseline.

the baseline from the location of the proposed station line, or by striking an arc. Then increase the length of the compass arm and strike two short arcs above the original mark on the baseline. Where they intersect will be directly above the spot on the baseline.

With the baseline, waterline, and station lines accurately drawn, the next procedure is to begin to project the actual lines, usually, but not necessarily, beginning with the profile. This is a simple procedure. Measuring precisely from the baseline or waterline, the measurements given in the table of offsets for each station are marked on the designated station line, the bottom and top of the keel, the chine (if a chine boat), the main sheer, top of the bulwarks, cabin trunk, or whatever segments of the boat are provided in the table. On each of these marks is then vertically driven a thin finishing type nail to sufficient depth to hold it firmly in the wood but leaving enough projecting to provide stiffness against a bent wood or plastic batten. Similar points for the keel, chine, sheer, etc. are then marked and nailed for each of the stations.

Several battens will be required—a fairly pliant one for short curves, a less flexible one for easy sweeps. The battens should be as long as convenient to handle, or as long as available. It is important that they be free of defects such as knots, uneven grain, or other faults that would interfere with their curving smoothly when bent.

Beginning with the sheer line, a batten is then bent so that it curves smoothly from sheer nail to sheer nail at successive stations. It may be held in place by driving another nail immediately adjacent to it (but not through the batten) at each station location. The batten should have enough length so that a minimum of six stations are spanned, preferably more. Then, when temporarily fixed in position, a sighting should be taken along its length to determine if the curvature is "sweet and true." If it is not, a nail should be pulled at the station, or stations, where there are lumps and hollows or other unseemly discontinuities, until the sweep is fair and easy. All laid-out lines should end up fair; that is, they should run their courses evenly, smoothly, and unoffendingly to a critical eye. The sheer line is then drawn along the batten, and the batten moved fore or aft, depending on the starting point, and the line extended in the same manner except that at least three points of the original line should be overlapped to insure easy continuity. When the entire sheer line for the entire length of the boat is completed, the full sweep should be viewed for possible unfairness and corrected again if needed.

The other lines for the chine, trunk, top of the deck curvature, keel, etc., are done in the same way. In the case of round-bottom boats, there may be additional lines to run, such as buttock lines, but the basic procedure is the same.

However, before the elevation or profile is completed, it will be necessary to draw in the stem and connect it with the keel or forebody of the boat and to expand the transom. Usually the designer will provide dimensions for the bow and bowsprit assembly, if there is one, or for locating points from which the stem curves may be achieved with battens precisely like the other lines, except that thinner and more pliant battens will be required for the shorter and more severe curves.

Before the transom can be expanded or projected to full size, it will be desirable to next develop the half-breadth. The half-breadth is a view of one-half of the boat from either side of the centerline looking from directly above it, or conversely, directly below looking up. The table of offsets provides dimensions for each station precisely as in the profile, except that instead of being given from a baseline or a waterline they are given from the centerline of the boat. For convenience, the profile baseline may be used as the half-breadth centerline. This will save time later on when the body plan or cross section is worked up.

Then, marking from the baseline at each station, the offset dimensions for the half-breadth are marked out and nailed, and then battens bent and lines drawn for the sheer, cabin trunks, bulwarks, chine, and keel just as was done for the profile. With this completed, the transom, or, more conveniently, half of it may be expanded full scale.

Usually the transom will be sloped and sometimes curved, and the problem is to translate this to a flat plane which, when templated, cut, and curved will fair precisely into the main body of the boat. At first inspection this may seem complicated but really is not. The first step, if the transom is not curved, is to strike the slope of the transom on the profile with the top marked and the bottom joining the keel at the proper place. Then, where the sheer line intersects the slope of the transom, a line is projected in either direction at 90° to the transom slope. Similar projected lines are struck parallel to this, also at 90°, for the chine or chines, if the boat is a multiple-chine one, and for waterlines if the boat is of round cross-section. Then going back to the completed half-breadth lines, pick off the distances for each of these points by measurement, or with a straight batten stick, from the centerline to the outside edge of the boat where they intersect the transom slope. These distances are then marked on the appropriate 90° parallel lines and may then be connected with a straightedge in the case of single- or multiple-chine boats, or with a curved batten in the case of a round-bottomed craft.

One other line must be struck—the deck curvature. This can be done simply by bending a batten from the top of the transom to the sheer. However, to achieve a smooth parabolic curve, the sheer 90° line should be extended the full half-breadth distance of the sheer on the opposite side of the transom-slope line. The batten may then be bent between the three points and the result will be a proper curve. With this accomplished, the result should be a development of half of the transom from which a full transom may be templated and cut.

This all, however, becomes a little more complicated when the transom is to be curved, as most of them will be, particularly in sailing craft. If one is lucky, the architect's drawings may include a fully expanded, fully dimensioned, curved transom; frequently, though, it is not given and it is up to the builder to arrive at his own.

A curved transom may be envisioned, practically, as a partial section of a cylinder, and in laying out a curved transom the thought must be kept in mind that a curved surface when laid flat, as for cutting on a piece of steel, occupies a larger area than the same projection, as described above, for a flat transom. In effect, because of the inherent arc in any portion of a cylinder, the projected lines, such as were described in the method for flat transoms, "stretch out" and must be compensated for accurately if one is not to end up with a transom too small to fit properly or which "pinches in." There are a variety of methods, some complicated, for arriving at the amount of "stretch out."

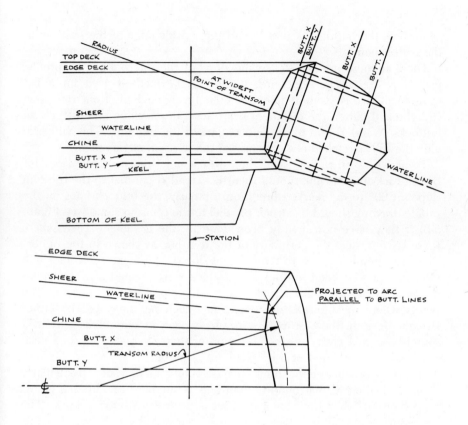

5-3. *The profile and half-breadth of the after end of a vessel with a curved transom.*

Probably one of the simplest can be explained by reference to the sketch of the after lines of a hard-chine boat shown in Figure 5-3. This drawing shows in separate detail the profile of the after end of the craft and the half-breadth of the same area. Also shown is the transom radius on the profile as specified by the designer. With this same radius, using the centerline of the half-breadth plan as the centerline of the arc, strike the radius at or about the widest part of the transom, in this case the sheer. Also shown in the half-breadth and profile plans are two buttock lines, *Y* and *X* (in an actual layout there may be several more, but for simplicity here the number will be limited to two). Bend a batten around the radius as it is shown on the half-breadth plan and mark on it the centerline, the buttocks X and Y, and the outside edge of the transom at the widest point.

Then, at right angles (90°) to the slope of the transom on the profile, project a straight line outward, similar to the method used for a flat transom. On this straight line can then be marked off from the now-straightened batten the distances from the transom-slope line to the two buttocks, X and Y, and to the widest part of the transom. This will provide the full "stretched-out" expanse of the transom at this point.

To arrive at other points on the "stretch out," the marked places for the buttocks on this line should then be extended parallel to the transom slope (at 90° to the marked line) and, similarly, the buttock lines on the profile drawing should be struck parallel to the transom slope (see Figure 5-3) if they have not already been done by the designer. Then where these last intersect the periphery of the transom, as shown in the profile, they are extended at 90° to the transom slope. These extended lines will intersect the expanded buttock lines, which were erected at right angles to the original radius line struck at the widest part of the transom. The points where the intersections occur may then be connected by either straight lines, in the case of a hard-chine boat, or curved battens in a round-bottomed craft, or a combination of these, to show the final periphery of the expanded or "stretched-out" transom.

In actual practice, depending on the contour of the boat, particularly if one is dealing with a round-bottom hull, a number of additional points must be established both for waterlines and for extra buttock lines. The procedure is exactly the same and can be repeated for each set of points required. Where waterlines cross the transom, project its intersection with the edge of the transom on the profile at 90° to the slope of the transom (parallel to the buttock lines). Then, on the half-breadth plan, again parallel to the buttocks, project the waterline from where it intersects the transom to the original radius-arc line at the widest part of the transom. This will then give the length of the arc at that point. The arc length is then transferred (by straightened batten) to the line at 90 degrees to the transom slope. The periphery point is marked and is ready to be connected to other waterline points or other points on the periphery, such as the chine, sheer, etc. (see Figure 5-3).

We have now produced the profile, the half-breadth, and the expanded transom of the boat. The drawings will also show a body plan or cross-section of the boat, giving the appearance of the body as viewed from midship to the stem and from midships to the stern. This may be worked out on the wood layout floor if desired, but unless more than one boat of

74

a design is planned and one wishes to make permanent frame moulds, this may be eliminated and the work done directly on the framing floor, where the actual frames are fabricated. Indeed, this latter practice is likely to be, in the long run, more accurate than the double effort of reproducing patterns or moulds and translating them to fabricated frames. The profile and the half-breadth provide all the measurements and information needed to begin actual fabrication.

6 FABRICATING THE KEEL AND THE FRAMING

The actual beginning of steel boat construction, like the laying down of the lines, should be governed by accurate work. Improper practices at this stage will pose all sorts of problems later. It is not enough simply to mark off some chalk lines on a wood or concrete floor and expect to end up with frames, longitudinals, sheer members or other parts that will be true or fair in respect to each other.

There are three basic reference lines that control the position of every segment of a boat: (1) a baseline or waterline, (2) a longitudinal centerline, and (3) a vertical centerline.

Every component and member must be precisely related to these three control lines and when they are, they will, automatically, be properly located in respect to each other. Therefore, at the very beginning, provision should be made at the sites of erection, and of fabrication, that these controls be fixed and available for ready reference at any time. The two most convenient and useful references are: (1) a tight, thin wire strung longitudinally above the main axis of the boat from which plumb bobs may be suspended, and (2) vertical centerlines and horizontal waterlines and/or baselines *scribed* at 90° on a steel plate or plates laid flat on the fabrication floor.

The steel plate need not be a permanent fixture, but can be made up from one or more pieces of future shell plating. These sheets should be, collectively, as wide as the completed boat and as high as the hull and keel as seen in cross-section, and they should be tack-welded together to prevent them from moving during frame fabrication. When joined, a baseline should be struck, or the bottom edge used as a baseline, provided, that is, that the bottom edge of the plate is true. The waterline should also be struck precisely parallel to the baseline, and the vertical centerline erected at exactly 90° to the base and waterline. These lines should be permanently scribed with a steel or carbide-tipped scribe; by so doing they will not be erased and can be relocated easily at any time.

The scribe is a most useful instrument and should be used constantly in preference to soapstone, chalk, or the crayon commonly used for marking steel. A scribed line is very accurate, and one can cut steel and grind to a scribed line to very close tolerances not possible with other marking methods. It may be argued that a scribed line is not easy to see, particularly with cutting goggles on, but this is not true. With any reasonable lighting and clean goggles, a scribed line is quite visible and has the added advantage of not disappearing from the heat or blast of a cutting torch. Also, unless the line has actually been cut out, it is still visible after the cut has been made and serves as a guide for accurate grinding to a precision line. I have cut many hundreds of feet of steel without difficulty and to close tolerances using scribed lines.

With the master floor plate down and scribed with the appropriate centerline, waterline, and baseline, the guide lines for the frames may be laid out one at a time, or in groups if preferred. This is done precisely as it would be if the body plan were laid out on the wood layout floor.

The simplest procedure is to use a straight wooden stick, square on one end, to serve as a baseline point. Mark the load waterline on the the stick and then, a frame at a time, mark off accurately from the profile plan and the half-breadth the locations of the bottom of the keel, the width of the keel, the top, the sheer, the chine, the edge of the deck, the top of the deck, the edge and top of the cabin trunk, extra waterlines, or any other points of significance. As each point is marked a brief symbol should be written beside it designating what it is, whether it is for the half-breadth or profile, and what station or frame is involved. Thus, typically, "6 chine HB" would indicate frame 6 at the chine on the half-breadth drawing. This will avoid confusion or error during transfer to the master floor plate.

With the stick so marked, the various points may now be transferred. Beginning with the keel, the stick can be matched with the permanent base and waterline marks on the steel master plate and the bottom of the keel marked by a punch mark to either side of the vertical centerline at a distance slightly greater than the actual width of the keel. The two punch marks are then joined by a scribed line, and then on this line the half-breadth width is marked off from each side of the centerline. These points are then punch-marked and will provide accurately the width and height of the bottom of the keel at that station. The top of the keel is achieved in the same way as is the chine (or chines if a multiple

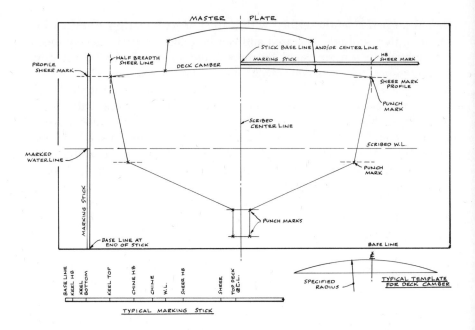

6-1. *A master plate, marking stick, and deck camber template.*

chine boat), the sheer, the location of the cabin trunk sides, or any other basic points in the cross section of the boat at that particular frame. Figure 6-1 shows a typical set of marks and lines, together with the use of a master stick to locate the sheer points. Once the various points are punched and marked they may be connected by scribed or chalked lines that will portray the shape of the cross-section.

The deck or cabin top cambers are usually given by the designer, and a template, as long as the width of the widest frame, can be cut to the specified radius and used successively for each frame. However, frequently, particularly in cabin tops, the radius may not be constant, as it is usually in decking and must be arrived at individually for each frame. Practically, unless there is some unusual configuration, the camber can be arrived at by simply taking a batten and bending it smoothly between the top mark of the cabin at the centerline and the paired, opposite points at the edge of the top of the cabin trunk. These curves will fair nicely from one frame to another as they follow a natural parabola.

At this point, we should now have a precise tracing of the periphery of the particular frame and of the keel outlined on the master plate. Some additional location marks will be required, and it is best to deline-

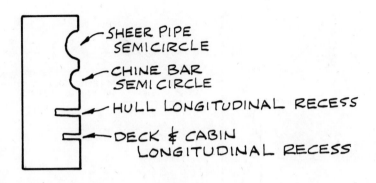

SHEER PIPE SEMICIRCLE

CHINE BAR SEMI CIRCLE

HULL LONGITUDINAL RECESS

DECK & CABIN LONGITUDINAL RECESS

6-2. *A recess template.*

ate these before beginning fabrication of the actual frame. Reference to the construction drawing will reveal, or should reveal, the locations of the longitudinals, the size and shape of the gussets, if any, and probably the positions of sheer pipe or guards, water cooling systems, or other recesses or protuberances. Of course, the frame can be fabricated and the various notches or recesses, such as for the longitudinals, cut after the frames are in place, but this is not likely to be nearly as accurate or as convenient as doing it while the frame is being put together, for reasons of distortion if no other. It is much easier to cut and weld, or straighten, if warpage has occured, while the frame, or its segments, is flat than after partial or full assembly.

Assuming, as is consistent with good practice, that longitudinals are to be used, and, also, probably a chine bar and a sheer pipe, it is convenient to make up a recess template for scribing these after their locations are marked. This saves time and ensures that each torch-cut segment will be correct. Figure 6-2 shows a typical template for this purpose.

Depending upon the designer, most longitudinals will be evenly spaced, typically, twelve to eighteen inches for boats between thirty to seventy-five feet, and will parallel the sweep of the sheer from the chine or waterline up. Bottom, deck, and cabin top longitudinals often parallel the centerline but may sweep in curves. In either case the locations should be accurately determined, either by laying their position lines on the profile and half-breadth plans or by other measurement.

With this done, the individual segments to make up the frame may now be cut. The first step is to make up whatever keel segment might be called for, such as a spacer piece to hold the sides of the keel apart (and together) for a box keel in a sailboat hull. The shape can be arrived at by either templating or laying a suitable piece of steel over the

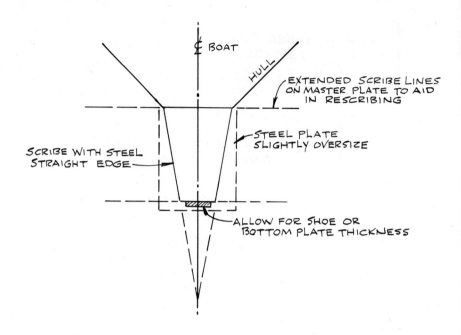

ℒ BOAT

HULL

EXTENDED SCRIBE LINES
ON MASTER PLATE TO AID
IN RESCRIBING

STEEL PLATE
SLIGHTLY OVERSIZE

SCRIBE WITH STEEL
STRAIGHT EDGE

ALLOW FOR SHOE OR
BOTTOM PLATE THICKNESS

6-3. Scribing the shape of a keel spacer piece.

scribed lines and rescribing from the original (see Figure 6-3). The boat's vertical centerline should also be scribed on the piece as a future refer-ence. The oversize plate can now be cut, as close to the scribed lines as possible, and then ground down to finish tolerances with a hand power wheel. The piece should also be beveled by the grinding wheel where it joins the remainder of the frame unless it is quite thin (1/8″ or less). This is to insure good welding penetration. This subject will be discussed in detail later, together with torch cutting practices in the next chapter.

With the completed keel piece cut, finished, and laid on the lines to match, the actual frame bars can now be cut. For simplicity of illustra-tion, a chine boat frame will be considered, and in this instance the simplest practice is first to cut from flat bar stock the paired bottom pieces slightly longer than final size. They are then laid on the scribed frame lines and adjusted until they match the outside frame lines exactly. A decision is then made about the cuts for the ends of the pieces. There is a tendency here with the novice to make joints as in wood with long overlapping edges, but this is usually not necessary in steel because, once welded properly, the joint is virtually as strong as the original members. The simplest practice then is to make the shortest cut that will

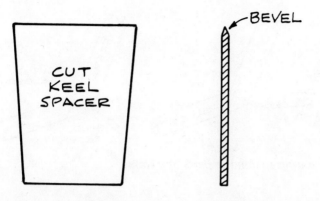

BEVEL

CUT
KEEL
SPACER

6-4. *A beveled keel spacer piece.*

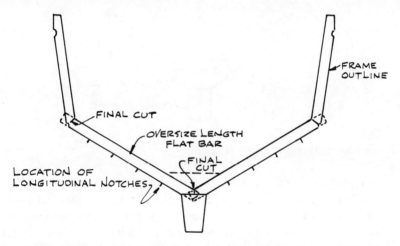

FRAME
OUTLINE

FINAL CUT

OVERSIZE LENGTH
FLAT BAR

FINAL
CUT

LOCATION OF
LONGITUDINAL NOTCHES

6-5. *A frame made from flat bar stock, with final cuts made after the parts are matched to the scribed frame lines.*

make a proper junction with the next mating piece. This is a better practice than overlapping the mating members, although overlapping can be strong enough. Overlapped joints in frames only add unnecessary weight and create a frame which does not lie completely flat and which, later, may pose finishing problems.

The shape of the cuts adjacent to the keel will be governed by the presence of, or absence of, a floor piece. A floor piece may carry fully

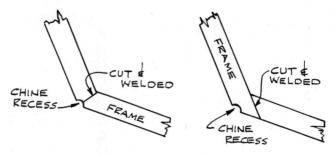

6-6.   *Two ways to join the parts of a frame.*

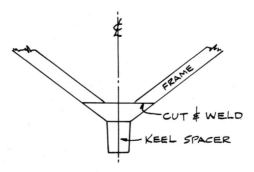

6-7.   *A floor that overlaps the frame.*

out to the periphery of the frame and the flat bar segments joined to the top, as in Figure 6-7, or they may be continued and the floor piece matched into them, as in Figure 6-8. The best advice is to use whatever rule of joining that requires the least cutting and welding. The same rule will apply to watertank ends or baffles that may be an integral part of a frame, as in Figure 6-9.

After the first pieces are cut and properly beveled at the weld joints, they may then be laid on the scribed lines and checked for accuracy of cut, and the longitudinal or other recesses can be marked off with the recess-template. The required notches are then cut with the cutting torch, the piece allowed to cool, and then laid again on the master plate. Quite likely, because of changes in stresses due to the cutting operation, the notched flat bars will no longer be straight, but will have a slight camber (see Figure 6-10). This will have to be corrected or ultimately the skin plating will show slight dimpling at each frame and may be unsightly. The easiest way to correct this is to place the piece on edge

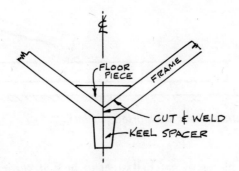

6-8. *A floor matched into the frame.*

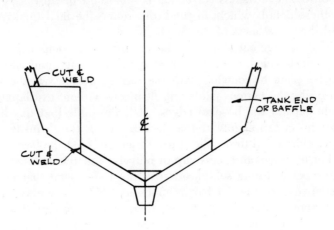

6-9. *Joining watertank ends or baffles to a frame.*

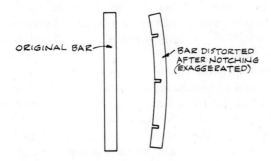

6-10. *Distortion in a flat bar after it has been notched.*

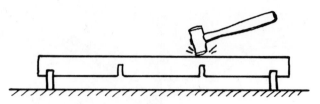

6-11. *Straightening out a distorted flat bar.*

between two pieces of notched steel to hold it vertical and tap lightly with a maul or hammer until the curvature is removed (see Figure 6-11).

While this may seem a minor matter, the distortion being only 1/8″ or 3/16″, nevertheless correction is important because it is the attention to these details which, in total, determine the final quality of the work and the smoothness of the finished hull.

Thus, a segment at a time, the several frame components are individually cut, beveled, corrected for shape if necessary, and laid down on the master plate to coincide with the scribed outline. If the work is done precisely, the various joints will fit nicely without overlapping or having wide gaps at the beveled edges. It is desirable that this be so because poor fit-up can aggravate the stresses and/or the shrinkage created during welding and throw the entire frame out of shape (see Figure 6-12).

For example, an excess gap of only 1/8″ at the weld zone can initiate a shrinkage during solidification of the weld metal that may distort the distant end of the flat bar as much as 3/4″ in a length of four or five feet, sometimes even more. So, then, it is important that the weld fits are good and that the individual segments lie flat and in precise position on the master plate. Before welding, if desired, they may be lightly tacked to the master plate to keep them from moving. I prefer not to do this because, if distortion occurs, it is best seen during the weld-up and corrected when first evident, rather than having the whole frame spring out of shape after full welding is completed and the restraining tacks have been cut away.

Among the components usually comprising the frame are the curved deck supports, cabin-top carlings, and the like. These deck pieces may be torch-cut out of flat plate if desired, but a more realistic practice, if the deck is designed to a uniform camber, is to order these pieces pre-curved cold to the specified curve. This insures that each deck beam is to the same radius and is usually much less expensive than the labor of cutting in the shop. Almost any steel distributor will have a source to have this done when the steel is originally ordered. Of course, notching for the longitudinals may create some change of shape, but this may be corrected readily by the same method as used in other components.

Unless the frame is quite small, after it is welded on the master plate, it will have to be handled and must be temporarily supported both before and during frame-up on the keel. Wide frames, for all of their ultimate strength, can be quite flexible and springy as they come off the floor and need some temporary stiffening if they are to retain their shape precisely. The most convenient way to do this is to provide one or more steel angles and lightly weld them to the frame. Most useful is a steel angle welded vertically with one edge positioned exactly on the centerline on the master plate. This not only keeps the frame from sagging vertically but also provides a place to clamp a spirit level to align the frame during erection on the keel (see Figure 6-13).

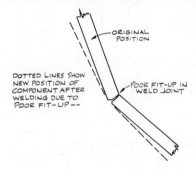

6-12. *The change in shape of a frame because of poor fit-up in the weld joint.*

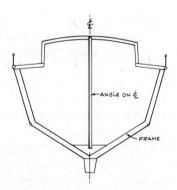

6-13. *A temporary steel angle lightly welded on the centerline.*

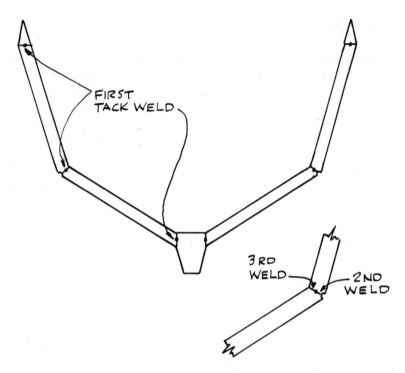

FIRST
TACK WELD

3RD
WELD

2ND
WELD

6-14.   Using tack welds to prevent distortion.

With all the pieces carefully placed on the master plate and the supporting angle, or angles, in position, the frame is now ready for welding. The problem is to accomplish welding without distortion and a careful welding sequence is highly desirable. If one should simply proceed from one weld joint to another and weld them together, the result, likely, would be unusable, or at best unusable without some heating and rebending.

While there is no certain sequence, I have developed one which has been successful and can be suggested pending a better method. This is to proceed from one weld joint to the next and place a small tack weld in the *center* of each joint and at the ends of the angle stiffeners (see Figure 6-14). This will tightly lock the segments together without pulling them appreciably one way or another. Then, when the first welds have cooled, begin at any given point and weld from the outside to the center, then quickly, without pausing, weld from the inside to the center. This equalizes the shrinkage stresses in both directions. The

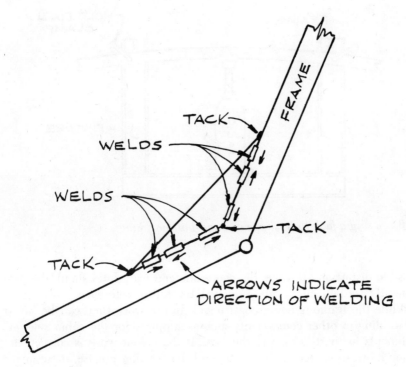

6-15. Welding a gusset.

remaining joints are done in the same way. When cooled, the entire frame can be lifted with a tackle and turned over and the sequence repeated on the opposite side.

The construction drawing may call for gussets at the chine or deck. Gussets may be overlapped, but it is a cleaner and neater practice to weld them flat on the same plane as the rest of the frame. Like the other joints the gussets should be cut, beveled, and fitted nicely before welding. If the gusset joints are long, it may not be advisable to weld the entire joint at once but instead to tack and make several short opposing welds (see Figure 6-15).

In many cases, gussets are a hold-over from wooden construction and not really necessary unless the area is to be subjected to stresses in excess of those exerted against the remainder of the frame. Unnecessary gussets merely take up space and complicate interior finish-work later.

With the welding done on both sides and the welds ground smooth, if desired, the frame should now be rechecked on the master plate for

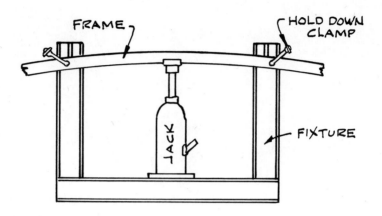

6-16.   Using a jack to re-shape a round-bottom frame.

possible distortion. If none, the centerline and waterlines should be permanently scribed and center-punched for future reference.

While the frame is being constructed, future work time can be saved by welding in other components such as supports for the cabin sole, attachments for partitions, and the like. If the layout work is correct, the frame fabrication free of distortion, and the erection precise, these members will fall exactly in place when the boat is fully framed.

The procedure for round-bottom frames is essentially no different, except that the frame segments will have to be torch-cut from flat-plate stock to the proper curvatures or cambered from flat-bar stock, either cold on a press of some sort or by local heating and bending. In general, torch-cutting is the quickest and most economical method, but some re-shaping will almost invariably be required because of distortion caused by the heat of cutting or the release of stresses inherent in the metal. For light re-shaping, an inexpensive press can be fabricated by welding up a fixture of channels or angles to hold the work and by utilizing a hydraulic or screw jack (see Figure 6-16).

If the piece to be re-shaped cannot readily be formed cold, a little judicious local heating with the torch will usually solve the problem. It is suggested that, in most cases, the local heating be done on the *compression* side of the metal and to no greater depth than necessary to accomplish the bend desired. This, ordinarily, produces a smoother curve than heat applied to the tension side. In severe bending, red heat applied to the tension side may cause local tearing or cracks. Another way of producing a curve is to hammer cold the outside of the arc in a succession of relatively light blows until the desired curve is obtained. Needless to say, frames for a round-bottom boat are more laborious and difficult to fabricate than for hard- or multiple-chine craft.

When the frames are complete they can be temporarily stored or stacked while the keel is being fabricated and the stem made ready. At this point, the master plate can be removed if floor space is at a premium, as it usually is, and stored out of the way. Unless a frame is damaged or done incorrectly, it will not be needed again.

The Keel

Depending upon the design of the boat, whether it is sail or power, for commercial or pleasure use, steel keels are used in a variety of forms and shapes. Commonly, they will be box keels—most frequently in sailing craft, made hollow to carry ballast loads—or bar keels, which are simple, solid, flat bars or plates erected vertically on edge and usually thin in cross-section. Some large powerboats may have no exterior keel at all except for a skeg aft and will depend, instead, on either a bar erected vertically on a flat, horizontal, keel plate or a conventional I-beam running almost the entire length of the vessel.

The simple, straight, bar keel or I-beam keel fabrication is uncomplicated, and little more is required than to cut them to the required length and to scribe carefully on them the location of the frames. Box keels are not so simple to make and should be given the same meticulous care as frames. Some box keels are open at the top for access to ballast or other storage; some are completely closed by a top plate; some are

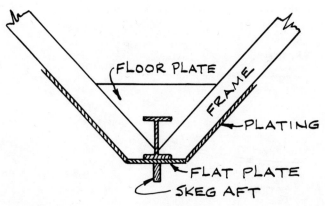

6-17. An I-beam keel.

used for fuel or water tankage. Also, some will carry a heavy bottom plate for weight or ballast reasons. Box keels may be fabricated by either of two basic systems: (1) by assembling the entire keel as a separate unit on which the frames, stem, and transom are subsequently installed, or (2) by erecting the frames with the keel spacers welded on, as described earlier, and attaching these to the keel bottom plate laid down first in position to the proper slope (if any), and subsequently plating the keel sides. The method used is mostly a matter of judgment and, also is governed by the size of the boat and by the handling equipment available. Where practical, however, I prefer to assemble the entire keel and all its components separately before framing-up.

Welding is so much easier when the entire assembly can be positioned in any direction, rather than trying to stand on one's head in an attempt to reach the deep and narrow recesses of the keel when it is in its final position, and immovable. Also such items as shaft tubes and the like can be placed with more accuracy and with less effort, when the assembly is movable.

The first step in assembling the box keel is to template the entire profile of the keel from the layout floor full scale so the shape may be transferred to the steel plates for cutting. If the layout was done full scale longitudinally, templating may proceed directly. If not, the keel should be laid out full scale over the original reduced lines, preferably in a pencil whose color is distinct from the rest of the layout.

Templating may be done with a variety of materials ranging all the way from stiff paper or cardboard to thin plywood or even sheet metal. I prefer thin "masonite" or hardboard, as it is sometimes called, because it is stiff enough for handling in large sections, can be drilled or bolted together easily, can be planed or sanded to a close line, and has about

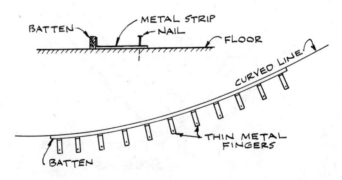

6-18.   *Using a batten with metal flanges to lay down a curved line.*

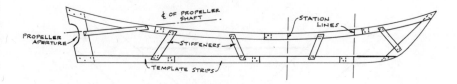

6-19. A template for a sailboat keel.

the same bending characteristics as steel. Also, it is not quite as likely to expand or contract with weather changes as some other template stocks. This is important because a template 20-feet long made up on a dry day can enlarge or distort overnight as much as 1/2″ if the humidity changes drastically.

The least wasteful method of templating a keel or other large member is to cut the template hardboard into strips 12″ to 15″ wide depending upon the size of the template required, or as wide as necessary to strike off the necessary curves. The individual strips may then be laid on the full-scale layout, nailed temporarily in place, and the lines rescribed on their surfaces. There are several methods of doing this: (1) drive nails on the station lines just as was done in the original layout work and re-batten and scribe, or (2) use a batten with numerous metal "fingers," bend it to the original curve, nail it in place at the finger ends, and then slip the template strips under it for marking (see Figure 6-18).

The marked template piece can then be cut to the desired shape, returned to the layout drawing, checked for accuracy, and again temporarily nailed. The adjoining pieces are similarly cut and laid down with an overlap until the entire assembly is in place. The overlapped joints can then be drilled and bolted securely with small bolts, together with whatever reinforcing pieces might be necessary to prevent distortion from handling. The final step is to mark off the station or framing lines, the centerline of the propeller shaft, or any other lines of importance to the final assembly.

During templating of keels which are relatively thick in one area and thin fore or aft, allowance should be made for this curvature. The extra length required may be secured from the half-breadth lines and compensated for. Otherwise the keel may turn out a trifle short or some of the frames may be a little out of their proper position. Figure 6-19 shows a typical template for a sailboat keel.

The template can now be transferred to the steel and the metal scribed ready for cutting, grinding, and beveling at the joints, if any.

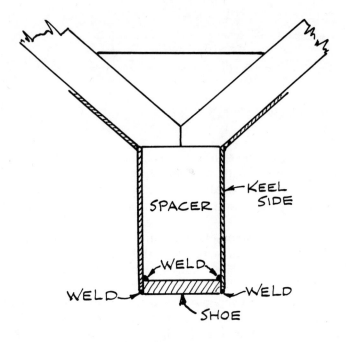

6-20. A square-bottom box keel.

The procedure for the fabrication of the keel assembly will vary, of
course, with the particular make-up of the keel, whether there is a heavy
shoe or not, whether the bottom is rounded or square, the shape of the
leading edge, and the like. Most box keels, fortunately, are square at the
bottom, which simplifies fabrication a great deal, and the sides are usually joined to a fairly heavy flat bar, sometimes several inches thick (see
Figure 6-20). This is a convenient arrangement for sailing vessels that
need weight at this point. However, if the design requires a rounded
bottom or rounded leading edge, this may be achieved by use of a split
pipe, whole pipe, or round bar section. (see Figure 6-21). Unless you
are building a racing machine, there are few advantages to a round-
edged keel to compensate for the extra labor and material necessary to
make one.

Probably, your most important job during the making of a keel is to
insure that the entire assembly is true and accurate. It might seem that
a structure as massive as a keel is unlikely to be otherwise, but this is not
necessarily true. Injudicious welding or overwelding can pull a keel out
of shape even when a heavy shoe is employed. Because keels are in-

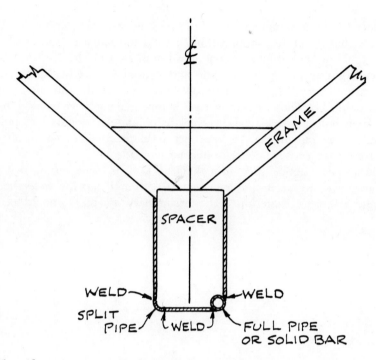

6-21. *Alternate ways of achieving a rounded-bottom box keel.*

An open box keel in a sailboat. Notice the handling of the transverse and longitudinal framing.

herently heavy, it is human nature to avoid moving them any more than possible during fabrication and thus to weld too much in one area at a given time. A keel to be any good at all must be straight; it may not be if you begin welding on one side and continue there without giving equal attention to the other, or if you do not reverse the direction of the welds or do not allow welds to cool before making new ones. I have seen keels with massive shoes, as thick as 3" and as wide as 12", pulled several inches out of true by improper weld practices in which all the shrinkage stresses were concentrated on one side.

The proper practice, then, in making up keels is to be certain that the various pieces are accurately cut to start with and that the weld shoe is straight to a true centerline. The preliminary assembly should be no

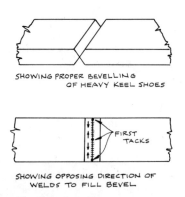

SHOWING PROPER BEVELLING
OF HEAVY KEEL SHOES

SHOWING OPPOSING DIRECTION OF
WELDS TO FILL BEVEL

6-22. *Welding heavy keel shoes.*

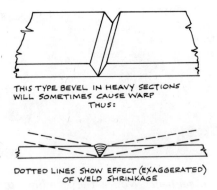

THIS TYPE BEVEL IN HEAVY SECTIONS
WILL SOMETIMES CAUSE WARP
THUS:

DOTTED LINES SHOW EFFECT (EXAGGERATED)
OF WELD SHRINKAGE

6-23. *Warpage in an improper bevel for a heavy keel shoe.*

94

more than tack-welded, enough to allow turning and positioning; then welding should proceed in small segments. Weld in paired, opposing or mated sections, never laying down too much weld metal at a time, aiming constantly at equalization or cancellation of welding shrinkage stresses by reversal of weld direction, never laying a new weld bead until adjacent old beads and the neighboring metal is cooled. If this is done meticulously, if the keel is turned constantly for best welding position as the work progresses, you will end with a keel that is truly accurate and not shaped side-winded. Frequently, one hears of boats that seem to steer preferentially in one direction; usually this is due to a crooked keel, to sloppy work at some stage of keel construction.

A note of caution should be added about welding very heavy shoe pieces together. In spite of their massiveness and bulk, they are very easy to warp out of shape and almost impossible, short of re-cutting, to straighten. They should be beveled at the joints from both sides, carefully fitted and tacked, then welded from opposing sides in quick sequence, as in the manner described for welding frames. They should then be turned over and the process repeated, then turned again until the bevels are filled (see Figure 6-22). An improper bevel in heavy sections will sometimes create warp (see Figure 6-23).

The entire keel assembly, with dividers, separators, propeller aperture, stern tube, and the like is now ready for erection and ready to receive the stem, transom, and frames. It has been assumed during this discussion that the boat will be built upright and in the position it will rest in the water, that the waterlines, both fore and aft, and transversely, will be level. There are some advocates of building boats upside down, undoubtedly, in certain materials this makes work easier. However, except in cases of mass production, I feel that the benefits of this for steel is questionable and the disadvantages usually outweigh the gain. The prime argument advanced is that welding is easier done downhand and that by having the boat upside down the outside seams are easier to do.

This I feel, is an untenable argument because (1) as welding progresses it should be done intermittently inside and out, and (2) upside-down welding is not as difficult as the practitioners of the art would have us believe. For the relatively small amount of upside-down welding involved, the labor of turning a hull upside-down and back again is simply not worth the effort. If a large production series of boats is contemplated, and large rotating jigs are employed to aid unskilled welders, this may be worthwhile but is of little value when the number of boats to be built is limited.

7 TORCH CUTTING AND WELDING

Before proceeding further into this discussion, it is desirable, if not imperative, that some attention be given to both welding and cutting techniques and that there be a reasonable understanding of both. The creation of a steel boat, its soundness, and its appearance, are directly related to these two arts. Failure to observe certain basic rules can be disastrous, or at least the genesis of a host of troubles.

The Cutting Torch

The cutting torch is a frequently misused and abused piece of equipment, but it is also a highly developed and precise instrument that will perform a variety of tasks if used with common sense. Not the least of these is its ability to cut metal quickly, neatly, and inexpensively. For making curved shapes, for beveling of heavy sections, piercing, and local heating, it is the most practical tool in the steel boat builder's kit.

In essence, the working part is only a well-adjusted flame. The mechanical torch and the gauges are merely devices to meter the ignitable gases and to direct and control their flow. The first step in understanding the cutting torch is to learn how to adjust its flame so that (1) it produces great local heat without waste of gas, and (2) it is controllable for cutting. For this, two ingredients are essential: (1) a properly proportioned mixture of gases, and (2) a clean cutting tip. The torch itself contains a trigger for actuating the flow of oxygen for actual cutting, a tip through which flows a mixture of preheating gases, and an orifice for oxygen flow.

The mixture of gases to the torch must be precise for best results; most failures in precision cutting are due to improper gas combinations. The most common fault of inexperienced operators is to use too high a fuel mixture (acetylene, propane, etc.) in relation to the oxygen. The industry freely supplies data cards that show the proper proportions for the size of tip in relation to the thickness of metal to be cut. The rule is that the thicker the metal, the larger the tip needed, and the more gas pressure required, particularly oxygen. The pressure of fuel gas (acetylene, propane), however, does not increase with metal thickness as quickly as oxygen, though, of course, the amount does. Typically, the gas pressures in relation to metal thicknesses are about as indicated in Table 2.

Table 2

Metal Thickness	Tip Size	Lbs. psi Acetylene	Lbs. psi Oxygen
⅛″	00	3	30
¼″	0	3	30
⅜″	1	3	30
½″	1	3	40
¾″	2	3	40
1 ″	2	3	50
1½″	3	3	45
2 ″	3	3	50

Very little acetylene pressure is necessary, and both oxygen and acetylene should, for reasons of economy, be kept at the lowest pressures practical to maintain quick and clean cuts.

A proper flame can be recognized by simply looking at it through the cutting goggles, which, for safety, should be worn at all times, including preliminary adjustment of the flame. Improper balance of gases creates a "feather," which can be instantly recognized. A feathered flame will not cut properly, although such a flame can be useful for other purposes, such as silver soldering or brazing. The proper procedure is to (1) turn on the acetylene first at the tank, (2) turn on the oxygen, and (3) adjust the gauges to the recommended pressures for the thickness of steel involved. (*Warning:* never lubricate or oil gas gauges; pure oxygen can be explosive in contact with oil). With gloves on and the torch in hand, open the acetylene valve first and ignite the gas with a flint lighter (do not use matches). The first flame will be yellow and smoky but the opening of the main oxygen valve and gentle adjustment of the secondary control will change the long, yellow flame to a blue one with a feather (see Figure 7-1).

Adjust the flame further until the light blue feather just disappears, and then press the oxygen trigger. If the feather reappears, adjust the

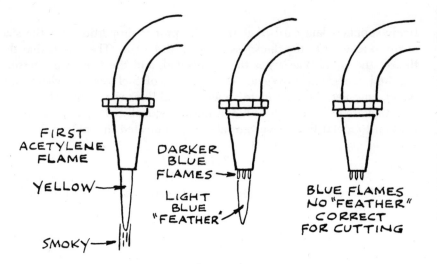

FIRST
ACETYLENE
FLAME

YELLOW

SMOKY

DARKER
BLUE
FLAMES

LIGHT
BLUE
"FEATHER"

BLUE FLAMES
NO "FEATHER"
CORRECT
FOR CUTTING

7-1. Adjusting the cutting flame.

control some more until, with the oxygen fully on, no feather is present. The torch should now be ready for cutting. If the flame "pops" and suddenly goes out, the pressure may not be correct or there may be dirt or slag on the tip. The cutting tips should be kept clean at all times with the correct size cleaners; an unclean tip will create a ragged cut or no cut at all. Precision cutting is possible only with correct proportions of gas and with clean equipment. Constant cleaning is a requirement of good work.

With the flame adjusted, the actual cutting can begin. The torch is brought into contact with the work until the preheating flames bring a small local area to red heat, then the oxygen trigger is depressed and the cut started. As rapidly as possible the torch is advanced; too fast and cutting stops; too slow and gas is wasted and excess slag is accumulated in or under the kerf. A little experience will reveal the correct speed; cutting should proceed at a smooth, constant rate. The making of precision cuts is primarily a matter of having the torch in comfortable or balanced control. Use both hands, one for the torch and one to steady and guide, and to relieve weight so the unit is free to move in any direction or to rotate as desired. Also, arrange the hoses so there is no drag or strain from them. With a little practice, there is no problem maintaining a cut to a scribed line or to within 1/64" of it. For long cuts, both the body and hands will need to be re-positioned frequently.

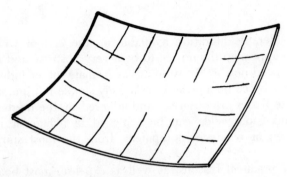

7-2. *"Dishing" of flat metal from cutting.*

When completed, the underside of the cut will usually have a small amount of slag hanging from it. This can be readily removed simply by stroking it with the flat blade of a chipping hammer or with the edge of a grinding wheel. If the slag is difficult to remove, or must be hammered away, the probability is either that the gas pressures were not correct, the cutting speed was too slow, or the torch tip was not clean. Precision cutting should always be done on a clean surface. Heavily scaled or rusty surfaces are not conducive to precision work, nor can good cutting be expected through heavily painted surfaces.

With proper cutting on clean work, to carefully laid-down scribed lines, very little subsequent grinding, filing, or other conditioning should be necessary before assembly. However, during cutting it should be remembered that the mere act of cutting produces heat. Heated metal expands and then contracts when cooled, and sometimes cutting will locally alter the stress patterns inherent in the metal. Cutting too much at once, or cutting parallel or adjacent surfaces while they are still hot can produce distortion. A good general rule is to allow newly cut metal to cool to room temperature before beginning additional cuts and to "balance" the sequence of cutting to minimize stresses set up by heat. This is not particularly a problem with large, wide sheets or plates but can occur with narrow pieces.

Cutting, because of progressive contraction of the cooling metal immediately adjacent to the cut, will sometimes curve or "dish" a flat piece of metal. This can be common with thin-gauge stock, 1/8″ or less; such "dishing," however, can be controlled by lightly tapping the edges with a hammer, thus locally expanding the recently cut metal until the plate flattens out.

Welding

There is considerable literature available on the arts of welding and, indeed, it can appear to the novice to be a very abstruse and mystifying technique. It need not be. In welding, as in many other industrial arts, good practice is based on a series of relatively simple but important principles. If these basics are observed and adhered to, the mystery quickly disappears and good welds can be achieved by whatever method of welding is used or whatever equipment, from the most simple to the complex.

Because for practical reasons, as well as expense, most boat welding within the context of this book will be done by electric-arc stick-type coated electrodes, the discussion will center around this method. The rules, however, are fundamental and will apply generally to other welding systems. The basic principles, not necessarily in order of importance, are these:

1. The composition of the weld metal laid down must be compatible with the metal being welded.

2. The metal to be welded must be clean and free of extraneous substances, such as other metals, slag, scale, rust, paint, or chemicals.

3. The metal to be welded should be fitted so that full penetration of the weld zone is possible, so that no voids or hidden cracks or other stress-raisers are created.

4. The method of laying down the weld metal should be such that (a) there is adequate heat to melt and fuse both the weld metal and its joint, (b) the direction of welding is such that there is full penetration of metal to the root of the joint, (c) that the weld is free of entrapped slag, gas bubbles, or other porosity, and (d) that the shape of the final weld bead is such as not to promote notch-stress failure or have an excessive contour that will be unsightly or require excess grinding for appearance.

5. The sequence of welding should be such as to minimize or eliminate undue distortion.

The selection of the type of electrode to use—whether the electrode is wire, as used in various types of automatic welders or gas-shielded "gun" machines, or, most versatile of all, the common stick weld-rod—should be governed by the composition of the laid-down weld metal produced from the electrode. It is important that the completed weld be as close in composition as practical to the metal to be welded and have as many of the properties of the original metal as possible. It would not do, for example, to lay down a weld of excessively high carbon steel in a mild steel joint, because, while that weld might look satisfactory and have

100

excellent tensile strength, it might also be brittle under impact or at low temperatures. Similarly, it would not be wise to lay down a weld of such composition that there might be preferential corrosive attack in the weld zone due to dissimilarity of the weld to the surrounding metal. There are a variety of weld rods available for the ordinary mild steels commonly used in boat work. They differ primarily in that they have very slight modifications of carbon content and flux coatings. Some flux coatings are less prone to produce spatter during the welding, some are reputed better for poor fit-up, some for easier slag removal, some for vertical down, or up, or overhead welding, some for fast deposition, and the like.

This may seem confusing, but to be practical, most boat work in mild steel can be done with class E6010, E6011, E6012, or E6013 electrodes. The letter "E" indicates metal arc-welding electrodes, the first two digits denote the tensile strength derived from all-weld-metal tension tests, and the last two digits indicate the usability. Almost all electrodes carry some such identification code. It is not within the scope of this book to provide all the code numbers or the special characteristics and properties of each type of rod. Any well-established electrode supplier can supply this information on request.

The use of any one type of electrode will depend to a great degree on the personal preference of the welder as well as the specific situation involved. I prefer, for example, E6012 because it is versatile in all positions and produces deposits with a minimum of spatter.

Indeed, a long dissertation could be written on electrodes alone. However, the decision about what to use will lie in the nature of the metal to be welded and the specific problem involved. For high-tensile steels, the manufacturers will usually recommend the proper electrodes or signify a choice. In selecting a weld rod, the architect's drawings should be checked as to whether the weld rods must meet certain specifications, such as delineated by the American Welding Society (AMS), the American Society For Testing Materials (ASTM), the U.S. Coast Guard, the Bureau of Ships, Lloyds, or other groups.

There are situations where the welding of dissimilar metals is required, particularly the stainless steels to mild steel for trim, rails, bulwark tops, stanchions, and the like. Here, the choice is to use a stainless rod generally of higher alloy content than the stainless alloy to be welded. This is to compensate for dilution of the stainless deposit and to provide ductility to prevent cracking where dissimilar metals are joined. Usually stainless boat trim is of the so-called 18-8 (18% chromium - 8% nickel) or 18-12-Mo (18% chromium, 12% nickel, 3% molybdenum) varieties. Ameri-

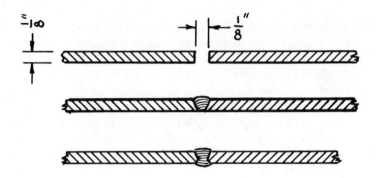

7-3. *A light-metal weld. (Top) Proper spacing. (Center) Cross-section after the first pass. (Bottom) Completed weld after the bottom pass.*

can Welding Society class 308, 309, 310, or 316 electrodes will take care of most situations. However, because the stainless steels comprise such a variety of diverse metals, care should be taken to insure (1) that the proper grade of stainless steel is used in the first place, and (2) that the rod type is applicable to the specific metals to be mated. Suppliers will gladly provide guidance if needed beyond the information available in numerous stainless steel handbooks and the standard welding textbooks.

Flux-coated electrodes should be kept dry. The use of wet or damp electrodes can be the cause of porous welds or even welds afflicted with what is known as "hydrogen embrittlement." Embrittled welds have little ductility and may crack or fail under impact or stress. For the same reason, all weld joints should be dry and free of entrapped moisture during the welding operation. In very damp climates, it is advisable at times to bake electrodes before use; an ordinary oven is quite suitable for this

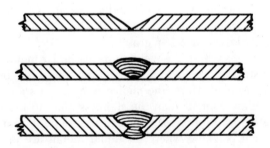

7-4. *A thicker metal weld. (Top) Proper bevel. (Center) Weld on one side. (Bottom) Completed weld after the bottom pass.*

7-5.   Completed thick-metal weld.

purpose. Electrodes should always be stored in a dry place, preferably in sealed containers.

Another cause of porous welds is failure to weld on a clean surface. Old scale, zinc or other coatings, paint, grease, liquids, or semi-solids can all be the cause of porosity. Any questionable surface or joint should be dried, wire brushed, or ground clean.

A great deal of attention should be paid to proper fit-up, since so many cases of weld failure or severe distortion can be traced to this cause. There is very little excuse for poor fit-up. If the original layout work is done properly, as has been stressed repeatedly in this book, and if accurate templating and cutting is done, the various parts and plates will fall nicely into the proper spacing for welding. I have frequently seen mating plates with 1/2″ or more of gap to be filled with weld metal. A common and sleazy practice, often resorted to by careless or indifferent workmen, is to fill such gaps with stick electrodes, or metal scraps or slivers, and weld them together. The result is always dubious and should never be permitted under any circumstances.

The proper spacing for good welding is governed largely by the thickness of the metal involved, with the criterion always being proper penetration of the weld metal with no cracks or voids at the roots of the welds when they are completed. As a general rule of thumb, light metals, 1/8″ or less, can be spaced a distance about equal to their thickness, or slightly less (see Figure 7-3). For thicker metal, 3/16″ to about 3/8″, it is desirable to bevel one side of the joint (see Figure 7-4). In heavier cross-sections, both sides should be beveled as in Figure 7-5 for full penetration, and several passes made when necessary to fill the beveled void. Of course, when multiple passes are required, thorough slag cleaning should be done between each pass to insure proper bonding and to avoid slag entrapment. Except for some massive pieces such as stem segments, keel pieces, and the like, relatively little work of this sort is required on the average boat within the purview of this volume.

Angle joints should be handled much the same way as straight joints and butted so that the corner of the angle may be fully filled with weld metal (see Figure 7-6).

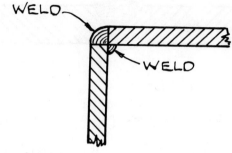

7-6. *Weld in an angle joint.*

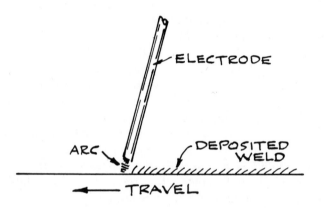

7-7. *An electrode tilted in the direction of travel.*

Because many of the readers of this book will be boatbuilders under-taking their welding for the first time, some mention should be made about the mechanics of laying down weld beads. Welding, in most cases, is not very difficult although some practitioners of the art would have us believe otherwise. This applies to upside-down welds as well as to welds in other positions. Indeed, in boat work, a great many welds will neces-sarily have to be made in the upside-down position. All it requires is a little practice.

Assuming that the proper machine settings have been made and that a good grade of electrode has been selected, the rest is primarily a mat-ter of a sense of touch and a gauge of distance. Because an electrode is being constantly consumed it must be fed into the work at a steady and constant speed and at such a rate that a constant gap between the arc and the work is maintained. It is important, then, that the welder be in as relaxed a position as practical, that his hand be steady but free to move, much as one would guide a pencil, except, of course, that the pencil is held in its middle instead of its end. As in torch cutting, the use of a second hand to provide steadiness is usually a help.

For some reason, novices frequently find starting an arc difficult. Sometimes the electrode will stick to the work; this will occur if the electrode is held against the work an instant too long. The proper technique is to touch the work lightly, much as one would strike a match with a light stroke; then the instant the arc forms, retract the electrode slightly, about 1/8" or so and begin welding. In a brief second or so, the best distance for molten metal flow will be seen and this distance should then be maintained for the duration of the weld. With a little practice, beginning and maintaining the arc will become second nature and almost automatic.

The angle the electrode is held in relation to the weld is also of importance because this will control, to a degree, not only the amount of metal laid down at any given spot but also the shape of the finished weld. While there is no blanket rule about this, usually, for most welds, best results occur when the electrode is tilted slightly in the direction of travel. Also, frequently, the electrode will be given a slight weaving motion, particularly in fillet welds. There are numerous exceptions to this rule, depending on conditions and the individual situation. Whatever electrode direction is used, the final criterion is the penetration and the appearance of the finished product.

A properly laid-down weld bead will possess a slightly convex, slightly rippled surface (see Figure 7-8). To be avoided are highly convex beads that overlap their joints or are lumpy, as they may act as stress-raisers and possibly initiate cracks if located in highly stressed areas or areas subject to continual vibration. Such beads also may entrap moisture or contaminants and eventually become focuses for corrosive attack. Such unsightly beads are usually due to either inadequate heat during welding or simple pile-up of excess metal due to inexperienced welding, or both. Amateur welders often believe that using plenty of weld metal at a joint produces a stronger weld, and they will produce heavy and massive beads. Actually, a heavy bead seldom is strong; a proper weld of correct contour is very nearly as strong as the parent metal. Adding excess and unnecessary metal may only introduce undesirable effects.

One of the indexes of a good weld being laid down is the facility with which the molten pool "wets" the surface of the weld joint. With proper

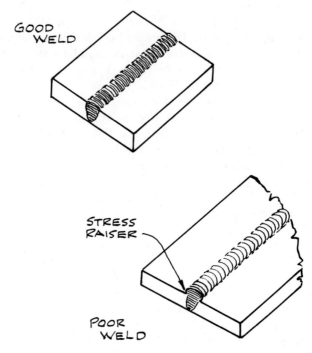

7-8. *The difference in appearance between a good weld and a poor weld.*

heat and a good arc, the molten metal can be seen flowing readily and joining smoothly to the weld zone. There is no tendency for the metal to "lump" or fail to become one with the mating surfaces. However, if oppositely the molten pool appears to become watery or to run like quicksilver, particularly in vertical welds, this is an indication of the entrapment of slag or other contaminants. The cure then is to stop immediately, clean or grind out the weld area, and begin again.

Weld-rod position as well as proper heat will also control the nature of vertical, horizontal, or upside-down welds. With proper voltage and amperage settings (best determined for each individual machine and individual situation), the molten metal coming from the electrode will seem to flow, and often even to "push" toward the weld joint. Thus a slight upward and forward tilt to the weld rod while doing horizontal welds will often eliminate undercutting on the upper side of these welds. Undercutting is caused by the sagging of the molten weld pool by

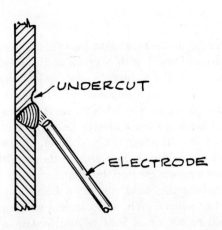

7-9. An undercut on the upper side of a horizontal weld.

gravity before solidification. It also may be caused by amperage that is too high and a molten pool that is too hot.

A slight upward tilt to the rod will make vertical welds easier when working from the top down. Now, certain welding codes do not permit vertical welding from the top down and insist on work being done from the bottom up. However, for small boats with light-gauge steel, a more satisfactory weld can be had by this method provided the welds are short (as they should be to prevent distortion) and are immediately stopped if there is any tendency of the weld metal to run. Just the right degree of electrode tilt and a slight weaving motion produces a sound, smooth weld that requires relatively little grinding to blend with the rest of the hull.

Surprisingly, upside-down welding with the weld rod held nearly vertical, but with a very slight forward tilt and a slight weaving motion, is easier than either horizontal or vertical work. Where bottom plating is to be upside-down welded, it is easiest to first weld inside downhand and then finish the weld vertically from the outside. Before doing so, it is important to clean out all slag created by the downhand weld before proceeding with the vertical upside-down part. This, is, of course, true of all welds done from opposite sides.

Frequently, where butt joints are made in plating, weld shrinkage will cause the spacing originally prepared to become too narrow for proper weld penetration. When this occurs, the joint should be opened up with the thin edge of a grinding disc or by other mechanical means. No welds should ever be made over tight butt joints, because the result will usually be an unsound weld with a crack at the root of the weld bead.

Shrinkage caused by the contraction of weld metal from the molten to the solid state is the prime bugaboo of steel boat builders. It is the main reason why so many steel boats are unnecessarily warped and "washboarded." Shrinkage must always be kept in mind while welding, and every means taken to minimize or compensate for its effects. While an individual weld may shrink only a mere thousandths of an inch or so upon cooling, the stresses created by that shrinkage can be enormous. The "pull" of a solidifying weld can often be measured in many thousands of pounds per square inch, and careless welding can distort a valuable hull beyond repair, or at least beyond repair as far as appearance is concerned.

As an illustration, if two steel plates are laid side by side, properly spaced for welding, and then welding is begun at one end and done continuously, the first few inches will irretrievably close the gap at the other, or even cause the edges to overlap and ride over each other, possibly for several inches. If the gap is then artificially forced open, the plates will buckle or create an unsightly warp.

This, in effect, is what would happen to one's new boat if proper welding sequence is not used or if the welds laid down were not arranged to oppose or counteract each other. New steel is an exceedingly strong material, but its yield strength can be locally exceeded by the accumulated forces of weld shrinkage applied in concentrated directions. Therefore, it should be a cardinal rule in small boat building that at no time, unless experience has dictated otherwise, are continuous welds to be made without regard to their total effect. Continuous, long welds are frequently made with success in large ship building, in steamers and military craft, where the relation of steel and ship size to weldments may make it possible, but in small boats it is usually disastrous—disastrous, that is, unless one intends to plaster one's boat with many pounds of putty or filler to round out the cavities. A steel boat, properly welded, will require no cavity filler whatsoever, and will end up as smooth as when the welding was begun. This can be achieved in large part by never laying down more than two or three inches of weld metal at a given point, by never welding adjacent to these points until they have cooled, by welding adjacent welds in opposite directions so their directional stresses and shrinkages are canceled, and by welding opposite sides in the same manner.

It should also be a fixed rule not to overweld a boat. A boat should have every weld necessary to insure its integrity under all conditions,

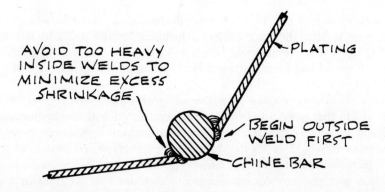

7-10. A joint where the side and bottom plates meet a chine bar. Here, the welding should be done on the outside first.

but no more. There is no point in using continuous welds where intermittent welds are more than adequate, or in using a 3/16″ electrode to fill a seam, which would properly be done with a 1/8″ rod, or "wash in" a big gap with an excess of weld metal when a proper fit-up would have been better. A great many poor-appearing steel boats have had the very be-devil welded out of them and would have turned out rather well if some common sense were employed.

There are certain types of weld joints that are more prone to excessive shrinkage than others. "T" joints and angle joints are in this category and so, also, are joints where relatively thin sections are welded to massive ones, such as the joints where side and bottom plates are welded to chine bars. In such sections, it is preferred practice to do the bulk of the outside welding first, where there is likely to be less shrinkage "pull," and then do the inside later with as small an electrode as reasonable compatible with the size of the plates involved (see Figure 7-10).

A word is in order here for the reader who has no intention of donning a welding helmet or of striking an arc, but who expects instead to hire a professional welder for his job. It should be borne in mind that a great many so-called "professional" welders are professional in name only, or only because they may work eight hours a day at welding on jobs that have no relation to the care which should be given to boat work. A great many are trained to lay down as much weld metal a day as possible in construction where production is an aim in itself. Many have little or no understanding of distortion or its causes, although they may be perfectly capable of laying down beautiful weld beads. One incompetent welder can ruin a multi-thousand-dollar boat in short order. If a man is hired because he has a welding "certificate" and is caught laying down continuous weld beads as fast as the machine will let him, fire him out of hand and get another if you value the appearance of your finished product.

This is not meant as an aspersion on professional welders, but it is a fact of life that many of them are not acquainted with the requirements of good boat work, particularly yacht work where appearance is of first moment. It would be better to take an inexperienced man and train him properly than to try and convert a thoroughly "brain-washed" production welder. Anyone can learn the mechanics of welding in a few days; good boat work requires, in addition, an ability to learn and a pride in workmanship.

8 SETTING UP THE KEEL AND FRAMING

Sooner or later, whether the finished boat is to be produced on a shop floor or outside with no cover, it will be necessary to move it either to launching rails or to the place where it is to be put into the water. Unless a mobile lift is available, it is very convenient as a first step to fabricate a cradle for this purpose and then set up the new keel on it rather than cradle the entire boat when it is finished. Both keel and frames are going to require temporary supports during frame-up and plating, and a cradle provides a useful base for this purpose, at least for a substantial section of the boat. I usually use a steel cradle because (1) it is quickly and easily put together and will stand a great deal of stress during moving, (2) it costs no more than one of wood of comparable strength, and (3) temporary or permanent supports can be welded to it or removed more quickly and easier than by bolting to wood. Six-inch H-beams properly spaced make a convenient cradle and are quite rigid, even for boats in the 50- to 60-foot class or more. Such cradles are normally made of two longitudinal "runner" beams and an appropriate number of transverse members.

Another preliminary convenience is to weld some short angles with the corners up on the transverse pieces where the keel is to be set (see Figure 8-1). the keel will then rest on narrow points, and this will later save jacking up the entire boat to sandblast the bottom of the keel where it rests on the cradle's transverse beams.

The cradle should be set up level, secured or wedged, so it cannot move during construction and then two plumb verticals should be erected at each end of the boat for holding a tightly stretched centerline for hanging plumb bobs. Of course, if the boat is built inside a building, the centerline can be strung from one end of the building to the other.

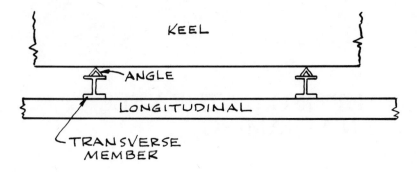

8-1. *Setting up the keel on short angles.*

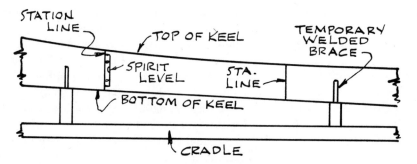

8-2. *Determining the proper slope of the keel.*

The fabricated keel, or as much of it as practical, may now be positioned precisely below the centerline and trued up so that it is not only centered on the centerline fore and aft but also vertical from the base to the top. If the keel is parallel to the waterline, it may be merely centered longitudinally and vertically on the level cradle, but if the keel is sloped from aft forward, as so many sailing craft keels are, it must be given precisely the right tilt. One of the simplest ways to arrive at this is to use the pre-scribed station lines, marked on the keel as suggested during the layout work, as guides. A vertical "level" may be held against these lines and the keel gently jacked up at one end until the level bubbles show the scribed lines to be truly vertical. When this occurs the keel slope will be correct (see Figure 8-2).

Once the keel has been exactly positioned it should be secured firmly by temporary chocks or braces welded so no further movement can occur during construction.

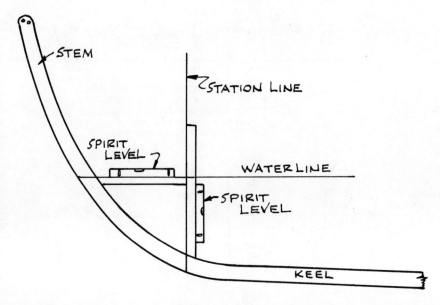

8-3. Two metal strips tack-welded to the stem to aid in aligning the stem properly.

This may all seem very obvious but, as has been repeatedly noted, the quality of a steel boat is predicated on accurate work. Precisely positioned keels and framing, held rigidly in place, will make subsequent work easier and quicker and the end result more pleasing. Also, it must be remembered, the stresses of construction can easily pull loosely fixed pieces out of alignment. With the keel locked firmly in position, the stem may now be raised. Here again, positioning is important. Centering with plumb bobs is simple enough, but obtaining the correct upward sweep can be troublesome and sometimes optically deceptive if sight alone is depended on. One convenient method is to temporarily tack-weld two strips of metal to the stem while it is being fabricated on the layout floor. One piece should be precisely parallel to the waterline, or baseline, and the other parallel or contiguous to a vertical station line (see Figure 8-3). The after end of the stem can then be set roughly in position where it joins the keel and the forward end raised until a level placed on the horizontal strip shows it to be truly level or the vertical one truly vertical. Then, when the stem is exactly centered longitudinally under the centerline and is joined to the centerline of the keel, it will exactly occupy the position it should in the finished boat. It should

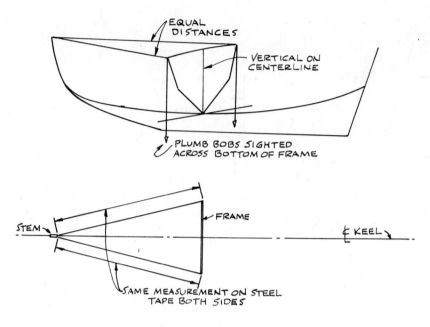

8-4. *Setting up a prefabricated frame on the keel.*

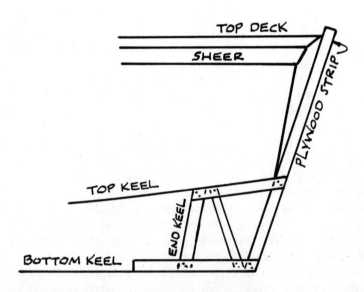

8-5. *Typical template for determining the slope of a curved sailboat transom.*

now be braced rigidly in position with temporary angles or other supports.

The first prefabricated frame can now be raised and set up on the keel so its bottom centerline coincides with the keel centerline. Again, a level can be used either against the temporary vertical support, suggested for frame fabrication, coincident with the vertical centerline, or on a straight-edge clamped or temporarly welded across the transverse waterlines. The frame is carefully inched up until it is level and vertical, both transversely and longitudinally. It can then be clamped temporarily in position with angles or other supports tack welded to the cradle, keel, or other convenient holding places, while the outboard edges are being positioned at exactly a 90° angle to the centerline of the boat.

This is not always as simple as it seems, because frames first set up sometimes have a tendency to be limber and may spring forward or aft at the sheer and at other outboard locations. One method of measurement is to fix a temporary nail or weld rod fragment to the top of the stem, attach a steel tape to it, and check that the opposite sides are equal and that a plumb bob hung from the outer edge of the frame may be sighted to correspond to the bottom of the frame where it rests on the centerline of the keel (see Figure 8-4).

It is not usually necessary to repeat this with all frames, but only one or two. I have found it convenient to raise the center frame first and then work forward and aft. The new frames going forward or aft, as the case may be, can then be spaced by simple measurement from the first erected frame. It is also common practice if the frames have projections, such as the sides of angles, to face these forward from the midsection of the boat to the stem and aft from the midsection to the stern. There is no requirement to do so, of course, if they serve their purposes better facing the opposite way. The general effect, however, is more ship-shape.

There are other methods of squaring the first frame: (1) ideally with a transit, or (2) by squaring off on the floor and dropping a plumb bob to the drawn floor line. But whatever means are employed, it is important that the frames all be vertical, transversely level to their waterlines, and square to the axis of the hull. They should also be firmly braced, because during plating and bending of the longitudinals, they may be under considerable pressure or stress. Steel angles make excellent bracing and are conveniently welded or removed by cutting.

The slope of the transom is usually easiest to arrive at by making a template of plywood or hardboard strips and raising the transom to fit. The template is derived from the layout drawing (see Figure 8-5).

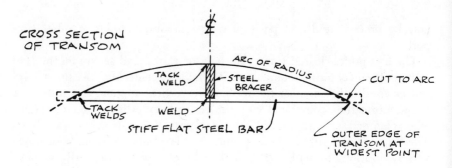

CROSS SECTION OF TRANSOM

ARC OF RADIUS

TACK WELD

STEEL BRACER

CUT TO ARC

TACK WELDS

WELD

STIFF FLAT STEEL BAR

OUTER EDGE OF TRANSOM AT WIDEST POINT

8-6.   *Fabricating a curved transom.*

A curved transom is best cut out and curved to its prescribed radius on the floor and then raised as a unit to its final position. Curving such a transom may be readily accomplished by striking the arc of radius across a flat bar of steel, cutting the curve at the ends with a torch, and then welding a bracer piece to the centerline of the arc (see Figure 8-6).

The bracer piece is then lightly welded to the centerline of the flat transom, which is then pulled with clamps until it joins the outer edges of the flat bar where it is temporarily welded in place. The transom will take a natural bend equal to the prescribed radius. The whole unit, bracer bars and all, can then be lifted in place, positioned as to slope and squareness to the axis of the hull, and thoroughly locked in place with angle supports. The bracer bars can be removed when the plating is done, and the transom will retain its original bent form. If any stiffeners are deemed necessary, they can be added then.

When the frames, stem, and transom are all up, thoroughly braced so they will not move, the sheer members, chine bars, if any, and longitudinals may be placed. Here again, careful work is important. Kinks or unfair bends in any of these members will be reflected in the plating and will show up as unpleasant defects in the finished hull, particularly if it is finished with a gloss paint.

The sheer members are the best place to begin, and they may take one of several common forms. Quite frequently, designers will use the deck itself as a sheer member, or a relatively narrow flat plate for that purpose if a wooden deck is to be used (see Figure 8-7), and will then split a section of pipe to be welded over the plating as a guard or rubrail. For some designs, particularly in modern-looking sailing yachts, no rubrail will be wanted and in these cases the flat plate alone is quite satisfactory. The sheer plate (or the deck plate) is derived from the layout floor, but remember that if the up-sweep of the sheer fore and aft is sub-

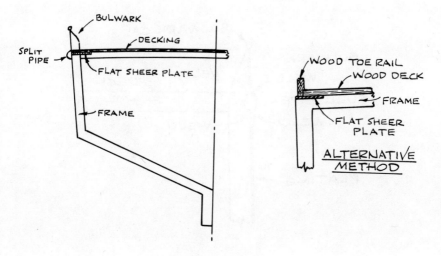

8-7. *Two ways of handling the sheer members.*

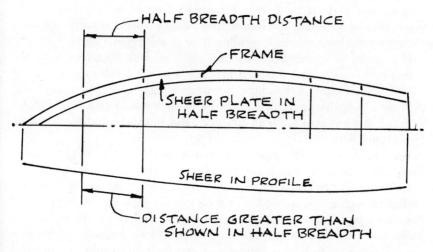

8-8. *Determining the length of the sheer plate.*

stantial, some additional length between frames must be allowed to compensate for the vertical curvature. Thus, the half-breadth curvature from which the deck plates are derived is not quite adequate when applied against the profile. So check the profile spacing between frames against the same spacing shown in the half-breadth. Otherwise the sheer plate may come out a little short (see Figure 8-8).

117

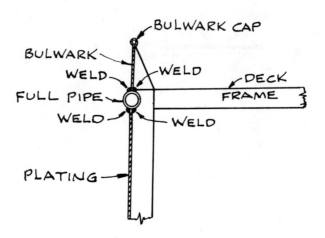

8-9.   A full pipe used as a rub rail (see also 4-8).

If a sheer plate is used, it is a simple matter of merely laying it in place, making sure that the frame lines coincide nicely with the squared frames themselves, and tack welding it so it will remain rigid.

If a guard is specified or desired, and the deck coincides with the sheer, as it usually does, the best practice is to use a *full* pipe instead of a split or half-pipe. A full pipe is much stronger and if bent cold will provide a smooth and natural curve between frames. Also it provides a convenient weld area for both the sides and bulwarks and for the deck (see Figure 8-9).

Bending a sheer pipe guard cold is not as difficult as might appear, even when the half-breadth curvatures seem considerable. Pipe will take a surprising degree of natural curvature before crimping, even heavy-wall pipe such as "Schedule 80." Of course, the pipe can be bent on the floor with pipe benders but this is not recommended, except in extreme cases. First of all, it is quite difficult to bend long lengths of pipe to a smooth sweep with a pipe bender and very easy to overdo it, causing a crimp that will be unpleasant to the eye. For appearance, the sheer curvature is one of the most critical parts of the boat.

Instead, it is better to weld together the full length of pipe required for each side of the boat, with perhaps a little extra. This should be done straight and flat on the floor and care should be taken that the weld joints are also true and straight. This may be accomplished easily by nesting the adjoining pipe ends to be welded in an angle and clamping them (see Figure 8-10).

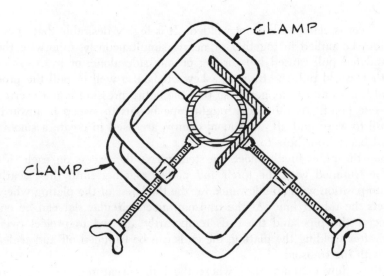

8-10. Pipe clamped in an angle during the welding of straight lengths.

Care should be taken that the welds are sound and that full penetration is achieved. Most black-iron pipe comes already beveled for welding; if not, proper end bevels should be ground. Also, a slight spacing between the pipe ends to allow for weld shrinkage will help. The joint can be partially welded, unclamped, rotated, reclamped, and finish welded. The result should be a straight, continuous pipe joint which, when the excess weld metal is ground off, is indistinguishable from the remainder of the pipe.

Now the entire length of pipe should be lifted at several points simultaneously so it cannot crimp because of its own weight, positioned roughly, and then nested in the midship frame slot previously prepared for it. In this position, the pipe will be hanging roughly parallel to the axis of the boat. It should now be clamped to the midship frame, checked to determine if it nests in its semicircular slot nicely, and then tack welded. *Do not weld it completely in place;* tack weld it only enough to hold it. This is important and is equally important at each of the successive frames. Failure to observe this will inevitably result in a crimped member.

Next, leave the pipe hanging from its temporary slings and raise the other pipe on the opposite side of the hull and similarly tack weld it in place. Then, progressively, one frame at a time going both forward and aft, pull in the port and starboard pipes together with clamps until the entire sheer is clamped but not welded. It is highly desirable that opposite sides be pulled in together or nearly simultaneously, otherwise the accumulated pull caused by working on one side alone, or in excess of the other, could pull the framing askew. It is also well to pull the pipe several frames at a time, gently so that the entire pressure is not exerted all at one point. As the once-straight pipe begins to sweep in towards the hull forward and aft, additional clamps are used to create a smooth natural bend from bow to stern.

When the pipes finally meet the stem piece, the excess on each side may be trimmed with the torch and pulled together until they neatly fall into position with an allowance for the thickness of the plating where it meets the rabbet line. At the transom, a semicircular slot can be cut to receive the pipe and the ends temporarily allowed to project over. Later, after welding the plating, the ends can be trimmed off and sealed flush with the transom.

In those few extreme cases where the hull curvatures are so severe the pipe cannot take the bend, the problem can be solved by carefully locally heating the *compression* side of the pipe with a torch while maintaining pressure. This will cause the compression side to "upset" slightly but will leave the outer tension side smooth (see Figure 8-11).

With the sheer members in and tacked only, the clamps can be removed and the chine bars placed in much the same manner. Chine bars are much easier to do, as they are much more flexible and lighter to handle. However, care should be taken that they are: (1) tack welded only (except at the ends), (2) straight to start with, and (3) nested properly in their slots. This last is to insure that the plating flows smoothly into the chine bars, does not leave an excess of bar which must later be laboriously ground off or, conversely, does not pinch the plating in. A small metal or hardboard gauge or template of the same thickness as the plating will be helpful (see Figure 8-12). The same plating thickness allowance should, of course, be made at the sheer pipes.

The flat, cross-sectioned longitudinals now follow and are done basically the same way as the sheer pipes and the chine bars. They may be more conveniently done a length at a time rather than full hull length, because they are so limber in their flat-sectioned direction. The joints, however, must be welded straight before they are bent if they are to bend fair later. Again, as in the case of the sheer pipes, it would seem almost impossible to bend them edgewise, but if their thickness is in reasonable relation to their width, it is not difficult at all. Typically, a 2" wide bar should be about 5/16" thick for an average boat of about 45 to 55 feet; this would be more or less in proportion for smaller or larger

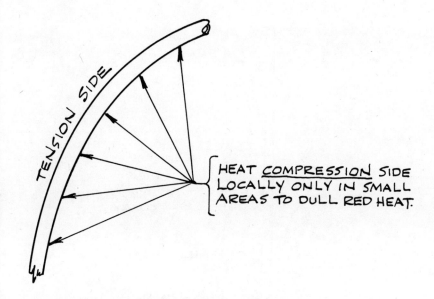

HEAT _COMPRESSION_ SIDE
LOCALLY ONLY IN SMALL
AREAS TO DULL RED HEAT.

8-11. *Using heat to bend a pipe to a severe curve.*

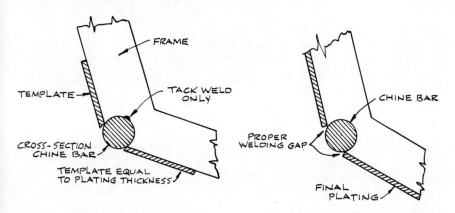

FRAME

TEMPLATE

TACK WELD
ONLY

CROSS-SECTION
CHINE BAR

TEMPLATE EQUAL
TO PLATING THICKNESS

CHINE BAR

PROPER
WELDING GAP

FINAL
PLATING

8-12. *Using a template to make an allowance for the plating at the chine bar.*

craft. If the bars are pulled in gently and simultaneously several frames at a time they will have no tendency to collapse or twist.

As the longitudinals fall successively into their pre-cut slots, they should be clamped up exactly even with the outer edges of the frames

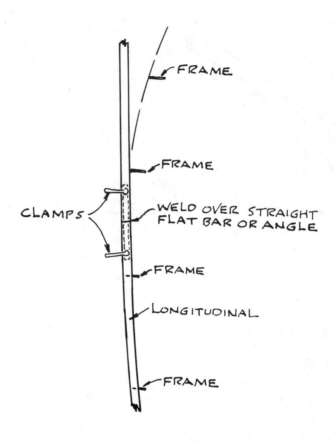

8-13. Welding adjoining longitudinal sections.

and, like the sheer and chine pieces, tack-welded only. Adjoining lengths may be welded together straight by clamping them to the flat side of an angle or other straight edge. Once welded straight, the weld joint area will bend exactly like the remainder of the bar length (see Figure 8-13).

As the longitudinals are successively placed, the hull will begin to resemble a basket-like grid of curved bars; it will also become more and more rigid, even with only tack welds to hold it together, until finally it becomes nearly immovable. Pieces that, at first, seemed almost as limber and as flexible as rubber now, because of their curvatures, are exceedingly stiff and strong. When finally welded after the plating is on, the accumulated strength is enormous.

The deck, unless it is to be of wood, will also be longitudinally stiff-

8-14. Exaggerated effect of the full welding of flat bulwark plates at the frames before plating.

ened but, usually, this is quite simple as the contours are relatively gentle. The deck will undoubtedly have several openings for hatches and the like; these can be framed in at this point; indeed, in some cases some longitudinals will terminate at hatch opening framings.

The hull is ready for plating when it is completely framed, with the sheer, chine, and longitudinals run as well as the bulwark cap pieces in place, if any. Bulwark caps can be pipe, in which case the same basic procedure used for sheer pipes should be followed, or may be flat plate, with or without a capping of decorative wood. Here, too, whether flat plate or pipe is used, tack-welding only should be resorted to at this stage. Full welding of flat bulwark plates at frames will cause them to assume a series of down-curving loops, which must later be straightened if the plates are to look fair (see Figure 8-14). It is surprising how a little "looping," if not corrected, can create an unsightly effect. Only 1/8" to 1/4" out-of-fairness may spoil an otherwise smooth-appearing bulwark, particularly when viewed along the length of the boat.

9   PLATING

With the plating, the "moment of truth" has arrived. This is the time when the new boat is either going to be sleek and smooth, as it should be, or is going to end up looking like a washboard, as so many needlessly do. Or, like so many carelessly built craft, it might require numerous pounds of filler to cover up the builder's ineptitude.

Possibly the first, and one of the prime, rules is to use the largest sheets possible consistent with the curvature of the hull, the amount of compound curvature required, if any, and your ability to handle those sheets. The fewer the plates, the less welding necessary, the less probability of unfairness at joints, the less time consumed, and the smoother the boat is likely to be. Quite often, plates 20 or more feet long are quite practical and, indeed, in certain designs, such as most sharpies, it is even possible to plate a whole side with a single plate, or only two plates. This applies to many V-bottom hulls, except for a small area near the bow. If there is doubt, a plating half-model will quickly show the limits. The objection may be made that long plates are difficult to handle, but this is not so if you provide two or more lifting points and use appropriate restrainers, such as clamped angles, to keep the plates from buckling during hoisting.

For example, I have produced several boats in the 50- to 75-foot class, working by myself or at most with a single helper, using only three sheets to a side or bottom. In boats with highly compounded curves of course, this is not possible.

Unless you happen to be a highly skilled layout man, of which there are only a handful in the country, capable of laying out a plate precisely from the original lines, it is recommended that all plates be carefully templated before cutting. The practice of laying a rectangular plate against a hull, as is done in some commercial yards, and torch cutting it to fit, is at best poor technique and usually results in sleazy work. So also, is the practice of first plating the bottom, allowing the chine edge to overlap the proper chine curve, cutting it to a probable curve, and then plating the sides, again allowing an overlap of an inch or so and beating it over the bottom plate by sledge and local heating. Several production yards have done this and the result is usually horrendous and a source of future trouble for the owners. I have had occasion to repair several hulls plated by this inadequate, if speedy, method.

Templating may be readily done with hardboard strips, about 1/8" in thickness, by clamping them temporarily in place, marking them, trimming them with a saw, sander, or plane, and reclamping them to an exact fit. Successive pieces can be bolted together until the entire outline of a projected plate is achieved. The periphery of the template is then joined with appropriate cross pieces and bracing pieces to prevent movement during transportation, and then the template is lowered to the floor. If the original curved template will lie flat on a level floor, the plate cut from it will fall readily into place on the boat. If not, some compound curvature is present, in which case the template will have to be changed or shortened, or local heating or other technique used to make the metal lie properly on the hull.

The template is now laid flat on the plate to be cut, clamped so it cannot move, and then the shape precisely scribed. During scribing it is convenient, though not necessary, to mark the station or framing lines, or other special points, for future reference. The template pieces may now be unbolted and used, with appropriate changes, for the next adjoining, or opposite, template.

The plate may now be cut to the scribed lines, the slag removed with a chipping hammer or grinding wheel, and the edges smoothed and cleaned with a grinder. Butt joints should be beveled for improved weld penetration unless the plates are quite thin, 1/8" or less, when precise spacing is used at the joints instead. I prefer to bevel from the outside surface on the sides and from the inside on the bottom plates, but the opposite is satisfactory so long as complete weld penetration is achieved later on.

While the steel is still on the ground, it is much easier and less time consuming to clean and prime the inside surfaces of the plates than do it later on when they are in place on the hull. Additional local cleaning and priming inside will, of course, be necessary after the hull is all welded and ready for finish painting, but this laborious job is made easier by doing most of the work before the plate is erected. The inside

9-1.   Partially plated hull showing temporary plate supports.

surface can be prepared by one of several means: (1) sandblasting, the preferable method, (2) disc-sanding or grinding off the scale, or (3) power brushing with a stiff, bristled wheel. It is important that all loose scale, oil, grease, or other dirt is removed so that a firm bond with the priming material, whatever paint system is used, can be achieved. The prime coat should not be so heavy that it will interfere with future welding but should be adequate to prevent atmospheric corrosion during fabrication. The several priming methods are discussed in a later chapter.

With the prime coat on and dry, the plate is now ready for erection. Depending on preference, either the sides or the bottom may be plated first. I usually plate the sides first because by so doing, a great deal of climbing in and out is eliminated and because preliminary clamping is easier. Usually, before a side plate is erected, some temporary arrangement will be necessary to hold the plate while clamps are readied and adjustments are made for a precise line-up to the exact welding space. One convenient method is to weld temporarily two or more short pieces of angle or flat bar to a frame, or the chine bar at a frame, and provide the angles with temporary vertical supports to the floor to carry the weight (see Figure 9-1).

The piece welded to the frame or chine should be tilted slightly up, so the plate, when dropped into it, will slide automatically into its approximate position and not be prone to work its way out while the plate is being bent or moved fore and aft.

With the plate on its vertical supports and still hanging from its block and tackle, chain fall, or other hoisting device, a series of clamps can be temporarily fastened on the upper edge. The plate will be drawn in evenly along its length toward the hull. When the plate is close to the hull, the hoisting clamps may be released and the plate brought within touching distance or nearly so. By this time, it will be evident that the plate probably will have to be shifted longitudinally a few inches one way or another. This also can be done by the use of clamps or a "come-along." Done with care, the plate will slide smoothly along its temporary supports until it is almost precisely in position.

Final positioning, however, will require full snugging up of the plate against the frames and longitudinals at all points, and this is best achieved by temporary welding a number of threaded rods at right angles to selected portions of the inside surface of the plate. Threaded rods are available at almost any hardware store and can be cut to any length needed. For plates 3/16" thick to 3/8" thick, 3/8" rods are adequate; heavier or lighter rods can be used as plate thickness increases or decreases. Also needed will be a number of short angles, long enough to span two longitudinals. The angles should be pre-drilled with appropriate holes to receive the threaded rods, which are then tightened by nuts evenly over the length and width of the plate as it is brought in to the hull framing (see Figure 9-2).

As the plate is drawn ever closer to its final precise location, and as it takes its curvature, it will likely require additional fractional-inch longitudinal and vertical adjustments. This is readily done by lightly and successively tapping the angles with a hammer in the direction desired and at the same time maintaining pull with a clamp or "come-along." By this method, plates may be positioned and held to precise location while they are being tack-welded at intervals along the periphery and at strategic points. No additional finish welding should be done at this time; this can be done when the hull is fully, or nearly fully, plated. Before tack-welding, however, careful inspection should be made to insure that every part of the plate is fair, that there are no discontinuities, cavities, or lumps. If there are, they should either be corrected or the framing inspected to determine if it is fair. If not, the framing should be adjusted before tack-welding is done.

9-2. *Partially plated hull. The port plate is snugged up with threaded rods temporarily welded to the bottom plating. Also note the temporary vertical frame supports aligned on vertical centerlines for accurate leveling with a spirit level.*

Even light tack-welding will quickly stiffen up the hull and, once done, corrections are not so easily made. Particular care should be taken along butt seams to insure that the plate follows the contour of the boat so there are no unsightly puckers or ridges at the joints. Once the tack-welds are made, the threaded rods and their component angles may be removed, most readily by the edge of a grinding disc, and used again on the next plate.

There are, of course, other methods of placing a plate on a hull, such as the use of props and wedges, but the threaded rod technique provides exact control at any and every desired point and is, in addition, flexible and safe. It should always be kept in mind that a large steel plate is a potential guillotine if it accidentally gets away. It is dangerous by its very size and weight.

The sequence of plating is not particularly critical; I prefer to do the middle plates first and work toward either end, but this is a preference only. However, it is desirable to install matching or opposite plates as

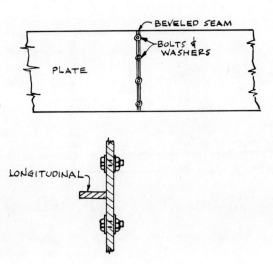

9-3. *Trueing up a butt seam with bolts and washers.*

you progress. This will insure that the framing will not be twisted preferentially to one side, or otherwise distorted.

As the plates are put on in sequence, going either forward or aft, the butt joints will have to be trued up for welding and, in so doing, some slight contraction during final welding should be accounted for. It is common to space a seam properly before welding and then find it closing up because of weld shrinkage as welding progresses, until the seam is locally too tight for full weld penetration. This can be controlled by inserting temporary spacers in the seam or making a small allowance in advance to take care of this. This is not much of a problem in plates with beveled edges, but is a problem with thin plates, 1/8″ or less in thickness. Short pieces of weld rod of the same thickness as the steel, inserted at a 90° angle to the weld, make excellent and convenient spacers. Where, in spite of these controls, undue contraction occurs and a too-tight seam is the result, the seam should be ground out with the fine edge of a wheel or disc. A seam with a hidden crack caused by inadequate weld penetration is potentially weak and should be avoided.

The butt seams must also be true to each other in respect to their curvatures along the hull. A simple but effective way of achieving this is to drill along the seam at intervals, insert bolts with washers and nuts, and pull them up tight (see Figure 9-3). This insures precise meshing of the mating plates until final welding is near completion, when the bolts are unscrewed and knocked out and the weld finished. Another

129

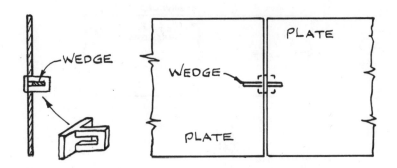

9-4.   Trueing up a butt seam with a slotted tee and wedge.

method of achieving the same result is to use a thin T-shaped piece of metal with a slot cut in it to receive a wedge (see Figure 9-4). These tees do a good fairing job but are often difficult to remove because of weld contraction, and often must be destroyed to get them out.

Most hulls, even those with carefully worked out lines, will have some local areas where plates will not fall readily into place by simple clamping or by the use of threaded bolts, where compound curvatures have been deliberately specified. This is particularly true of some bow sections, such as on bottom plates where a "dead-rise" bottom must fair into a vertical stem section. There are several approaches to the problem: (1) pre-form the plate before erection by hammering and heating or cold pressing, (2) template the plate as accurately as you can, draw it up as close as possible by clamps and threaded rods, and while maintaining pressure, strip heat selected areas so that it pulls into place, and (3) slit the plate at strategic points to permit local bending where it was not possible before. Such slits are later grooved and welded together again. A fourth approach is to lap-strake or butt-weld a series of narrow plates. While this method is often used, I do not care for it because, in the long run, it creates more work than it saves and is often inconsistent with the remainder of the hull.

With a little patience and the judicious use of an acetylene torch plus a number of threaded rods, it is often surprising how a seemingly impossible twist or curvature can be induced into a plate or small segment of it. Another method is to heat a section and quench it with a water spray, but this is almost impossible to describe in words as the conditions will vary so much with each plate as to make experience the only teacher. In general, I have found this method to be of only limited value. When strip heating coupled with clamping or other pressure is

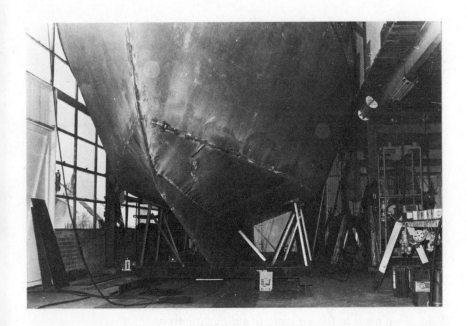

Forming a difficult forward bow section. The starboard plate has been completely shaped. The port plate has been cut on different angles and locally strip heated to bring it into approximate position. As the heating progresses, it is pulled tight with inside-mounted threaded rods.

resorted to, the plate edge will locally "upset" as the red hot strip is squeezed together and will be slightly thicker than the remainder of the plate. Once clamped and tack-welded, the local area may be easily ground smooth and continuous with the rest of the hull (see Figure 9-5).

Bottom plates are relatively easy to position. Carefully templated and cut, they can be merely laid flat under the hull and raised to rough position by use of a couple of U-bolts temporarily welded to the inside of the sheet. Blocks and tackles or other lifting hooks are then fastened through these and the plate raised flat under the hull until it is close enough for temporary threaded rods to be attached. These are then evenly screwed up, just as was done on the side plating, until the plate is snug and coaxed into precise position. Once in place the plate can be tack-welded and the threaded rods and U-bolts removed for further use.

Where bottom plates are to be attached to a box-type keel, they should be templated and positioned so that just the mating corners of the keel and bottom are touching (see Figure 9-6). This permits a nice V-joint

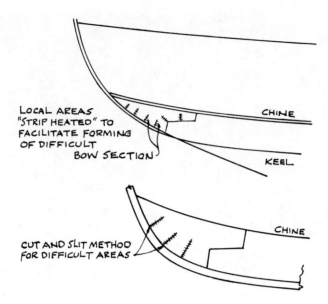

9-5. *Two ways to form a plate to a difficult curve.*

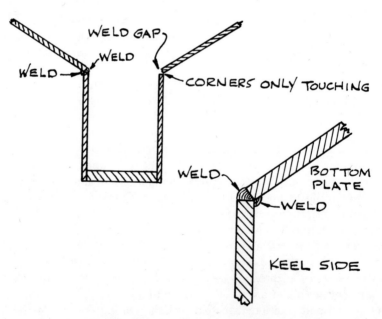

9-6. *Positioning and welding the bottom plate to a box keel.*

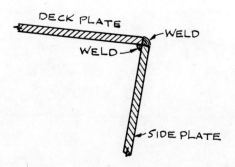

9-7. *Positioning and welding a deck plate to a side plate.*

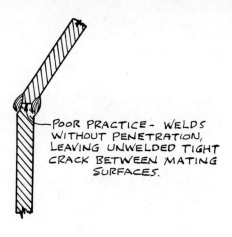

—POOR PRACTICE - WELDS WITHOUT PENETRATION, LEAVING UNWELDED TIGHT CRACK BETWEEN MATING SURFACES.

9-8. *A poor weld with no penetration of the weld metal.*

for welding, which ultimately may be done from the inside with full penetration of weld metal. A single bead outside should then complete the joint, making it both strong and leakproof. The same principle applies to other plating joints, such as at the gunwale if a flat plate is used, or for bulwark caps (see Figure 9-7).

It is not good practice merely to let joining plate edges overlap each other and to depend on welds in their corners to hold them. Such welds inevitably contain concealed cracks, which conceivably, some day, due to vibration or other stresses, may propagate and lose their integrity (see Figure 9-8).

There are, of course, numerous welds, such as intermittent welds along longitudinals and frames, where full penetration is impossible, or at best

Hull plating completed on Manteo. *Note the full pipe guard-rail and the use of only three plates to a side.*

impractical. But all welds that are necessary for watertightness or in which strength is both critical and essential should be welded *fully* to the roots of the weld and proper positioning, beveling, or other preparation insured to make this possible. During plating, this is essential for all chine and keel joints, the transom junctures, the stem welds, and all butt joints between plates.

Deck plating, usually of lighter stock than the sides or bottom, is relatively easy to install and is handled in much the same manner. Like both bottom and side plates, it should be snugged down evenly on its transverse and longitudinal supports before tack-welding, and here again the sheets used should be the largest possible consistent with the shape of the deck and with economy. Also, careful templating is recommended. Many deck plates will require slotting in the way of the bulwark supports to make them fit, and only careful templating will provide correct spacing on the flat sheet on the floor before cutting.

Sometimes, because of the increasing resistance of the steel to bending as it is curved to the radius of the deck, there is a tendency toward ridging of the center seam along the axis of the hull. A simple way of curing this to provide a centerline longitudinal to which the edge of the plates can be clamped and welded (see Figure 9-9). The edge of the deck plate is templated and cut to meet the upper corner of the longitudinal, and the opposite plate is handled the same way. This leaves a gap equal to the thickness of the longitudinal which is filled with weld met┄' and later ground smooth. The under corners are given a light

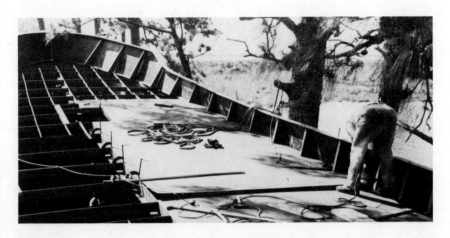

Early stages of deck plating on Manteo. *Note the bulwarks and method of framing.*

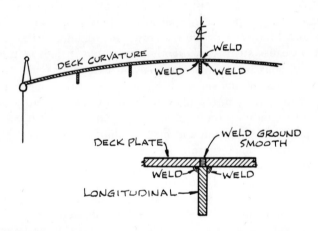

9-9. *Welding to deck plates over a centerline longitudinal to prevent ridging of the center seam.*

weld bead, and the total result is a strong weld and a smooth deck. For the same reason, it is good practice to terminate other deck seams over either longitudinals or transverse members rather than between them. An uneven deck quickly catches the eye and is unsightly. Attention to a few details such as this, coupled with even "snugging-up" of the plates before welding, usually provides a clean, unrippled, and unridged surface as smooth as any wood or plastic deck.

With the sides, bottom, bulwarks, if any, and the deck on and thoroughly tack-welded in position, the cabin trunk and/or deckhouses can be placed. However, quite often a great deal of labor and subsequent climbing in and out can be eliminated by doing some of the interior steel work at this point while the hull is wide open and accessible. Some of the interior fuel or water tanks can be made and the engine beds fabricated. Also, if desired, the engine, or engines, can be roughly installed. It is much easier to drop an engine through an open deck than to try later to fish it through an opening just barely large enough to receive it. The engines, of course, should be carefully covered to protect them from weld spatter, dirt, paint, or other fabrication debris.

The plating of cabin trunks and deckhouses follow much of the same procedures outlined above. However, most cabin trunks and deckhouses will have a number of openings in their sides for windows, ports, and the like. Before cutting them, some consideration should be given to the effect of the openings on subsequent fabrication, particularly where the cabin sides are appreciably curved. In recent years, the trend has been to rather large openings, especially in power pleasure vessels with very little metal between windows. Now, this seldom creates a problem of strength because steel is inherently strong, but it does at times make smooth, continuous bending difficult—even if bending is no problem, it can be the source of unevenness from subsequent welding. If there is doubt about the ability of the plate to curve evenly without local crimping, it is best to plate up the member as a total unit and to cut the windows and ports *after* erection and final welding. This is mostly a matter of judgment and common sense.

It should be remembered also that most cabin trunk sides have a slight slope inward toward the top as well as a curvature from fore to aft and that allowance for this should be made in the template. Boats with straight cabin sides look boxy and offend aesthetically.

When the plates now on are smooth, tacked, and properly spaced for welding, the final welding can now begin. This is the point where an expensive vessel and a lot of effort can be ruined almost irretrievably by sloppy work or ignoring the basic rules. To reiterate once more, the basic rules are: (1) do not overweld, (2) do not weld continuously along any seam; unless experience dictates otherwise, do not lay down more than two or three inches of weld at a time, (3) do not make an adjacent weld until the first weld has thoroughly cooled, (4) constantly reverse direction to cancel out contraction stresses, (5) work equally from inside to outside to prevent preferential contraction in any one direction, (6)

Forward deck of a 51-foot schooner during construction. Note the bulwarks and longitudinal framing of the cabin trunk.

Looking toward the bow of a 51-foot schooner. This clearly shows the arrangement of the transverse framing, longitudinal framing, and plating.

insure full penetration of all important welds where watertightness and integrity is essential, (7) clean all welds before making an adjacent one, (8) be particularly cautious as to the amount of weld where the weld is to fill an acute angle or a right angle.

The final weld-up can begin almost anywhere at the middle or the ends of the boat so long as the rules are observed. I prefer to strike the first beads along the outside of the chine and sheer to create a slight preliminary contraction pull towards the convex side of the boat and so "anchor" the first stresses in that direction; I then proceed equally inside and out as suggested above. Also, the transverse members, the frames, bulkheads, or other cross-section segments should be left unwelded, except for a few tacks, until all or nearly all of the longitudinal welding is done. This applies particularly to the area between the sheer and the chine, and the chine and keel, less so on the deck. As the welds at the chine, sheer, and keel cool, they contract and exert a surprising amount of pull. Sometimes this can be so great that the frames between these points will be bent laterally to some degree and must be corrected by local strip heating and straightened while still hot with clamps and some type of stiff, straight steel such as an angle. Failure to observe this precaution will often, especially in thin-hulled boats of about 1/8" plating or less, create an unpleasant rippled or washboarded effect.

In the case of bulkheads that are too rigid to bend laterally, or too rigid to be corrected if they do, there is no choice but to weld them as carefully as possible as you proceed with the rest of the hull. However, bulkhead washboarding can be controlled by deferring most of the bulkhead welding until last and then doing only very short skip welds, only about an inch at a time with complete cooling in between. This, of course, is very tedious and requires a lot of slag cleaning between welds, but the result is well worth the effort if aesthetics are of any value, as they should be.

All plate joints that are of essential structural importance should be welded both inside and out except in those few cases where it is physically impossible to accomplish, when care should be taken to insure full penetration from the outside by beveling, grinding, or other means. However, longitudinals, frames, and deck beams need be only welded intermittently. Complete welding of these, except in very special vessels, is unnecessary and undesirable and would inevitably result in a washboarded hull. This is especially true of transverse members.

The question, of course, is how much welding constitutes intermittent welding? There are no set rules about it, and it is mostly a matter of common sense. Typically, in a vessel with a 3/16" skin, 2" welds placed alternately on opposite sides and separated by about 2" gaps between welds would be about the maximum before some noticeable distortion would be visible. Intermittent welds of this sort in their accumulated effect are immensely strong, and frames and logitudinals so welded become extremely rigid. Much of the wrinkled appearance of improperly welded steel boats is due to overwelding of the frames, by welding them con-

Engine in place and integral water tank partially assembled.

tinuously, or by piling on far more weld metal than required for structural strength. Strangely, people who would be quite satisfied with wood planking screwed or nailed every six inches or so seem vaguely perturbed about intermittent welds, which are many times as strong as intermittent fastenings.

As welding of the hull approaches completion and most contraction has already occured, it is proper to begin placing other plate members, such as watertanks, fuel tanks, holding tanks, or other equipment that is installed integral with the hull. Of course, these could be welded in simultaneously with the hull plating, but I have found that less ultimate distortion will occur if they are welded later and the plates templated to fit the fully contracted vessel. Also, tanks pre-fitted before hull welding often pose welding and cleaning problems because of space limitations. It is better to weld all the main parts of the hull while one can get at them before trying to squeeze into a narrow box or trying to weld upside-down into impossible corners, which are hard to see, let alone reach. In

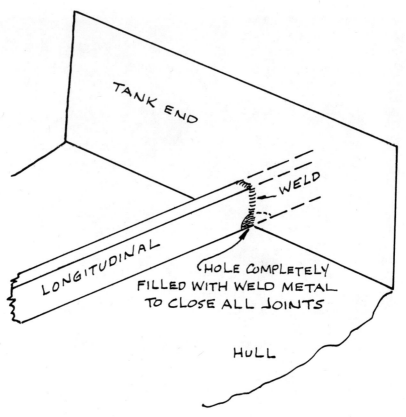

9-10. *Sealing the joint where a longitudinal passes through a tank.*

large boats with large tanks, this is no problem, but in small vessels there are difficulties.

All water and fuel tanks, of course, should be welded both inside and out, and special care should be taken where longitudinals or frames pass through the tank sides or ends. Diesel fuel in particular has a nasty habit of seeping out of the most minute seams or cracks, and it is imperative that none be allowed to creep under intermittently welded longitudinals or frames. This may be prevented by cutting a hole in the base of the member where it joins the hull and the tank skin. This hole is then filled with weld metal to seal the bottom ends of the longitudinals or frames and at the same time seal the tank skin and hull (see Figure 9-10).

All tanks should be provided with generous holes for both cleanout and inspection and should be capped with watertight lids. Such clean-outs may be easily fabricated by simply cutting the desired size hole in the top, making a matching oversize lid out of plate, clamping the two segments together, and drilling a suitable number of bolt holes. Bolts are then inserted and pulled up tight. The underside of the bolts may then be welded and so made liquid-proof. The entire component with the lid still bolted may then be welded to the tank, using the same basic welding sequence for other parts of the hull. After welding the lid may be unbolted and a suitable gasket of rubber, neoprene, or other substance inserted for complete final seal. Welding of the tank top without the lid first bolted in place will often permit excess distortion and make subsequent closure questionable or difficult; the bolted lid acts as a partial restraint against distortion.

Another item that may best be done after most of the hull welding is the engine bed, or beds, for reasons of welding access if nothing else. Surprisingly few engine beds are adequately done and the most common mistake in metal-hulled vessels is to mount all, or portions of, the bed on the hull plating and to depend on the skin of the vessel alone for support. Now, structurally, in most steel boats, the strength of the plating is more than adequate to take care of the weight or stresses of the engines, but it should be borne in mind that metal, like most other materials, is subject to fatigue and that an engine vibrating a few hundred thousand cycles an hour is flexing the metal on which it rides an equal number of times. While these vibrations may be microscopic in scale and well within the elastic limit of the metal, they nevertheless, by sheer accumulation, may reach the limit of the steel to absorb them and initiate minute cracks that will propagate and ultimately fail or create weeping seams, rusting, and progressive decay. I have had occasion to weld up several boats that had developed local cracks because the builders for convenience, or in ignorance, had installed the beds partially or wholly on the hull plating alone.

Properly built engine beds should derive their main support from other structural parts of the boat, preferably from transverse frames, longitudinals tied into frames, or, better yet, bulkheads. This does not mean that engine bed plates should not be welded to the hull plating at all, for they may be, but instead the basic vibration load should be dispersed and distributed through the frames, bulkheads, longitudinals, and similar structural members. Thus, a proper engine bed will span two or more frames, bulkheads, or longitudinals, which will distribute vibration over a wide area rather than localize it on a relatively thin, flat bottom plate.

Once the load is carried by the proper structural members, there is no objection to further stiffening of the bed by suitable plates welded to the hull skin. These basic principles apply equally to boats made of wood, fiberglass, ferro-cement, aluminum or other metals.

Localized flexion of metal should be considered in other parts of the plating, especially where heavy concentrated loads are involved or where temporary stresses may exceed or approach the ability of the hull plating to absorb them. Such places as mast steps, where the masts are mounted on deck, boat davits, winch or capstan mounts, mooring posts, and propeller shaft struts, may require doubler plates to distribute stresses. They are nothing more than relatively small plates cut to suitable size and welded to the deck or hull where needed.

Like the engine beds, however, they should span, if at all possible, two or more basic interior structurals. Merely doubling the thickness of the deck plating alone may be of little value and, in fact, may increase local stress and accelerate fatigue instead of inhibiting it as was intended. A too-small doubler is not much better than no doubler at all; doublers if they are needed at all should, within reason, be of generous dimensions.

10 FINISHING THE HULL

With the basic plating done, it is likely, unless the boat is an extremely simple one, that there will still be a number of items to be welded, cut, or made up. Also, before the final cleanup in preparation for corrosion protection and painting, the welds must be ground smooth and thoroughly inspected for pinholes, entrapped slag, or other possible defects.

Grinding, in essence, is a simple operation, but it can be noisy, fatiguing, and tedious unless a few aids are employed to relieve the weight of the grinder and provide control without undue muscle strain. The average boat will have several hundred feet of welds to be ground, and without some mechanical assistance the job becomes a bit of a chore. The average grinder or sander will weigh ten to twelve pounds; after some hours it will seem much more. Downhand welds, as on the deck, are no problem but vertical or horizontal welds along the outside of the hull can be tiring. A simple solution is to suspend the grinder from a hook, short chain, and line from some point above the hull or from the sheer or bulwarks. Thus suspended, the grinder is free to move back and forth or up and down as desired with no strain other than light guidance. The chain links will allow quick change of position vertically (see Figure 10-1).

Generally, best results are achieved with any of the several varieties of discs specifically made for grinding welds and available from any welding supply house. They are usually about 1/4″ thick and about 5″ to 7″ or more in diameter. They remove weld flash quite rapidly, remove a great many feet of excess weld metal, and with care will last a surprisingly long time. They are usually bonded with a tough resin-impregnated fabric and will stand a considerable amount of abuse. With care, the edges may be used to smooth fillet welds and grind out defects in welds for re-welding. Weld grinding is most efficient with a light pres-

Fifty-one foot schooner Pipestrelle *ready for sandblasting and zinc-spraying. The bright horizontal grind marks indicate the location of interior longitudinal framing welds. These are ground to produce a glossy surface free of raised impressions from interior welding.*

sure and at the speeds recommended by the wheel manufacturer. In no event should these speeds be exceeded, because the wheel may shatter and cause injury. No grinding should ever be done without a proper face mask or eye protection. A slight oscillating motion of the wheel provides a smooth cut and a more even surface than a fixed wheel position. Grind welds nearly flush and finish them with a flexible sanding disc suitable for metal. Do not overgrind; an overground surface is unsightly and more eye-catching than an underground one, particularly where glossy paints are later used. A properly ground weld will fade into the adjoining surface and be indistinguishable from the rest of the metal.

When grinding stainless steel trim or welds joining stainless to other metal, the wheel pressures should be light enough to avoid locally overheating the stainless surface. Carelessly done, the red heat from grinding will create a heat scale that is difficult to remove and which, later, on exposure to salt air or water may cause local rusting. Similarly, care should be taken to avoid grinding carbon steel particles into adjoining stainless steel surfaces. When in doubt about such possible impregnation, the final finish can be done with emery by hand or the carbon particles removed by selective local use of dilute nitric acid against the stainless steel surface, followed by a freshwater rinse. The acid should not be used on carbon steel but restricted to stainless alone. It may be used for the same purpose where stainless has been filed, drilled, cut, or otherwise contaminated by micro-particles of iron.

It is disconcerting to have one's expensive stainless trim suddenly rust. The fault usually lies not in the stainless steel itself but is the result of

144

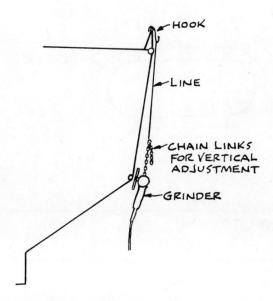

10-1. Suspending a grinder to ease the strain.

minute bits of ordinary steel that have become attached to or imbedded in the bright metal by other mechanical operations. While grinding in the vicinity of stainless steel it is wise to tape it or otherwise shield it from flying sparks that can readily ruin an otherwise spotless surface. Grinding sparks, incidentally, can also ruin glass, so be sure portholes or other glass-surfaced objects are nowhere in the vicinity of grinding operations; if they are, they must be properly protected.

In addition to the seam welds, the outside surface of the hull over the interior longitudinal and frame welds will have to be lightly ground. The reason for this is not very evident when the hull is in its original scaled condition but becomes plain during the final painting. The heat of welding inside raises the exterior surface a very slight amount over each interior weld. This may amount to only a few thousandths of an inch, but later when glossy or semi-gloss paints are applied, the raised areas become suprisingly prominent and destroy the visual continuity of an otherwise slick surface. First lightly running the flat of the grinding disc over the surface will expose the locations of the raised areas; they may then be made even with the rest of the hull by lightly stroking them with the edge of the disc. This is one of those extra touches that, while minor, distinguishes a superior product from its more carelessly finished counterpart.

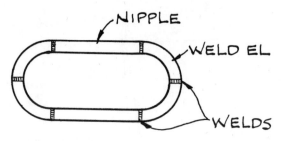

10-2. *A hawse fitting.*

10-3. *A simply constructed scupper.*

Among the various items that must be cut at this stage are the scupper holes for deck drainage and hawse holes for chain or rope. It is almost impossible to purchase stock hawse fittings suitable for small steel vessels and these must, perforce, be fabricated by the builder. Very satisfactory ones may be produced out of standard black malleable iron pipe fittings in almost any size desired. Made of four "weld-els," or two returns and two short pieces of pipe of the same diameter welded together and ground smooth, they make a light, strong unit, easy on rope and satisfactory in appearance (see Figure 10-2). Set halfway into the bulwark plating, they merge nicely into the hull and become an integral part of the boat.

Scupper holes may be simple cuts for drainage, may be edged with pipe or rod as desired, or maybe embellished with grids to prevent small objects from being washed overboard. One very simple but satisfactory scupper consists of a combination slot and larger opening. Large amounts of water are freely disposed of and the slot retains small loose objects (see Figure 10-3).

The edges of such simple, cut scuppers should be smooth and preferably rounded for retaining paint. Paint will tend to chip on sharp corners when abraded. Other scuppers may be rectangular, oval, or almost any configuration consistent with the design of the boat. Where they are of appreciable size, they should be provided with some sort

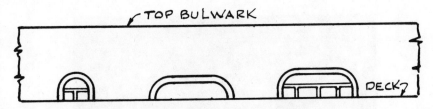

10-4. *Typical scuppers with rod edgings and gratings.*

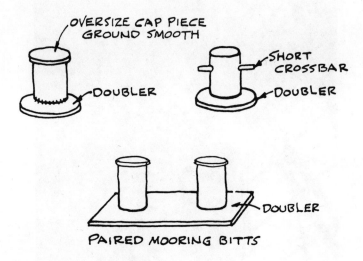

10-5. *Various types of steel bitts.*

of edging, usually a round rod bent to the appropriate shape (see Figure 10-4) and welded integral to the hull. Similar edging is appropriate for other bulwark openings, such as leads for spring lines or other lines.

An appropriate number of mooring bitts will likely be called for, and they may conveniently be fabricated from pipe cut to length and capped with a flat disc of metal welded on and ground smooth. Bitts may or may not be equipped with a cross bar to prevent rope from slipping up and off, or the disc top, if allowed to overlap the pipe, can serve the same purpose. If a cross bar is used, it should not be permitted to project too far. Overlong cross-bars serve only to snag lines, particularly on sailing vessels, and can be more of a nuisance than a benefit (see Figure 10-5). A piece of stainless for the cross bar adds a nice touch; if used, it should be welded to the bitt with a stainless electrode.

147

Billet and trailboard supports of a clipper-bowed schooner. Carved wooden trailboards will be bolted over the steel supports. The opening for the bowsprit has not been cut yet.

Steel mooring bitts can also be used to serve as ventilators while at anchor. The caps can be made detachable and a ventilator screwed or slid on; the bottom can be made to protrude through the deck or a hole cut into the deck at the foot of the bitt to allow passage of air. Steel mooring bitts are exceedingly strong and cost far less than conventional cast ones. Cast bitts should not be welded unless they are cast *steel;* ordinary cast iron may become brittle in the weld zones and crack. Cast bitts of iron or bronze, of course, may be bolted on.

Steel allows a great deal of freedom in the installation of chain plates or shroud attachments, and, in fact, ordinary chain plates such as those designed for wood or fiberglass boats need not be employed at all. The fastenings for shrouds and similar rigging may be welded directly to the hull or the deck, to segments of the framing, or to steel pieces made to fit between the bulwarks and the deck. Of course, thorough weld penetration should be insured in all such attachments and sharp notches should be avoided to eliminate setting up stress-concentration points. Ordinary steel padeyes made especially for welding and available through any marine supply house make excellent and inexpensive chain plate fittings, especially for deck attachment. Also, the hull plating itself, extended and drilled in the way of the shrouds, is quite suitable, or a piece of flat bar stock can be used as long as the total width of the shrouds can be welded to the deck edge. If the boat has bulwarks, another approach is to cut and weld a piece to fit the angle between the deck and the bulwark sides and then drill it for turnbuckle jaws and pins.

All of these methods are neater and stronger than old-fashioned chain plates and less likely to fail. Conventional chain plates have a habit of eventually working loose or of cutting through the glass or timbers they are bolted to. The same applies to bobstay and bowsprit fittings. A properly welded fastening integral with the hull is almost always stronger than a bolted one.

Also where bowsprits are concerned, expanded metal grating is much safer than old-fashioned foot ropes and, done properly, looks quite as good. If used, it should be welded in along with other weld attachments at this point. In those sailing boat designs that call for clipper bows, the billets and trailboards may be readily duplicated in steel or in combinations of steel and wood. Billets in steel boats are usually for decoration only and are best made up hollow of two thin plates spaced for lightness to whatever thickness might provide the best appearance. The billet is then welded to the stem as a unit and should be all but indistinguishable from the old-time wooden ones (see Figure 10-6).

The billet also serves as an attachment for the forward ends of the trailboards, which are swept backwards and curved to merge into the sides of the hull. Long wooden trailboards, or boards that are possibly subject to damage from anchor or mooring lines, should be supported underneath by a thin plate cut to shape and curved like the finished trailboard. The final carved, gold-leafed, and painted board may then be later bolted to this. Of course, a steel trailboard can be used and the scroll work laid out by raising the surface with a weld rod. However, this rarely looks well and is, at best, only a substitute for the real thing. If trailboards are to be used, they should be as handsome as possible.

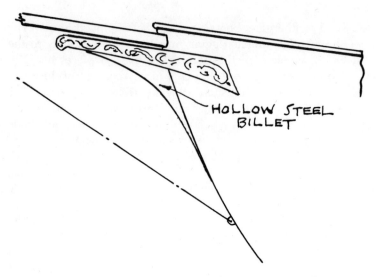

HOLLOW STEEL BILLET

10-6.   *Trailboards mounted over a steel billet.*

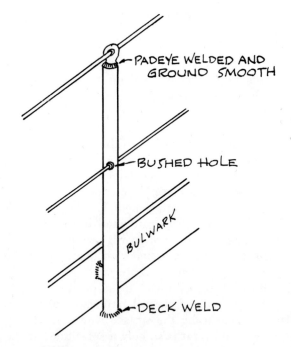

PADEYE WELDED AND GROUND SMOOTH

BUSHED HOLE

BULWARK

DECK WELD

10-7.   *A simple steel stanchion.*

150

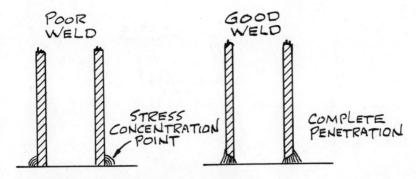

10-8. *Welding stanchions to the deck.*

The steel boat is ideal for the attachment of rails and lifeline supports, and these may be as simple or as complex as the ingenuity of the designer can devise. Unless rails are to be removable, they should be welded on at this time rather than through-bolted, and all through holes for wire cable or bolts for wood capping drilled also at this time to prevent subsequent local "bleeding" of rust. Manufactured stanchions for lifelines while often very pretty, are also costly and the steel boat builder, if he is not enamored of chrome and gilt, can make up attractive stanchions or rails of common stock materials at a fraction of the price of manufactured ones. One of the simplest, and quite strong, methods is to use ordinary pipe or tubing cut to length, capped with small circular welded-on padeyes to receive the top wire lifeline. Intermediate wires are passed through drilled holes (see Figure 10-7).

The holes should be drilled a little oversize and bushed with copper or other soft metal liners to take chafe from the wire. The soft bushings may be flared slightly at the ends to prevent them from working their way out. The deck welds should be smooth, substantial fillets; highly convex welds should be avoided because they create notch-type stress-concentration points that might fail if sudden excess weight is thrown against the stanchion. Properly done stanchions are almost impossible to break, even with the full weight of a falling body in a seaway. The same welding practice should be observed at the deck weld joints of the vertical members of railings (see Figure 10-8).

Removable rails or stanchions may employ pipe sockets to receive them; the sockets are welded to the deck in the same manner but they should be provided with small drain holes so water and ice will not accumulate and split them or accelerate ultimate corrosion. Matched holes

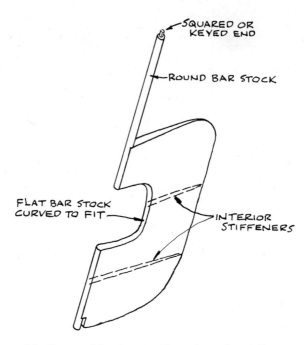

SQUARED OR
KEYED END

ROUND BAR STOCK

FLAT BAR STOCK
CURVED TO FIT

INTERIOR
STIFFENERS

10-9.   *Typical hollow rudder for a sailboat (see also 4-6).*

between the sockets and stanchions should be drilled to hold retaining pins. Here again, all drilling should be done at this stage rather than as an afterthought. This applies also to any other openings where raw steel edges will be exposed.

At some point in this sequence, the rudder will have to be fabricated and hung, the propeller shaft tubing welded in, and provisions made for stuffing-box attachments or for shaft bearings and struts. The steel vessel lends itself very nicely to installation of all of these items without the weaknesses so common to their installation in boats of other materials.

For sailing vessels with relatively large rudder areas, the lightest and strongest method is to make the rudder hollow with the leading edges welded to round solid bar stock or to hollow, preferably heavy-wall, tubing. The after edges may be carried to a relatively thin feather edge no more than the thickness of the two opposing plates. A few interior stiffeners may be required, if the rudder is large, to give it a smooth, elliptical cross-section if this is desired. Because of its inherent strength, steel allows considerable freedom in the shape of propeller aperatures with-

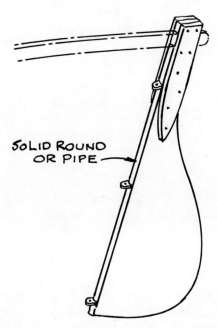

SOLID ROUND
OR PIPE

10-10. Typical hollow outboard rudder for a sailboat with decorative wood cheek pieces.

out danger of rudder failure. In such cases, the rudder stock is simply cut out in the way of the aperature and the aperature curve fashioned from flat bar stock or stock cut from plate (see Figure 10-9).

Rudders mounted inboard will usually require the upper end of the stock to be squared to receive a quadrant or one of the standard worm- or cable-actuated steering devices. However, hollow outboard rudders depending on a tiller may be equipped with decorative wood cheek pieces to receive the tiller (see Figure 10-10). The cheek pieces are simply bolted through the steel and a filler piece of wood inserted in the top of the rudder before welding to absorb the pressure of the bolts.

The method of hanging the rudder will, of course, depend on the design of the boat and whether the rudder is inboard or outboard. For inboard rudders that have the lower end fastened to the keel, a simple, satisfactory, and inexpensive way to hang them is to weld or through-bolt a short piece of heavy-wall tubing or pipe to the after end of the keel, first sealing the bottom of the pipe with a circular piece of sub-

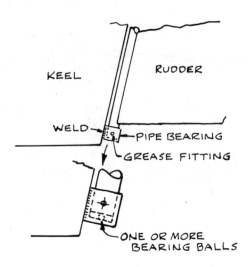

KEEL

RUDDER

WELD

PIPE BEARING

GREASE FITTING

ONE OR MORE
BEARING BALLS

10-11. An inboard rudder fastened to the keel at the lower end.

stantial plate. The inside diameter of the tube or bearing should be a
few thousandths larger than the outside diameter of the rudder stock, so
the stock will slide easily when turned. Also, turning can be facilitated
by inserting one or more loose ball bearings for the rudder stock to ride
on and by equipping the socket with a grease fitting for annual or semi-
annual lubrication with water pump grease (see Figure 10-11).

For the inboard end of such rudders, a tube, or pipe, of the same inside
diameter as the bearing should be welded through the hull at the proper
angle and either carried (preferably) above the waterline or, if this is
not possible, equipped with a suitable rubber-sleeved stuffing box, or
both. Such simple construction costs only a fraction of the expensive
bronze castings commonly employed to achieve the same results. Bronze
rudder fittings should not be used unless they are carefully insulated
from the hull (see Chapter 11).

Outboard rudders may be equipped with steel (not cast iron) pintles
and gudgeons, either purchased or welded up, or be hung with bolts
and paired, drilled fittings made to fit the situation (see Figure 10-12).
Paired fittings insure that the rudder will not jump loose in a jolting sea
or during momentary grounding.

For some reason, in a few localities, it has become the custom of a
few builders to provide their hollow rudders with filler holes and drain
plugs so they can be filled with oil, theoretically to prevent interior corrosion. This seems an unnecessary and undesirable practice because it

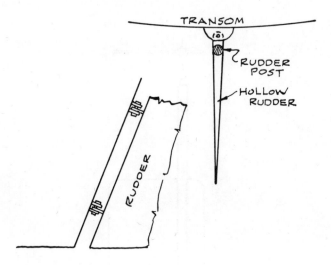

10-12.   Hanging an outboard rudder.

only adds excess weight where it is not always wanted and does nothing for corrosion prevention. A completely welded and sealed rudder will not corrode inside because any rusting whatsoever would quickly use the little oxygen available and further attack would be inhibited. Hollow rudders cut open after years of service are as clean inside as the day they were put overboard.

Powerboat rudders are usually simple affairs, generally much smaller than those for sailboats and are frequently "balanced" by addition of a proportionately small blade ahead of the rudder post (see Figure 10-13). Also, most are located inboard immediately aft of the propeller, though, of course, not always so. Many are of cast bronze, stainless steel, or other metal; few are of wood. Most are of solid construction rather than hollow and are made, in steel, by simply welding blades cut from flat plate to a steel rudder post. They may be made of ordinary mild steel or stainless. If the latter, a matching grade of stainless should be used both for the blades and the post and should be of either extra-low-carbon stainless, such as Type 316 L, or a "stabilized" stainless steel, such as Type 321 or Type 347. These grades are preferred because their carbon is either quite low or because it is "tied-up" chemically and will not precipitate out in the weld zone and create an area of possible accelerated grain boundary attack by sea water. For welding, either extra-low-carbon or matching "stabilized" electrodes should be used so the welds are compatible with the rest of the stainless steel.

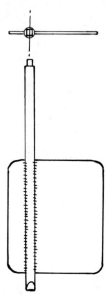

10-13.   *Typical powerboat rudder — a flat plate welded to a post (see also 4-5).*

Many such rudders are simply hung in a steel tube welded through the hull with a collar to sustain the weight and rubber bearings inserted top and bottom and with or without a stuffing box. Heavy-wall tubing is suggested because such tubes are seldom inspected between haul-outs and the rudder seldom removed once in place. A stuffing box at the top is highly desirable because of the frequently severe surge of high water pressure created by the propeller wash, particularly in high-speed craft. Bronze rudder shafts and rudders are permissible if preferred, provided they are carried in rubber bearings and insulated from the hull at the stuffing box, either by a flexible rubber sleeve or by other non-conducting material.

The propeller shafts will also be carried through steel tubing welded integral with the hull and, similarly, should preferably be of heavy-wall stock. Such tubing should allow generous spacing between the shaft and the tube and have sufficient inside diameter to allow the insertion of bearings at either end if this is specified. Shaft tubing should be carefully aligned before welding by use of a tight alignment wire from the centerline of the engine coupling to the outboard end or, alternately, an easy way, by placing the engine on its bed, temporarily connecting up

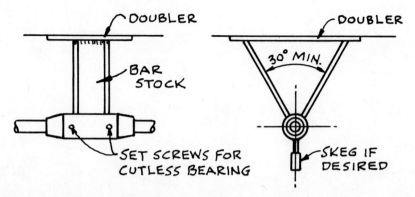

DOUBLER

DOUBLER

BAR STOCK

30° MIN.

SET SCREWS FOR CUTLESS BEARING

SKEG IF DESIRED

10-14.   Fabricating the struts.

the entire shaft assembly, including the tube, through a pre-cut hole in the hull, wedging the tube into precise alignment around the shaft, tack-welding it in position, and then completing the welding after the shaft has been removed. This is convenient if the engine has already been put in place before the deck was closed over. All that is later required is a final close engine re-alignment when the boat is in the water.

Very long shaft tubes may require some sort of small water scoops or other system of water circulation to insure that a fresh supply of cooling water reaches the stuffing boxes and associated shaft bearings. These scoops are generally not necessary for slow turning shafts in limited shaft tubes but may be essential for high-speed operations. They, too, should be welded in at this time.

Another type of through-hull tubing that should be welded in at this time are cockpit drains, and they should always be slanted aft toward the bottom. Otherwise, they will act as scoops and send a gush of water into the cockpit when the boat is underway.

At, or prior to, the time the propeller shaft tubes are lined up, the propeller struts, if any, should be installed. Like the tubes, they must be aligned precisely. They may be readily manufactured from heavy-walled tubing of sufficient inside diameter to receive a Cutless bearing and to be tapered at the ends for streamlining. The struts are conveniently made from flat bar stock beveled on the ends for the same purpose (see Figure 10-14). They may be used singly or, preferably, in paired V-formation with about a 30-degree minimum angle between struts. Also it is highly desirable to use a doubler plate welded to the bottom to absorb the shock of possible groundings, fouling of lines, or underwater

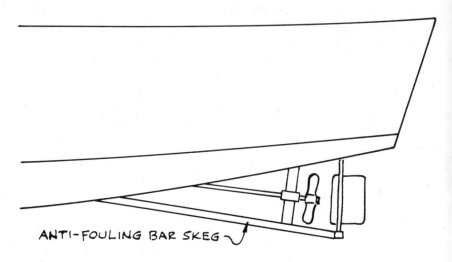

ANTI-FOULING BAR SKEG

10-15. A skeg used when there is no keel in the vicinity of the propeller.

debris. For further protection in twin-engined hulls where there is no
keel in the vicinity of the propellers, a skeg or anti-fouling strut can be
used (see Figure 10-15). This may be welded out of flat bar stock of
appropriate size and welded to the bottom of the stern bearing.

Along with the propeller assembly, the engines, unless they have a
closed heat-exchanger system, will require some type of cooling water
intake, either in the form of a tube welded to the hull or a sea cock.
Such intakes may be individual for each engine or be drawn from a
common sea-chest, along with other sea water requirements such as the
water for fire hoses, saltwater showers, and the like. A sea chest is usually nothing but a rectangular box with a grated bottom welded to the
hull and open at the bottom to the sea. The bottom grating is bolted in
and is removable for cleaning when necessary. The various intake lines
lead from the box via appropriate shut-off valves as convenient. A preferable arrangement is to weld a tube of generous diameter vertical to
the hull, provide it with a grated bottom to prevent intake of debris,
carry the tube above the waterline, and seal the top with a bolted
pressure lid. The several water intakes are welded to the periphery of
the tube as desired. The advantage of this type of sea-chest is that the
top may be removed for inspection and cleaning of the interior without
the danger of sinking the boat or the necessity of going overboard to
clean the gratings of accumulated seaweed or other clogging materials.

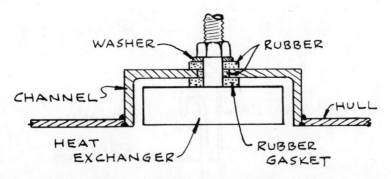

10-16. Insulating the heat exchanger from the hull.

If the engines are to use a closed freshwater cooling system and conventional, manufactured heat exchangers, commonly made of copper or copper alloys, the exchangers may be conveniently streamlined into the hull by welding in channels of appropriate size and closing the ends. Copper heat exchangers should be insulated from the hull by suitable rubber or neoprene washers (see Figure 10-16). Another approach, in increasing use in tugboats and other commercial vessels, is to weld split-pipe sections along the axis of the hull and circulate the cooling water through these. This is both inexpensive and practical.

Among the other items to be welded before the hull can be prepared for final cleaning and painting are the air intake tubes for the water and fuel tanks. Without them, the tanks would become air-bound and be difficult both to fill and to empty. Commonly they are of small diameter compared to the filler pipes but differ from these in that they are carried through and above the decking and then bent into a U so no rain or sea water will drain into them (see Figure 10-17). Some larger types will require spring-loaded check valves that permit intake of air as the tanks are emptied but halt the exit surge of liquids put in motion by a heavy sea. Filler pipes are usually finished flush with the deck, though not always so, and will end in threaded, watertight caps which are unscrewed for use and then replaced.

Closed engine rooms will also require air intake at some point through the hull or decking and unlike the air vents for fuel tanks, will have to be of quite generous dimensions. Diesel engines in particular gulp in huge quantities of air and will not perform at their best unless air is freely provided. In a great many pleasure boats, venting is accomplished by providing a screened or louvered slit in the side of the boat near the

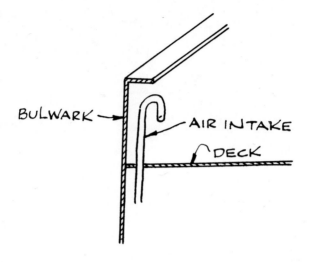

10-17. Arrangement of an air intake tube.

sheer. While this may be satisfactory for weekend cruising in quiet waters, it is decidedly unsafe for ocean work or even in temporary squall or storm conditions in inland waters. Engine room air intakes should always be as high above the water as practical, should be provided with louvered water traps and drains, or should be turned down so they will shed a boarding wave or spray.

The design of the air intake will depend on the configuration of the boat, the size and capacity of the engines, and the space available for venting. In large boats, there is much to be said for the old-fashioned stack for both intake and exhaust but, of course, most modern power-craft owners frown on this very practical and safe device. Air vents can assume numerous forms so long as they resist the intake of sea or rain water without inhibiting the inflow of air (see Figure 10-18). They may be welded up of light stock and prettied-up, if desired, by an edging of stainless.

Coast Guard regulations also require the venting of engine rooms for safety, especially where gasoline is the fuel. There are a wide variety of manufactured ventilators and blowers available. The openings and holding fixtures for these, too, should be cut and placed at this time as well as those for the exhaust system. Most powerboat exhaust pipes exit through the transom and can be either of carbon steel or stainless. If stainless, the same rules for welding as for rudder assemblies should

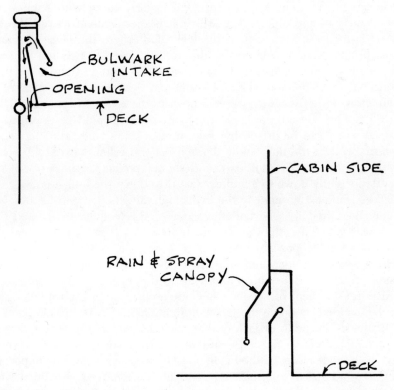

BULWARK
INTAKE

OPENING

DECK

CABIN SIDE

RAIN & SPRAY
CANOPY

DECK

10-18. Typical air intake arrangements.

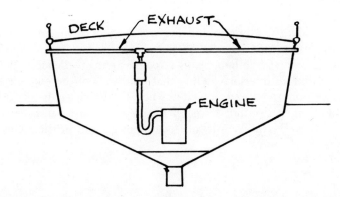

DECK   EXHAUST

ENGINE

10-19. An exhaust system with two openings on either side of the hull at the sheer.

be observed. In some sailing craft, particularly those with engines installed nearly amidships and in which it is inconvenient to run the exhaust through the after end of the boat, and where the vessel is sometimes heeled while under power, the exhaust may be installed on each side of the engine room close to the sheer.. The paired exhausts are then connected to a common Tee and muffler so that even if one exhaust is completely under water the other is open to the air (see Figure 10-19). If such a system is used, the interior exhaust piping should be arranged so that no water can be driven by wave pressure down into the engine. A loop or bend in the line below the level of the exhaust manifold is one simple approach. The outboard end should project an inch or so and be tilted slightly down to avoid exhaust drip down the hull sides.

There is almost no limit to the items and gadgets that can be attached to any boat, and it is beyond the scope of this volume to try and discuss them all. The important point, however, is that *all* permanent fixtures — all holes, ports, windows, drains, vents, or other openings — be welded in or cut open and smoothed before final preparation for corrosion protection is begun. Failure to do this may in the future create focuses for incipient rust spots, which are a nusiance to control but which can be avoided by doing the job thoroughly first. There is little point in meticulously finishing off a hull and then destroying the first and most important protective finish by subsequent mechanical work that could have been done easier in the beginning. In the same vein, it is important that all weld spatter, no matter how small, be removed. Retained weld spatter is one of the prime causes of early local rusting in steel boats. These sometimes tiny bits of extraneous metal or oxide make a continuous, pore-free paint system difficult to achieve, and once salt water reaches them they act as focal cells for local accelerated corrosive attack. After the welding is all done and the welds ground, the hull should be thoroughly inspected to insure they have been removed by grinding, chipping, or whatever other means is convenient or efficient. It is suggested also that all interior welding that might affect the exterior skin of the boat be done now and not later when the finish coats are on. The heat of welding will either burn off the new exterior paint, cause it to blister, or, at the least, cause it to become porous and brittle. This is just ordinary common sense.

11 CORROSION, PREVENTION, PAINTING

This is the point where, after having gone to a great deal of trouble and expense to produce a satisfactory hull, a considerable number of builders have failed either through ignorance, disregard of certain fundamental rules, indifference, carelessness, or lack of pride in workmanship. Their rusty products, streaked with brown stains, ugly reddish spots, or blisters, or pockmarked with pits, may be seen everywhere steel boats are found. This is a pity because it is all so unnecessary. The techniques are all at hand to insure almost indefinite life for steel boats. Modern chemistry, coupled with the basic knowledge of the causes of corrosion, has supplied the materials for the job and the means to prevent corrosion from becoming a problem. Several times in this volume, I have reiterated that the life of a steel vessel should be nearly unlimited given reasonable care and attention during the years and careful *first* treatment at the time of building.

In spite of the hostile elements to which all boats are subject, as corrosive or destructive as almost any normal environment on earth, there is still no real excuse for a steel boat becoming unsightly because of rust or literally eroding away beneath one's feet. Most important is that the boat in its very inception be given proper treatment; neglect of any or all of the basic rules will inevitably result in trouble either aesthetic or, in severe cases, structural. Properly built in the beginning and reasonably maintained, the steel boat will require relatively little annual care, and the time that could be lost in expensive maintenance could be used instead for sailing or cruising.

Corrosion
There should, first, be some understanding of the nature of corrosion, of the causes of rusting and of metal decay, and of the several forms

they may take. Metallic corrosion in its ultimate atomic physical causes is now conceded to be fundamentally electrical in nature. It is an electrical-chemical exchange of electrons that takes place whenever an electrolyte is present to create a flow of current, however minute or microscopic it may be. Any two dissimilar materials, whatever their chemistry, will in their inherent atomic structure, possess differential electrical, or energy, potentials, and when placed in proximity and in the presence of moisture, however dilute or small in quantity, will likely create an exchange of ions or sub-atomic particles and change the nature of the materials by alteration of their basic chemical structure. By just such sub-microscopic means does iron become rust, or iron oxide, or iron hydroxide, or any other chemical combination of iron and other materials. The physics of such reactions may be very complicated and some of it barely understood, although a very considerable literature is available on the subject.

On a larger and more visible scale, metal corrosion can be conceived, initially, as the creation of a single, or of a number of, electrolytic cells on the surface that act much like the cells of a battery with positive or negative plates suspended in an electrolyte (an acid). The cells may have their inception in a steel boat from contact with any dissimilar substance, a speck of dust, a fragment of other metal, a salt, any foreign chemical — or even a droplet of water containing excess of oxygen. Immediately, there is a preferential exchange of electrons or ions; a particle of metallic iron picks up a quantity of oxygen and becomes iron oxide or rust. The particle in turn becomes a cell of different potential which accelerates the creation of further ion exchange and the formation of additional cells and additional rust until ultimately the full ion exchange is complete and there is no more iron to be converted.

That this is so may be readily demonstrated by placing a mirror-clean piece of iron in a container in a perfectly dry atmosphere. With no electrolyte (moisture) to facilitate the creation or flow of currents, no cells are formed, no ion exchange takes place, and the metal will remain essentially unchanged for centuries. Conversely, a boat may be thought of as resting in an electrolytic sea (salt water is very efficient electrolyte), anxious to facilitate ion exchange and convert the boat to a mass of brittle rust.

Most rusting of steel, though not all, is a process of progressive oxidation accelerated by the presence of salt water, the electrolyte. It is an obvious corollary, then, that if one can seal off the metal from both water and oxygen, there can be only limited chemical-electrical ion exchange and no corrosive attack will occur, or that it will be so severely inhibited as to be of relatively little importance. This is one of the basic premises of many of the rust-inhibiting paints; they are intended to insulate the metal from both the electrolyte (the sea), oxygen, and foreign materials.

There is, however, another aspect of the corrosion system that should be considered, although it is really only another facet of the same basic phenomenon. When two dissimilar metals or materials are in contact in an electrolyte, the ion-electrical exchange is always preferential to one or another. That is to say, one side of the energy circuit will possess a greater potential attraction than the other, and the flow of ion particles will be towards that side which is the most potent. Thus, if iron and zinc, for example, are placed together in contact in salt water, or an other electrolyte, the zinc particles will flow towards the iron; they are "sacrificed" preferentially and, in salt water, become complex zinc oxide compounds, while the iron remains intact and essentially unharmed. This chemical or "ion-energy" preference is common to all metals, and they have been rated according to their position to each other in what is termed the "Electromotive Table or Series." Each metal is more "noble" or less noble than some other metal; a less noble metal is always sacrificed to a more noble one when placed in contact in an electrolyte. Gold, for example, is more noble than iron; iron would be sacrificed to it; oppositely, zinc, aluminum, or magnesium are less noble than iron and would be surrendered in favor of the iron. The sacrificed substances become "anodes"; the nobler ones are termed "cathodes."

This is why zinc collars and plates are placed on propeller shafts, rudders, and similar parts of boats. They are anodes and sacrifice themselves so the other, more noble parts of the boat may be free of corrosive attack. This is why, also, some of the protective paint systems for metals contain sacrificial substances, such as suspended zinc or aluminum, on the theory that they will provide some anodic benefit and so inhibit corrosion. Practically, while such paint systems do work to a degree and while they may act as good sealants against water, oxygen, and foreign substances, they are not in themselves sufficient and fully adequate no matter what the advertising or sales promotions may say.

With this somewhat oversimplified explanation of the nature of metallic corrosion, a few basic premises become clear and provide a few fundamental rules from which to formulate a guide to evaluate any method of proposed corrosion protection for metal boats. They are:

1. The boat hull, before any corrosion protection system is used, must be clean of all extraneous matter, of mill scale, slag, dirt, grease, or

other organic material and of chemical residue or dirt or scale entrapped in crevices or tight voids that might act as future electrolytic cells.

2. The hull should be free of any induced or inherent electrical circuitry that would speed up or accelerate the electrolytic effect always incipient in any boat floating in salt or fresh water.

3. Because no paint system so far developed is completely immune to scratches, abrasion, or other mechanical damage, as well as safe from peeling, blistering, or other local non-adherence, or protected from discontinuities such as "holidays" or bubbles, some anodic substance must be used to prevent local corrosive attack until the failures in the paint system can be mended or corrected.

4. No dissimilar metals should be used in close contact unless they are electrically insulated from each other or otherwise sealed from ion-exchange.

5. The paint system must be compatible with the hull itself, other paints, and the basic anodic material employed, and it must be electrically inert, or at least passivating, in its effect or, in addition, anodically beneficial in content. It must also provide a continuous, non-porous film that will effectually seal out oxygen and, hopefully also, water and at the same time be adherent, tough, and relatively inert to sunlight, oil, the organic solutions common to many waters, as well as a wide variety of water pollutants.

Until some superior protection system is invented, which at this moment seems unlikely, neglect of any of these five premises will ultimately pose problems; they are all of equal importance, necessary, quite practical of achievement, time-tested, and proven.

Corrosion as it occurs in steel and aluminum boats usually assumes at least one of many common forms, and they should be recognized for what they are and handled accordingly.

General Rusting and Scaling Rusting and scaling are caused by a general overall oxidation that takes, ordinarily, the form of a relatively uniform layer of corrosion. The rust may be soft and loose or, conversely, hard and tight. Such rusty scales may quickly deteriorate and accelerate the formation of additional scale. Sometimes, rather rarely, they will slow down or inhibit further rusting and act as natural sealants or passivating agents. It is these passivating rusts that are depended on in certain of the high-strength steels in unpainted buildings, bridges, and the like, in relatively mild atmospheric conditions. However, except for their strength, such passive rusting steels are of no value in boats, and anyone who convinces himself that by use of such a steel his corrosion problems will be eliminated or even appreciably minimized is due for a shock. This does not infer that such steels in boats are not useful, for they are, but not because of their rusting characteristics.

Crevice Corrosion As the name implies, crevice corrosion has its inception in tight seams, in narrow crevices, under slivers, or in other tight places. The crevices, no matter how small or how tightly compressed, once wetted either by atmospheric moisture or sea water, become, in effect, an electrolytic cell, and often corrosion will proceed quite rapidly once started. Usually, however, such corrosive attack becomes quickly apparent in the form of bleeding rust or stain, which can easily be traced to its source. The obvious control is to eliminate all crevices beforehand or, if they cannot be ground out or otherwise removed, to seal them permanently against moisture.

The stainless steels, interestingly, are quite susceptible to crevice corrosion, but for a somewhat different reason than ordinary steel. These alloys depend for their corrosion resistance on a micro-thin film of chromium oxide, which forms on their surfaces the moment they are exposed to air or oxygen. This film is highly passive to most chemicals and has the advantageous property of instantly healing itself if the film is scratched or otherwise mechanically damaged — so long as it is in the presence of oxygen.

However, when stainless steel pieces are closely paired with themselves or other materials, including wood, in the presence of corrosive liquids, especially chlorides (sea water) and an electrolytic cell is set up, the steel quickly becomes "starved" for oxygen and will no longer automatically mend itself. When this happens, rusting occurs just as in ordinary steel but, most likely, at a much slower rate. This is why owners of boats with stainless steel moulding screwed tightly against other materials are sometimes dismayed to find their expensive trim drooling rust. The outside, of course, open to the air remains bright and shiny; the oxygen-starved inside is breaking down into iron-chlorides or related chemicals. Such trim must either be sealed completely from moisture or so shaped and fastened that oxygen may reach it. A common method is to use moulding in the form of an ellipse (see Figure 11-1) rather than flat. This allows oxygen to reach all of the back side except a small area at the edges.

Pitting Corrosion Pitting can be the most aggravating type of corrosion if it is allowed to start. In some instances, it can occur and be well advanced locally before it begins to show appreciably. Pitting ordi-

ORDINARY FLAT MOULDING

ELLIPTICAL MOULDING

11-1. Of these two mouldings in stainless steel, the bottom one is less susceptible to corrosive attack as the result of oxygen starvation.

TYPICAL PIT   FUNNEL TYPE

SHALLOW LATERAL PIT

11-2. Three different types of pitting corrosion.

narily will start from some very minute fragment of foreign material adhering to the surface, from a bit of weld spatter left on, from a pinhole or other small discontinuity in the protective paint system, or even from a non-homogeneity in the metal matrix. A minute cell will be created, but instead of spreading laterally across the surface, will progress directly into the body of the steel. Quite often the corrosive attack will follow the grain boundaries of the metal, eating its way around the individual grains until they are loosened or converted to oxides. It is a phenomenon common to galvanized gas tanks; a small pit begun inside, works its way completely through an otherwise sound container. Most pits are simple U-shaped depressions, sometimes shallow, frequently deep. Some can be funnel-shaped with the small part of the funnel leading to the surface (see Figure 11-2).

Where pits occur, they are normally due to an unclean original surface before the protective coats were applied, discontinuities in the finish, or the presence of convex-shaped contaminants, such as weld spatter. When they occur adjacent to a weld, or in a weld, the cause may be traced to an improper grade of weld rod that deposited a dissimilar metal, to entrapped slag, pinholes in the weld metal, grain-boundary deposition of non-metallics, or low-melting-point constituents segregated by the heat of welding. Such precipitation (of carbides) in stainless steel has already been discussed. Once created, the only way to eliminate pits is to grind them out individually or en masse, repair the surface with weld metal or, if they are shallow, clean them thoroughly by sandblasting or other means. Pits, however, should not be a problem if the anti-corrosion rules are adhered to.

Galvanic Corrosion Galvanic corrosion can be divided conveniently into two basic categories: (1) erosion that occurs when two or more dissimilar metals are placed in unprotected contact or close proximity, and (2) accelerated decay from electric currents artificially induced into the hull from an extraneous source. They may usually, though not always, be distinguished by the fact that the attack occurring from the proximity of dissimilar metals will commonly be preferential, that is, most severe in the less noble metal and probably confined to the immediate area of the dissimilar materials. Artificially induced galvanic attack, in contrast, may occur wholly within a single metal, may be spread over a considerable area, or may be highly localized with no apparent relation to the part of the boat where it may occur, although it may be centered around areas of high electrical conductivity, such as bronze propeller assemblies, copper-alloy heat exchangers, depthfinder fittings and the like. Quite commonly, such attacked areas may be quite bright when the boat is first hauled out of the water, indicating rapid ion-exchange constantly exposing new unoxidized metal as it proceeds. Also, such areas commonly have a peculiar granular appearance quite different from ordinary corrosion. When they are found, you should look at your electrical circuitry to be sure that some part of the system is not grounded either through the hull or the engine, or that the boat is not electrically shorted to the dock.

With the present tendency of the yachting fraternity to use large amounts of electricity on its rounds from the electric plugs of one marina to another, induced galvanic attack is an ever-increasing hazard, not only in steel and aluminum boats but in other types as well. Stray current of the high voltages used are not selective and will erode fastenings just as easily as steel plates. A completely closed electrical system fully insulated from the boat is a must no matter what sort of craft is involved.

These comments might lead the reader to believe that no dissimilar metals at all should be used, but this is not the case. They may be, and are used constantly and quite successfully, so long as the fundamental precepts are observed and they are adequately insulated from each other. Fortunately, this is not difficult to do. Of course, if there is any choice, there is no point in introducing a dissimilar metal. But often it is impossible to use one metal only, particularly in such items as heat exchangers or propeller shaft assemblies. Steel propellers, for example, are not commonly available on the market, and even if they were, would not necessarily be desirable. Bronze propellers are no problem when properly installed in a steel boat.

Sandblasting

Before any dissimilar metal units are installed, the basic hull will have to be prepared to accept them and the boat will have to receive its first course of corrosion protection, which is to clean it thoroughly outside. Cleanliness in this case does not mean dusting it off and wiping it down, or even sanding or grinding it bright. It means instead that it must be *sandblasted* clean so that every square inch of it is down to raw metal unsullied by the slightest speck of rust, grease, dirt, or scale; so that every nook and cranny is bright, every crevice devoid of entrapped soil, and every trace of contaminant gone.

There is no other reasonable way to achieve this except by sandblasting, no other method of getting in the narrow corners or indentations or between the close spaces, nor any procedure half as efficient or as quick. And, even if there were, even if spotless cleanliness could be somehow achieved, the result would still be inadequate because the surface, even if mirror-bright, would not be correct for the second, and equally as important "anodic" process. For this, a roughened, as well as meticulously clean, surface is essential, and sandblasting provides it as no other practical process can.

Sandblasting at best is an unpleasant chore. It is a noisy, gritty process and probably the biggest drawback for the fastidious. The mechanics of it are simple enough: sand is blasted either from a tank equipped with flow and pressure controls, or sand is picked up from an open container such as a large bucket or tub and then blasted. Of the two, the tank is the more efficient and is recommended unless the job to be done is a small one. The air is provided by a standard air compressor of generous capacity, and the sand is fed by a hose from the tank or container through a hard cast-metal, metal-carbide, or ceramic nozzle from which it is directed at the work. The nozzle is held about six inches away from the surface and moved back and forth in a series of short reversible strokes as the sand blasts away the dirt and scale and leaves a velvety, white or grey, somewhat granular surface. Done properly, the surface should be uniform in texture and color with no residual streaks of imbedded scale or other contaminants. Any unskilled laborer can master the mechanics of the operation in a few minutes.

However, for the purpose involved, there are certain requirements which must be met. The flow of air must be at least 100 cubic feet per minute unless the operation is to take forever, and the pressure at the nozzle must be at least 65 psi, preferably more, in the order of 75 to 100 psi. The efficiency of the entire operation depends on a generous and uniform supply of air, and the sand will not cut properly unless it strikes the metal surface with great force. It is true that cleaning is possible with less pressure but more is involved than cleaning alone. The surface must be specifically roughened while it is being cleaned, and this is directly a function of air pressure.

Air pressure is also a function of nozzle size. The purpose of sand-blasting nozzles is not only to direct the stream of air and sand in a confined pattern, but also to increase the velocity of the sand. Thus while the air hose carrying the sand from the tank may be over an inch in outside diameter the size of the nozzle opening may be only one-eighth of an inch and seldom more than one-quarter, unless there is a very large air supply beyond the capacity of the average portable air compressor. It is important that the nozzle opening be kept small; as nozzles are used, they become increasingly larger in inside diameter because of abrasion and beyond a certain point should be discarded and replaced. Cast metal nozzles may last for an hour or so; the carbide and ceramic ones have longer lives.

The type of sand used is critical. It is a waste of time to use ordinary beach sand, or any sand that is soft, damp, or uneven in size. Beach sand, while cheap, is rounded and smoothed from wave action; it will not cut and will not roughen the metal surface properly. Only crushed, sharp, hard, washed and dried, graded silica sand free of feldspar or other mineral constituents which tend to break down and remain on the surface in visible quantity, or its equal,* should be used. It removes the

---

* Aluminum oxide, 20 to 50 grit, is also satisfactory but usually more expensive then silica sand.

ENLARGED CONFIGURATION OF
SURFACE BLASTED WITH
ORDINARY SAND --

SAME SURFACE BLASTED
WITH SHARP SILICA SAND

11-3.   The effects of sandblasting with ordinary sand and silica sand.

toughest scale and indents the metal evenly with thousands of sharp-toothed depressions per square inch (see Figure 11-3).

Sharp silica sand is readily available and may be bought in bulk or in 100-pound bags, the most convenient way of handling it. Bagged sand from any reliable source is clean, carefully graded by grit size, and uniform. It may be obtained in a variety of particle sizes from very fine to quite large. Fine sand does a good cleaning job but does not provide proper "tooth" for subsequent coatings; sand that is too large tends to clog the sandblast dispenser and is too slow for efficient use. A mesh size between 20 and 40, U.S. Standard Sieve Series, is suggested with a minimum of 40 percent of the sand retained on a 30-mesh screen.

It is equally important not only that the sand be dry but also that the air from the air compressor be dry and free of oil. The equipment, somewhere between the compressor and the dispenser, should include a trap (standard equipment) to remove any water vapor in the line. Sandblasting should be limited to those hours when the humidity is low. This is particularly important in seacoast areas where at times the atmosphere is so loaded with moisture that a newly sandblasted surface may visibly rust in an hour or less. In any event, no more sandblasting should be done to a given area at a given time than can be completely protected by the anodic coating within four hours, preferably less. No sandblasted surface should be allowed to remain uncoated overnight or even for short periods if the conditions of humidity increase. A preferred practice is to run through a tank of sand (usually about one to one and a half hours, depending on tank size) and immediately coat the new surface before it can become contaminated with atmospheric moisture.

Sandblasting, it should be noted, is a potentially hazardous operation if safety precautions are not observed. It should never be done without a proper sandblast helmet or without either a face mask to remove dust from the air or, alternately, a supply of clean air to the helmet. Many helmets have air hoses attached for this purpose. Silica sand should never be inhaled; prolonged breathing of it can cause silicosis, a disease of the lungs.

Never, under any circumstances, should a sandblast nozzle be directed at anyone, or your own body. Sand can cut like a knife and a very short blast to the face could cause serious damage to the eyes. Also, compressed air can be dangerous if you are careless with it. All equipment should be carefully bled before it is disconnected, and only hose designed for the purpose should be used.

Flame-spraying

As the hull, a section at a time, is sandblasted, and before it can become contaminated with moisture, it should be anodically protected by flame-spraying of either aluminum or zinc. I regard this "anodic treatment" as of the essence. It is essential for both long life of the boat and for freedom from annoying minor incidental corrosive attack from abrasion, scratches, or other mechanical mishaps that will inevitably occur unless the boat never leaves the launching dock. Both zinc and aluminum act as anodic materials; they are lower in the "Electromotive Series" than steel and serve to protect it in the presence of sea water, the ever-present electrolyte in which every boat rests.

It may be argued that flame-spraying, in view of some of the modern paint systems, is unnecessary, needlessly expensive, and, at the extreme, a matter of gilding the lily. It is true that there are a number of steel-hulled vessels which seem quite adequately protected without it, but critical examination of each case will reveal that the owners either lavish constant care on their boats, immediately touching up each rust spot as it appears, maintain their craft in fresh waters, such as the Great Lakes, or keep them under constant cover; many rue the day they did not go an extra step further to avoid the constant touch-up work. Each year, craft are brought to my yard by owners seeking correction for annoying problems which should never have occurred in the first place. No matter how good a paint system may be, or how carefully it may be applied, sooner or later it is going to be scratched or chipped, or it will locally blister, peel, or crack. Unless it is immediately taken care of, the inevitable streak of rust appears and becomes unsightly; neglected, it becomes a potential source of trouble. Few boats are hauled for painting more than twice a year, most only once; unless there is an auxiliary method of protection to carry over between hauls, the defect becomes aggravated, the unsightly spot more so. Beyond the general anodic protection it affords to the entire hull, flame-spraying provides anodic local protection from painting defects for at least a year and slows down the possible damage to such a degree that correction is easy, the expense minimal.

The cost of flame-spraying in the beginning, aside from the cost of the equipment, is negligible compared to the expense of future maintenance without it. No matter what system of paint might be used, the hull will still have to be sandblasted outside: no exterior paint system so far devised is completely satisfactory over a scaled or soiled surface. The main cost of flame-spraying is in the surface preparation, that is the sandblasting, which must be done anyway. The actual spraying of the anodic zinc or aluminum takes little longer than paint spraying; it proceeds at about the same pace, and the cost of the zinc or aluminum and the compressed air, oxygen, and acetylene required can be measured in only a few cents extra per square foot. Tabulated in terms of future maintenance dollars, let alone annoyance, failure to make use of it does not make economic sense.

The actual spraying is no more difficult than spraying paint but attention to a few more details is required. In essence, zinc or aluminum wire is fed into a gun* which contains a compressed air turbine, which in turn drives a set of knurled rolls that grip the wire and feed it through the gun at a constant rate. The wire speed can be adjusted by controls to be as slow or as fast as desired. Slower speeds provide a fine spray; faster speeds, a slightly coarser spray. For economy, the speed is adjusted to provide the fastest rate consistent with the spray fineness desired and still maintain full and complete melting of the moving wire. Along with compressed air, oxygen and acetylene is fed into the gun at predetermined pressures controlled by the same type of gauges used for the acetylene cutting torch. Typically, for 1/8" zinc wire, about 15 psi acetylene pressure to about 16 psi oxygen is used with an air pressure of about 65 psi. This will deposit roughly about 980 square feet per hour to .001" thickness. In practice, the hull should have between .003" to .004" total, or more if desired, so the final square footage will be about one-third to one-quarter less.

The actual operation of the gun is relatively simple, but care should be taken that the flame is properly adjusted either by sight or by automatic flow-meter control. Flame adjustment is much like that of the

* Available only through METCO, Inc., Westbury, L.I., N.Y.

11-4. Zinc spraying a hull.

cutting torch and may be regulated precisely by increasing or decreasing the oxygen pressure in relation to the acetylene until the maximum flame is achieved. Improper adjustment will cause the flame to "pop" and go out or will fail to melt the rapidly moving wire at the optimum speed. The adjustment is not difficult but must be correct.

The wire is then moved through the flame by the rolls and is melted and blasted by the air pressure in a fine spray onto the newly sandblasted steel. There it instantly solidifies in a silvery white finish about the texture of very fine sandpaper. The gun is used like a paint spray gun, with reciprocal motions back and forth to insure full coverage. For convenience, the wire may be fed continuously from a reel or laid out in straight lengths for easy feeding by hand. Once the metal spray has been deposited, it is firmly fixed in place by the thousands of minute interlocking "teeth" or depressions created by sandblasting. It will not spall and is almost impossible to remove by a hammer or similar mechanical blows. It becomes fully and integrally bonded to the metal. Its beneficial effect is immediate; within seconds after deposition, a hose can be turned on the hull with no effect other than a slight darkening of the zinc.

During spraying, goggles or a face mask should be used to protect the eyes, and unless you are working in the open air under conditions of full ventilation, a filter should be used to prevent breathing zinc dust or fumes. Better yet is to use a face mask provided with clean, fresh air. Zinc oxide fumes can be unpleasant and in some severe cases produce temporary illness. Also, the hands or other parts of the body should be kept away from the business end of the gun. The flame is intensely hot and the temperature of the spray is above the melting point of zinc or aluminum.

Other than these precautions, the actual spraying is uncomplicated, but every square inch of the exterior of the vessel should be adequately coated, with particular care given to corners, tight places, or areas where water or moisture are likely to lie or be trapped. All edges should be thoroughly sprayed, as well as places subject to frequent future wear or abuse. Once the boat is coated, it is not necessary to paint immediately. It can be delayed for hours or even days if necessary, but it is recommended that painting be done as soon as practical and that the newly sprayed surface be kept clean of dirt and grease. Greasy handprints can cause later paint blistering. It is my custom to begin painting as quickly as possible before moisture or contaminants can accumulate and spoil an otherwise immaculate surface.

Painting

There is, probably, no other item of steel boat construction that is subject to as much diversity of opinion, misconception, quaint folklore, or just plain ignorance, as painting. Every builder is also the target of a generous measure of dubious advertising, sales promotion, and unlikely claims by hopeful manufacturers. Each year some new product guaranteed to solve all marine corrosion problems is introduced to the market, has its hour in the trade journals, and quietly disappears. Also, surprisingly few boatyards or repair shops have any real knowledge of the selection and use of metal paints, and many are quite inept at prescribing or applying the proper types, although they may be experts in the use of paints for boats of other materials.

There are certain criteria which must be met for steel vessels that do not necessarily apply to paints suitable for wood, fiberglass, or even ferro-cement. Many of the common paints on the market are not only unsuitable for steel but also may actually, in the long run, be damaging. The paint system selected not only must be decorative but also must be primarily preservative — or at the least neutral. Thus, the basic requirements from which to judge any steel paint system are these:

1. The paint must adhere. No paint system is of much value if it does not stick tightly; it cannot peel locally, blister, or slough off. There

11-5.   A zinc-sprayed and partially painted hull.

are any number of paint-like materials in the plastics field that might seem suitable but they possess no tenacity at all, or very little. The same applies to most oil-based paints when applied to steel below the water-line. It makes no difference if adherence is achieved by a primer or directly by the main coating itself, so long as it can be depended upon.

2.   The paint system must be compatible with steel as well as with the anodic coating (zinc or aluminum) employed. That is to say, it must not contain materials that react disadvantageously chemically or physically, inhibit or destroy the anodic coating, attack the steel itself, or set up a galvanic response, either locally or in general. It must be compatible, above the waterline also, with ordinary decorative marine paints.

3.   The paint must be continuous and nonporous in nature and be free of the tendency to create small voids, bubbles, pinholes, and the like. It should also be of such a consistency to form an effective barrier, when dried, against oxygen and water.

4.   The system must be neutral or non-conducting to galvanic or in-duced electrical currents.

5.   The paint must be readily and easily applied by ordinary painting methods and easily renewed when required.

6.   The paint must be readily available from marine supply places in any major port or maritime country in the world. There is no benefit in using a system, no matter how good, unless it can be purchased easily and without special attention from some lone manufacturer who makes only a limited amount for local, special, or experimental consumption.

7.   The system must be compatible with anti-fouling paints and be shielding from the chemicals of these paints. Certain anti-fouling paints,

including those containing copper, if applied directly to an unshielded steel hull, will have a deleterious effect. The paint system must act as a barrier as well as a vehicle for anti-fouling ingredients.

8.   The paint system should be reasonably resistant to sunlight as well as to the ordinary chemical pollutants, oils, detergents, etc., common to harbors and other contaminated waterways.

9.   The finish after drying and/or curing should be smooth enough for final decorative finish. Some of the proprietary systems featuring thick, heavy barrier coats, while adequate for barges and similar commercial vessels, are by no means smooth enough for yacht use.

10.   No paint system which has not withstood the test of time in actual use should be considered unless the owner is willing to serve as a guinea pig. It is a long way from laboratory testing to full-scale proven service. A good corrosion-protection system should be good for years of use with only seasonal touch-up and repair. This, of course, does not include the overlying anti-fouling paints or the decorative color paints, which will have to be renewed regularly.

11.   The paint must be flexible to withstand thermal expansion as well as tough to be resistant to abrasion and mechanical damage.

All of this is quite a bill of requirements for any paint system to fulfill and why selection should be considered with *all* these points in mind. Ordinary paints will just not do the job and should not be expected to.

There are any number of proprietary paint systems on the market, each with its brand name and each with some sort of special or semi-secret formulation or sequence. Most, however, are variations of two or three basic systems and they serve either as relatively simple barrier coats against oxygen and water or as carriers for anodic particles which act, theoretically at least, as corrosion inhibitors. Some of the basic systems are:

The Vinyls The vinyls have the distinction of being the longest corrosion-resistant paint system in actual use and have an excellent service record on many hundreds of ships, both commercial and pleasure, since they were first introduced to the trade about 1947. I have used them since their inception with almost complete success. Boats painted over 20 years ago have remained essentially intact except where the paint was damaged and had to be renewed locally. The vinyls are quite compatible with anodic flame-sprayed metals, such as zinc and aluminum, and their electrical resistance makes them useful with controlled cathodic protection. Like nearly all the protective paints, their success is contingent upon an adequate film thickness; the film thickness specified by the manufacturers must be adhered to. Those failures which do occur (no paint system is ever 100 percent perfect) may almost always be traced to inadequate surface cleaning or to an incomplete film overlay, such as "holidays," bubbles, and similar discontinuities.

There are a number of proprietary variations in the vinyl systems, in color and in the quantity and content of the suspensions. The vinyl resins themselves are fairly clear, but as they are normally supplied, they are opaque because of additions of red lead, zinc, or aluminum particles, or zinc chromate or other additives. Some of the suspensions are intended to act as inhibiting anodic materials, others as mere colorants so that, as extra coats are applied, discontinuities in the film become visible and can be corrected.

Because most of the vinyls do not adhere too well when applied directly over a smooth metal surface, an adherent type of "washcoat" primer is almost always specified. These primers commonly have a vinyl base but contain, in addition, a phosphoric acid diluent and pigments, usually zinc chromate and lampblack, which impart a dark green color. The phosphoric acid acts as a mild etchant and creates a better bond between the metal and the coat. These primers are somewhat watery in their consistency and are simply "washed on" by sprayer, brush, or roller. They dry quickly at ordinary temperatures and are ready for recoating within an hour. Their pot life is short, however, and they should be used within about eight hours of mixing.

With the primer dry, a typical application of vinyl would then be to paint successively with alternate coats of different colors, for example red and aluminum, until five coats are built up, sandwich style, to a total, not including the anti-fouling paint, of about twelve mils. Properly done, this should insure a good, tough film impervious to water and oxygen and which should last many years.

Because of the labor involved in applying five coats, not including the primer and subsequent anti-fouling or decorative paints, some manufacturers have developed vinyl-based systems requiring fewer coats. Selection of these systems is, of course, subject to proof and the data supplied by the manufacturers. In practice the five-coat system has worked well.

Now, where the service conditions are not severe, as in freeboard locations, above-deck areas, and weather-protected interiors, and where there is to be an overlay of decorative paints, the number of vinyl coats may be reduced to three, but if there is doubt the five-coat system should be used.

The vinyls are quick drying, depending upon temperature (one to two hours between coats) and may be applied over dry surfaces at a considerable range of temperature (5° to 100° F), which is not true of a great many other paints. They may be brushed, sprayed, or rolled, but attention should be given to the manufacturer's literature for limitations in this respect, particularly in regard to spraying.

The anti-fouling paints used over the vinyls should be compatible with them. They usually are vinyl based both for compatibility and adherence. Ordinary anti-fouling paints may not adhere properly and, if they do, they must be removed for renewal of any of the original vinyl for local repairs, or for subsequent use of a vinyl-based anti-fouling paint. Above the waterline, however, any number of conventional paints may be used quite satisfactorily over vinyl.

Inorganic Zinc Compounds These coatings, subject in recent years to some manufacturers' trade publicity, are commonly made up of self-curing ethyl silicate and a generous percent of zinc flakes or dust. They depend on the anodic effect of the zinc for cathodic protection of the steel and are usually applied as primers directly over the steel. Additional coats of inorganic zinc may be added or followed by any number of combinations of coats of vinyls, epoxies, alkyds, or even chlorinated rubber, depending on the manufacturer and the nature of the manufacturer's individual system. There is some diversity in the claims of the various companies about their products under conditions of total immersion in sea water. Some state that inorganic zinc compounds are not recommended for continuous saltwater immersion, or for resistance to alkalis or acids; others claim full success if they are followed by other coatings. Most agree that they are satisfactory for above-waterline use, for interiors, holds, and the like. Their main appeal, compared to the regular five-coat vinyl system, is that fewer coats and hence less labor is required. However, often a "tie-coat" between the inorganic zinc and subsequent coats is required for proper adherence. Each manufacturer's product or combination is subject to proof, to the test of time, and the inclinations of the builder. Because there are so many variations of combinations it is not possible for me to comment on each.

The Epoxies Here, again, are a diversity of coating systems which vary according to the manufacturer. For the most part, epoxies are coal-tar epoxy resins requiring a polymide catalyst to activate and cure them. They usually can be applied directly over a clean metal surface, unless otherwise specified by the manufacturer, commonly in a two-coat system followed by a vinyl anti-fouling paint below the waterline and manu-facturer-designated colors above. They are somewhat more abrasion resistant than the vinyls or the inorganic zincs, over which they are some-times coated. The disadvantage of the epoxies is that their application is critical, with limited pot life and limited recoating times necessary for good adherence of one paint coat to another. They are not as simple to use as the vinyls and require attention to detail during application. Their main value is in applications where abrasion and wear is a problem.

Miscellaneous Along with the three systems just described above are a number of other systems of more or less value. Some of them are in-tended for large commercial ships where corrosion-resistance is not as critical because of heavy plate thickness and where some deterioration can be tolerated with equanimity, or where dockyard cost is of import-ance (usually a false economy). The outlook for commercial vessels is often quite different from that for yachts. Systems adequate for freighters or barges cannot be tolerated in small vessels with only 1/8″ plating, for example. These paint systems are mentioned here primarily for the sake of the record:

Bituminous-based paints having high concentrations of aluminum, like the inorganic zinc compounds, depend on aluminum for its anodic effect below the waterline. Commonly applied in a sequence of coats over a "washcoat primer," they are followed by resin, fish oil, pine tar based copper oxide anti-fouling paints. They do not meet the criteria established previously for yachts, but are frequently used on commercial vessels because of relatively low cost.

The same comments apply to the *plasticized hydrocarbon resins and pitches* containing iron oxide pigments. While often used because they are inexpensive, they are inadequate substitutes for the vinyls and other more efficient anti-corrosives.

Modified alkyd paints contain red lead, iron oxide, and zinc chro-mate. This family of paints is of no value underwater but is used fre-quently as a primer for interiors or areas of relatively mild exposure. This type is not to be compared with the vinyls or other superior paint systems.

There are a number of *coal tar and asphalt solutions and emulsions,* but they are rarely used for boat work, except for certain commercial uses and then usually over epoxies or other undercoats.

I have had no experience or valid data for comment on *chlorinated rubber systems*. Builders contemplating their use will have to rely on the manufacturers' information. The chlorinated rubbers are frequently used in Europe where they are reported to be successful and about on a par with the vinyls. However, they are not readily obtainable in the United States from the usual marine supply sources.

Undoubtedly, as time progresses, new paint systems will be developed that may be superior to those now in use but, at the time of this writing for the class of vessels dealt with in this volume, the vinyls are the most versatile, certainly the simplest to apply, and the most practical for the small steel boat builder. They are available everywhere, may be bought in small or large quantities, and fulfill the criteria established. They have withstood the test of time.

Some special comment should be made about anti-fouling paints. There are a number of types and a wide variety of special formulations. Frequently, some remarkable claims are made that might tempt the steel boat builder or owner to experiment. There is nothing wrong with this, for this is how we learn. However, before any steel-hulled vessel is coated with an anti-foulant, particularly a newly developed one of alleged miraculous virtues, a few questions might be asked. They are: (1) is it compatible with the corrosion-protective system already on the boat, (2) will it adhere to that system and not flake off, peel, or blister, (3) is it likely to set up an unfavorable galvanic action that might diminish the corrosion-resistance established, (4) does it require a special primer or "tie-coat," to bond it to other coats, (5) is it unduly toxic, (6) is it commercially available, (7) under what conditions has it been proved?

Recently some new anti-foulants have been developed that are so toxic that you cannot touch the bottom for days after painting without danger of skin burns. They cannot be applied without unusual safety precautions, such as wearing chemical-impervious masks and gloves or even refraining from smoking. The fumes are dangerous and clothing contaminated with the substance must be disposed of.

These anti-foulants, combinations of coal-tar epoxies and tributyltin acetate, allegedly possess long life and are reported suitable for steel hulls when applied over approved base coats or systems. But they should not be used haphazardly or without rigid safety precautions. Because they are relatively new, they are still subject to the test of time.

Most conventional anti-foulants are cuprous-oxide combinations in a variety of carriers ranging all the way from fish oils and resin-based materials to the vinyls. But whatever the combination, whether it is based on copper, mercury, tin, or other marine poisons, it is very important that it be proper, not only in its relation to the steel itself but also to the coatings which give it support and which shield it from the hull. Reputable manufacturers supplying metal corrosion-resisting paint systems also supply matching anti-foulants.

Through-Hull Fittings

With the hull thoroughly protected both inside and out with a vinyl or other paint system, the various through-hull fittings, valves, water intakes, shaft assemblies, etc., can be installed. Theoretically, in view of the galvanic effects of dissimilar metals, these fittings should be of steel coated with zinc or aluminum. Practically, however, for reasons of procurement, this is not feasible and, in some instances, not really desirable. Some number of dissimilar metals will have to be used, and actually, with proper precautions, there is no reason why they should not. The important matter is that they be insulated from the hull or shielded by some means so that no galvanic attack is possible, or if possible so minimized as to be of no importance. This is not as difficult as might, at first reading, seem.

It would be quite improper, for example, to screw a bronze valve to a steel pipe welded to the hull. Sooner or later it will give trouble; but a bronze sea-cock bolted to the hull over a pad of rubber, neoprene, or other flexible insulator will pose no difficulties so long as the bolts, too, are carefully insulated. It has been my custom to drill the bolt holes oversize, cut short lengths of insulating tubing, such as micarta, insert them in the bolt holes, provide insulating washers for the nuts, and then flood the whole bolted assembly with one of the rubber or rubber-like setting compounds. Once pulled tight, the bolts are effectively sealed off from water and oxygen, and when the exposed heads are thoroughly coated with vinyl or another barrier-coat material, they are effectively insulated (see Figure 11-6). In over twenty years I have not had a single failure.

There are, of course, plastic through-hull fittings available and from the viewpoint of corrosion-resistance their use is ideal. However, like all plastic products, their strength and fatigue life is quite low and they are subject to failure particularly in areas of sustained vibration and especially in threaded sections. I have had several boats brought to me on the verge of sinking because of notch-stress failures of these fittings.

As a further protection against galvanic effects, especially from induced electric currents, introduced by the boat's electrical system or from exterior sources, it is suggested that all non-steel tubing, including engine intakes, leading to and from through-hull fittings be equipped with short lengths of rubber, neoprene, or other insulating sleeves, preferably above the waterline. This will prevent any accidental transmission of stray currents to the fittings and/or the hull.

The same rule applies to propeller shafting. As has already been mentioned, shafts should be run through rubber-lined bearings and the inboard stuffing boxes should be of the flexible rubber-sleeved types. And, where for some reason this is not desired and fixed bronze stuffing boxes are specified to be bolted to the interior components welded to the hull, the same rules of electrical insulation used for through-hull fittings should be applied.

Some shaft bearings call for grease cups and grease for lubrication; in no case should graphite ever be used as a substitute for grease. Graphite is an almost perfect conductor of electricity and one of the worst cases of galvanic failure I have ever seen was directly traced to this mistaken practice.

Outboard bronze bearings to be introduced into strut tubes and the like should be sealed with insulating rubber-setting compounds or their equal. While this makes their removal a little difficult, it eliminates any appreciable galvanic attack in the tubes. As an additional precaution, propeller shafts should be equipped with zinc corrosion collars. Zinc anode plates on the hull may be used if desired, but if, as should be, the hull is flame-sprayed with zinc or aluminum, they are not necessary.

If appreciable corrosive attack becomes visible after the first haul-out, it is likely that either the protective paint system is inadequate or there are stray induced currents causing the trouble. It would be better to isolate the cause and eliminate it than to depend on anodes to correct an improper situation. The use of anodes on shafting, however, is a different matter, because here one is dealing with bare, uncoated metal on at least some segment of the shafting or the propeller itself. It is almost impossible to keep paint on propellers.

Dissimilar metal attachments on decks and above the waterline are much less likely to show galvanic effects unless they are constantly wet. They should, however, be sealed at their points of attachment by insulating materials to protect them against crevice corrosion, the retention of water in bolt holes, and the like. This applies equally to wood bolted over steel. Mating surfaces that are impervious to water and remain dry do not suffer corrosive attack. Wooden decks, plywood and the like, should also be sealed completely from water and oxygen at every faying surface on the exterior of the hull and in those interior locations that might accumulate excess moisture.

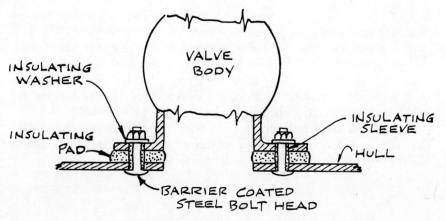

11-6. Insulating a fitting from the hull to protect against galvanic action.

Because of the complexity of the electrical systems on many boats, no attempt is made here to describe in detail all of the possibilities of corrosive attack from induced or stray electric currents. They are legion. The essential point is that all electrical circuits should be completely closed ones, that no part of the boat should be used as one side of the circuit, no matter how low the voltage or amperage, and that all fastenings of electrical systems to the hull be so installed that they cannot abrade insulated wires and short out to the hull. This applies equally to the engine circuitry, lights, generators, radar systems, television sets, radios, and all the other countless electrical gadgets, necessary or unnecessary, which modern craft are likely to contain. It also applies to ship-to-shore mooring attachments, including wire-rope mooring cables or chains, as well as to ordinary electrical connections. A steel boat properly insulated from its electrical system will pose no related corrosion problems.

Among the developments of recent years are cathodic protective systems for boats in which adverse galvanic currents of the hull are more or less automatically detected, measured, and then deliberately reversed in equal amount to cancel them out and thus restore galvanic equilibrium. They have been successful in some boats suffering galvanic troubles, indifferently so in other cases. They should not be viewed as a panacea for electrical troubles or even for other corrosion problems but rather as a luxury that the individual owner may or may not wish to indulge in. One of the hazards of this system is that if the power source fails, the flow of current can then reverse itself and accelerate rather than control the corrosive attack.

In my opinion, the steel boat, properly built, properly maintained, and properly insulated from its electrical sources, does not need instrumentation of this sort. However, if an owner insists upon loading his craft with every conceivable electrical device without regard to the insulation of his circuitry, then these devices may be of value.

There is no substitute for doing the job correctly in the first place. Corrosion prevention is mostly a matter of common sense, understanding the rules of the game, and adhering to them.

12　FINISHING OUT

The finishing of a steel boat does not differ markedly in any respect from the finishing of vessels of any other material.

In sailing craft, the rigging and sail plans are wholly within the desires of the owner and the requirements of the architect. That they are attached to a steel boat is of no special note beyond the fact that the shrouds, bowsprit lines, and the like are fastened to fittings welded integrally to the hull, rather than bolted on. In every large craft, steel masts can sometimes be used, but ordinarily, for weight reasons, other materials are more suitable.

Even though the finishing out of a steel vessel is basically similar to the completion of other boats, some consideration here to engine installation is advisable, if for no other reason than that it is often a carelessly done feature no matter what class of craft is involved. There are, of course, innumerable engines available of almost every conceivable size, shape, and horsepower, and the selection is pretty much up to the ideas of the designers, the requirements of the boat in respect to its proposed function, and/or the personal feelings or quirks of the owner.

A great deal of engine troubles in recent years, beyond inadequate installation, has been the tendency, especially among yacht owners, to vastly overpower their boats. The sight of an otherwise trim craft all "hunkered down" in the water and pulling a monstrous stern wave is all too common, as is the use of all sorts of "trim tabs" to compensate for either poor design or too much engine for the boat, or a combination of both. Surprisingly few boat owners seem to realize that, beyond a certain point, the addition of extra horsepower provides only a minimum advantage in speed, if any, and greatly augments both the capital expense as well as the operating costs, and at the same time makes the boat less livable and more prone to give them headaches and trouble.

The launching of the 75-foot centerboard ketch Clementine *from the Gwynn Island Boat Yard.*

It is not proposed here to provide a full-scale dissertation on engines or even engine selection, but instead to point out that when the prospective owner or builder is considering the purchase of an engine system and is faced with the engine manufacturer's often glowing literature, some basic thoughts should be kept in mind. One thing to consider is the effect of that engine on the trim of the boat. This can be of particular importance in auxiliary sailboats where weight can be critical. It is often tempting to contemplate, for example, using a fifty-horsepower engine instead of a twenty if space is available, but a careful look at the weight figures will indicate that the effect on trim may be very undesirable. Added to that effect will likely be a loss of space for auxiliary machinery, such as a generator, if one is desired, and this applies equally to power vessels. Space on any boat is at a premium and often more so in an engine room than any other location.

It should be remembered that all engines must be available for both maintenance and repairs, and there is nothing worse than trying to correct some engine fault, or even attempting some simple task like changing oil, in a space so small that even a midget would have difficulty. Some of the monster powerplants in small boats are almost hopeless to service once they are installed.

Another item that seems to escape new boat owners until it is too late is that the incidence of noise (and this has no relation to steel boats versus craft of other materials) is often directly proportional to horsepower, particularly in diesel installations. The racket produced by even a properly functioning diesel in the engine room can sometimes be horrendous, and there are many boats in which this is so great that normal conversation in the living quarters or on deck is all but impossible.

All engines must be properly and fully ventilated if they are to function properly and if engine odors are to be kept free of living quarters. Indeed, the very efficiency of all internal-combustion engines is predicated on their having adequate air intake and adequate exhaust systems. One cannot expect to box up an engine in a semi-sealed room and have it perform properly, or, in the case of gasoline engines, to be even reasonably safe.

To be efficient, the engine system should be adequate for the boat and for every reasonable task the boat is required to do, but no more than that. There is no virtue in overdoing engine systems and usually there are numerous disadvantages.

Assuming that both the owner and the designer have settled on an adequate and reasonable engine and engine-room layout, the final efficiency of the whole will depend on (1) the adequacy of the engine bed, (2) the alignment of that bed with the centerline of the shaft, (3) the final alignment of the shaft and the engine itself, (4) vibration control, (5) proper and complete installation of fuel tanks and feed lines, (6) simple and direct control mechanisms, and (7) a closed-circuit electrical system, if one is required.

The subject of engine beds has already been discussed briefly and it has been pointed out that the beds should always span three, preferably more, structural members and not be carried on the hull plating. It should be noted also that, with very large and heavy engines, the beds should at least be double the length of the engine and, if practical, carried from bulkhead to bulkhead of the engine compartment. Also, wherever possible, the engine beds should carry transverse stiffeners to absorb the thrust of the engines in a rolling sea. Where possible there should be transverse stiffeners (usually cut from flat plate) directly under the engines and also stiffeners outboard of the engines (see Figure 12-1). Lightening holes may be cut in the stiffeners to reduce weight and also to allow access to drain plugs and for cleaning beneath the engine itself.

The engine beds should be built with at least 1/2″ clearance between the top of the bed and the actual final position of the engine mounts. This will allow for corrections in final alignment by the use of shims. There are a variety of shim devices that may be used, from simple strips

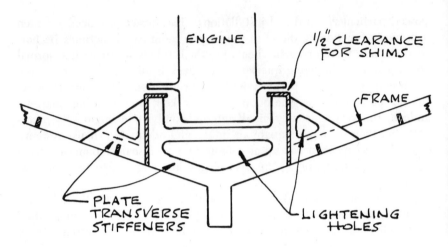

ENGINE ½" CLEARANCE FOR SHIMS FRAME

PLATE TRANSVERSE STIFFENERS LIGHTENING HOLES

12-1. Cross-section of an engine bed showing the method of transverse stiffening.

of metal to wedge-shaped paired metal units with threaded bolts for precision adjustment. Another method is to use threaded bolts tapped into the bed with suitable locked nuts to fix them in permanent position. With these, once the final alignment is achieved with the boat in the water, a temporary dam of clay or asbestos is shaped around the bolt area and molten babbit metal poured to form a fixed, permanent alignment. This is used mostly on fairly large commercial installations.

If rubber engine mounts are planned, and they are among the better methods of controlling noise and vibration, it would be desirable to check the dimensions of the mounts before final welding of the top of the engine bed. They may require more spacing than the conventional 1/2" allowance used for ordinary shim methods. The use of such mounts, while highly desirable, make mandatory the use also of flexible couplings between the shaft and the engine, and all other connections in the installation such as fuel lines, exhaust lines, water piping and the like. But this is a good idea anyway and is recommended no matter what the engine bedding system may be.

Probably the most important factor in engine installation is correct and precise engine alignment — a task often carelessly done. Improper alignment can be the cause of a whole host of troubles: excess vibration, accelerated shaft and bearing wear, fatigue failure of shaft and engine parts, breakage of fuel or oil pressure lines, and plain annoyance. Align-

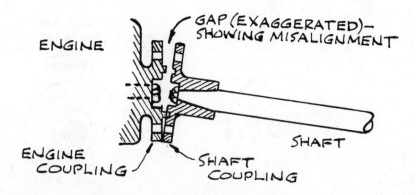

ENGINE

GAP (EXAGGERATED)—
SHOWING MISALIGNMENT

SHAFT

ENGINE
COUPLING

SHAFT
COUPLING

12-2.   *A misaligned engine-shaft coupling.*

ment is really quite simple and requires only a feeler gauge and a little patience. Indeed, if no feeler gauge is available, it can be done quite accurately with several strips of thin paper cut from a single sheet.

The technique is quite uncomplicated and consists of first placing the assembled shaft in its bearings with the shaft coupling in contact with the engine coupling just as if they were ready to be bolted together. A quick inspection will show visually if the two couplings are in near mating contact. If not, a gap between them will be evident at some point around the periphery of the couplings (see Figure 12-2). This will indicate that the engine will have to be tilted up or down or swiveled right or left on its bed. Adjust the engine until the gap disappears and then rotate the engine and shaft to determine if the spacing between the couplings remains constant at all points. If not, readjust again. Then tighten the engine bolts evenly and check the gap, if any, again. If unequal spacing occurs, once again shift and shim the engine and retighten the bolts until the gap at all points of rotation by sight appears equal.

The engine is now ready for final precision alignment with a feeler gauge. This is done by inserting one finger of the gauge between the couplings and "feeling" the amount of drag as it is pulled out. If the mating surfaces are in precise juxtaposition the amount of drag will be the same at all points of rotation; if not, the gauge will slide too readily at one point and resist at another. Continue to shift and shim the engine as described for visual adjustment until exact alignment is proved with the feeler gauge at every point of rotation with the engine bolted down. A maximum of three-thousandths of an inch on the feeler gauge can be permitted for most installations; less is better. Alignment should be re-

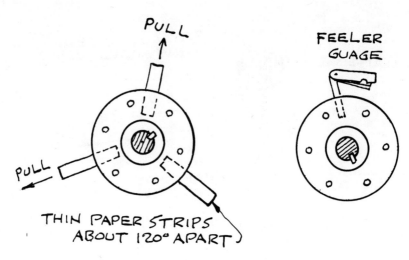

PULL

FEELER
GUAGE

PULL

THIN PAPER STRIPS
ABOUT 120° APART

12-3. *Cross-section of mated couplings showing the use of paper and a feeler gauge.*

checked after the boat is in the water because the hull may change shape slightly. In steel boats, however, this is seldom a problem.

When no feeler gauge is available, three strips of thin paper can be introduced between the couplings at about 120 degrees apart, and the couplings pushed lightly together until they just hold the strips in place. The strips are then gently pulled and the amount of drag, just as in the feeler gauge, will reveal differences from spot to spot. Adjustment should be made until the pull is equal at all points and at all points of rotation (see Figure 12-3).

Fuel tanks should be given careful attention if for no other reason than safety which depends on their integrity. Gasoline tanks are potential bombs and any leakage either from the tanks or fittings are extremely hazardous. Mention has already been made of the use of steel tanks built integral with the hull, and they are particularly valuable for diesel fuel. Diesel fuel is compatible with steel — just plain, ordinary steel — but galvanized sheet or fittings should not be used, although galvanized tanks for gasoline have been used for many years. Similarly, copper tanks are not desirable for diesel use because of the chemical reaction of the sulphur compounds common to diesel fuel. Stock fuel tanks of almost any capacity are available commercially or may be made up to fit the hull. They are made of any of several alloys, including nickel-copper, copper-silicon, copper (tinned inside), and fiberglass laminated with "fireproof" resin. The shell thickness needed will vary, of course with the capacity of the tank and with the strength of the material selected. It should be remembered that fuel is quite heavy and one should not expect to solder up a fuel tank of substantial capacity out of paper-thin stock and not have it collapse or go out of shape. Fuel tanks should be sturdy, dependable, and capable of being firmly strapped and bolted in place. They should also be fitted with baffles at no more than 30" intervals maximum to control surging in rough water. The open area of the baffles, should not exceed about 25 to 30 percent of the baffle area and should have generous limbers at the corners to allow free access and flow of fuel and air. Gas tanks should be completely closed, except for air and fuel intakes and outlets, and should, in addition, be constructed so that the outlet fittings extend close to the bottom of the tanks and a cut-off valve provided at the tank exit.

Diesel tanks can be provided with cleanout plates, but these should be closely bolted (spaced about seven times the plate thickness and with bolts at least twice the plate thickness) and provided with good grade gaskets compatible with diesel fuel. Rubber is not suitable, but neoprene is satisfactory. Diesel tanks will require, also, a return oil fitting.

All fuel lines leading to or from the tanks should be compatible with the tank material and with the fuel used — copper or nickel-copper, for example, for gasoline; iron or steel for diesel. All fuel lines must be flexible, or at least made as much so as possible by the use of suitable loops in the lines to minimize fatigue or by the use of flexible, reinforced non-metallic hose near the engine. All lines should be securely fixed or insulated with neoprene so they cannot chafe, and fuel tank straps should be similarly insulated.

Fuel fill lines should be at least 1-1/2" in diameter and should be as direct as practical to avoid "air-blow" during filling. The air vents should be reasonably generous, about 5/8" I.D., and should be looped downward outboard and provided with screens to prevent intake of water and trash.

The exit fuel lines should be equipped with appropriate shut-off valves and, in the case of fuel tanks below the engine level, with check valves to prevent drainage of fuel back into the tanks. In addition, diesel tanks should possess a small sump and drain cock at the lowest part of the tank to remove accumulated moisture from condensation or other sources.

There are three basic types of engine cooling systems. The oldest and

The sixty-two foot twin diesel yacht Manteo.

traditional one is simply to pump raw sea water through the engine and out the exhaust. In fresh water this is ideal, but in salt water, particularly with many of our modern high-speed, hot-running engines, the life of the engine is shortened by accumulated rusting and build-up of salt deposits. An alternative is to use a heat-exchanger system, which pumps sea water through a heat exchanger, which cools the closed, circulating, fresh water of the engine. The raw sea water is then returned overboard without entering the engine itself, either directly or full or partially through the exhaust. This system requires two pumps, one to circulate the raw sea water, the other to circulate the cooled fresh water closed within the engine. The other alternative is to use a keel-cooler in which the closed, fresh, engine water is circulated through tubes outside the hull; the cooling is accomplished by contact with the cool sea water flowing by the exposed tubing. Here again, two pumps may be required, one to move the fresh engine water, the other to push sea water through the exhaust if it is to be water cooled.

Whichever of these systems is to be used, it must be borne in mind that, even though they do not differ essentially in their installation in steel craft from boats of other materials, most commercial heat exchangers employ copper or copper alloys for their tubing because of its excellent heat conductivity and, as has already been pointed out, this metal must be insulated from the hull. If, as suggested earlier, the water-circulating system is incorporated into the hull as integral steel units, such insulation is not required.

Exhaust systems may be either wet or dry. Most dry exhausts will exit

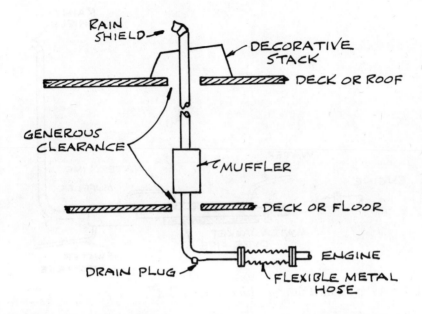

RAIN SHIELD

DECORATIVE STACK

DECK OR ROOF

GENEROUS CLEARANCE

MUFFLER

DECK OR FLOOR

DRAIN PLUG

ENGINE

FLEXIBLE METAL HOSE

12-4. A dry exhaust system.

through a vertical stack and will vent well above the upper deck. Because they may become extremely hot (up to 1000° or more), generous clearance should be allowed (about 10" minimum) where they pass through decking or flooring. And, where there is adjacent combustible material, the stack should either be shielded by suitable metal screening or by insulation. Under no conditions should a dry exhaust pipe be welded fully to a deck, floor, or roof, because the accumulated heat will radiate for a considerable distance, cause buckling or, because of constant contraction or expansion, initiate ultimate failure of either the exhaust pipe or the weld.

A typical properly installed dry exhaust will have a metal flexible hose between the engine and the stack to minimize vibration and will be insulated with asbestos pipe insulation to keep heat down in the engine room (see Figure 12-4). Commonly, the muffler will be mounted vertically in the stack so that its heat will be dispersed easily. If it cannot be so mounted, it will probably have to be insulated too. In many commercial boats, the entire vertical dry exhaust system, muffler and all, is mounted exterior to the cabin and hull with suitable brackets to hold it away from the cabin trunk. If this is done, the hot pipes should be shielded with pierced metal or expanded metal mesh.

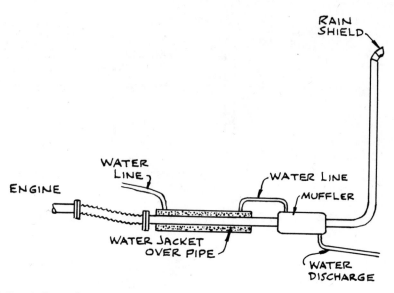

12-5. A dry exhaust system with a water jacket.

Where a direct stack is impractical or not desired, another method of handling dry exhausts is to provide a water jacket for the hot pipe between the flexible metal hose at the engine and the muffler. Cooling water is pumped through the jacket and led overboard (see Figure 12-5).

A great many exhaust systems are of the "wet" type, in which raw sea water is injected into the exhaust pipe and muffler, usually directly from the engine exhaust manifold. Wet exhausts have the advantage of being relatively cool and less prone to vibration because most of the piping can be made up of flexible rubber or neoprene "steam" hose. In operation, the exhaust water is blown out through the entire system by the force of the exhaust gases, thus cooling the system as it goes. Essentially, wet exhausts are of two types: (1) those for engines above the waterline, and (2) those for engines located below the waterline. In either case, provision must be made to insure that sea water is not forced back into the engine by wave action or other water surge. This is usually accomplished (1) by introducing one or more loops in the line (see Figure 12-6), or (2) in the case of engines below the waterline by the use of a stand-pipe above the waterline (see Figure 12-7).

In those vessels in which space is extremely limited or in which there is no room for looping or for a standpipe, some sort of check-valve close

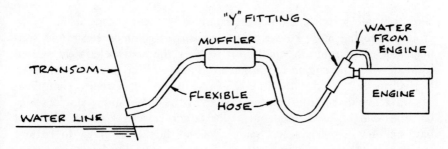

12-6. *An exhaust system with loops in the hose to prevent water from being forced into the system.*

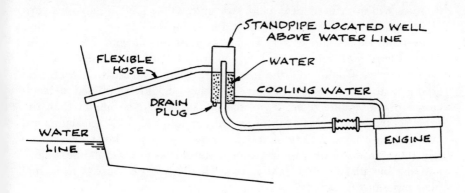

12-7. *An exhaust system using a standpipe.*

to the exit end is necessary to prevent intake of sea water to the engine. Also, in instances where there is any question of sea water flooding into the exhaust system during tie-up, a gate valve should be provided for safety.

Ideally, the preferred metals for exhaust systems are monel or Type 316 stainless steel for gasoline engines; cast iron, monel, or Type 316 for diesel. A variety of commercially produced mufflers, including neoprene, are available. Neoprene mufflers, of course, are useful only on wet exhaust systems; they are light and will not corrode. All steam hose connections should be made with stainless steel pipe clamps.

It is beyond the scope of this book to discuss all the endless variations possible in the electrical systems of any proposed boat beyond reiterating here that all systems should be completely closed and at no point grounded to the hull. However, for reasons of common sense and simplicity, it is desirable in small craft to have the boat's electrical system coincide with the engine requirement. Small craft engines are commonly electrically started with either 12-, 24-, or 32-volt systems. Complications are avoided if the lighting system is the same and a single set of batteries can be used. Of course, for larger vessels, separate banks of batteries may be desirable. Some thought should be given to battery location, particularly in small boats. Batteries are quite heavy and must be thoroughly secured, preferably in strong, immovable cases lined with lead or other substances not affected by battery acid. Also, battery cables should be kept as short as possible for efficiency.

Some comments are appropriate here about engine room ventilation. Engines will not run at peak efficiency unless they have a generous supply of intake air, and, for safety, the fumes incident to engine operation — gasoline vapors and battery fumes — must be efficiently disposed of. At least four vents are required on power craft, two for exhaust and two for air intake. Commonly, the intakes are located forward on each side of the boat and the exhausts aft, and they should be ducted to each corner of the engine room. Also, the intakes should be higher than the exhausts by at least six inches or so. Any number of deck ventilators are available in a wide variety of styles — cowl, half-cowl, low-cowl, etc. — and they are made of a diversity of materials — bronze, stainless steel, and flexible plastic. For safety, they should not be located near fuel filler pipes or fuel tank vents.

Ducts to fit most vents are readily available in copper, galvanized iron, and fireproofed, wire-reinforced fabric. Ducting should be generous in cross-section, at a minimum of about one square inch per foot of beam.

It is essential that gasoline-powered boats have at least one of the exhaust vents equipped with a non-sparking electrical exhaust blower. The blower motor must be vapor-proof and be of sufficient capacity to change the air in about five minutes. In sailboats with deep Vee-bottoms, it is desirable that the ducting be led to the lowest part of the bilge (but free of any bilge water). The Coast Guard will gladly provide full information on the ducting rules and requirements for all types of boats and volumes of engine compartments.

There are a wide variety of engine instruments and controls available on the market in about any category of expense the owner wishes to indulge in. Essential are (1) an oil pressure gauge, (2) an ammeter, and (3) a water temperature gauge. Useful instruments are a tachometer, oil temperature gauge, and a fuel pressure gauge. Most engine manufacturers supply suitable instruments for their particular engines. The selection of engine controls, throttle, clutch, etc. is restricted only by the design limitations of the boat and the owner's pocketbook. In general, the simpler and more direct the controls, and the less dependence on complicated hook-ups, the better. Most engine controls fall into two basic types; double lever, where separate handles control throttle and shaft rotation, and single lever, in which one handle does both. The single lever is less likely to cause confusion and with it one cannot engage the clutch with the engine in high speed in neutral.

One of the items that seems to bother prospective owners of steel vessels is the belief that steel boats are hotter (or colder) than craft of other stock and so will require insulation. This is not necessarily so, although, of course, any vessel intended for cold weather or semi-arctic use will have to be protected inside from extremes of temperature. For moderate or warm climates, this is rarely so and the best procedure is to rely on adequate ventilation or choice of hull color. A white hull or deck will be quite cool to the touch, even in tropical conditions, whereas a dark color will produce, conversely, a great deal of interior heat. However, where insulation is deemed necessary, there is a large variety of materials to choose from: cork, fibred-glass wool, styrofoam, to name only a few. They come in a variety of forms, from sprayed-on types imbedded in one sort of mastic or another to blocks of sponge-textured substances and wools, either loose or in batts.

In placing or selecting any of these materials, there are several considerations that should be weighed. Insulating materials must not retain or pick up moisture or condensation by absorption or entrapment. Some insulating substances act like modified sponges if wetted, and once water is absorbed it is difficult if not impossible to remove. They must be sufficiently bound together, or to the hull, to stay put during exposure of the vessel to a pounding sea. Many of the wool-type insulations shake down into wads of matted fiber if not restrained, and some will rain unending particles of itchy fragments through holes in acoustic ceilings if the holes are not sealed. Insulating materials must not be allowed to spoil the appearance of an otherwise good-looking interior if not covered. This is the fault of the sprayed types. Usually they are irregular in finish, rather messy in appearance, and, by virtue of their rough finish, great dust and dirt catchers that are difficult to clean or paint. Practically, the sprayed types can be done only by professionals with specialized equipment; most such outfits are distant from most boatyards and

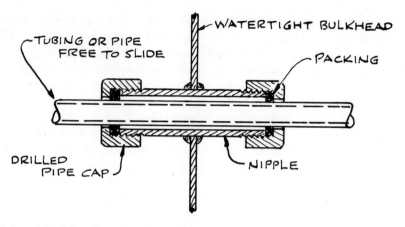

12-8. *A bulkhead stuffing box.*

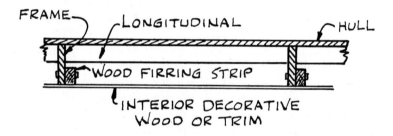

12-9. *Using wood furring strips for adding interior decorative material.*

are expensive for the results obtained.

Where the builder or owner wishes to insulate, but not cover, the interior hull with a double ceiling or partitioning, for space or other reasons, sheet cork cuts neatly to size and when installed fully against the hull with contact cement, is neat and attractive, whether left natural or painted. There are other sheet- and tile-type insulating substances that can be installed in the same way.

By and large, the need for insulation has been much exaggerated. Insulation should be used only as necessary for comfort under the conditions the boat is expected to operate under. The practice of sealing the entire inside surface with insulation and thus inhibiting the free flow of air to the hull is, in my opinion, undesirable and conducive to other potential problems. Overdoing the insulation makes periodic inspection of the hull difficult, takes up valuable space, and only adds to the weight that must be carried around, either in the form of the insulation itself or its covering. Below the waterline, insulation is almost never needed and is undesirable. Below-waterline areas should always be free to the circulation of air and inspection at all times.

Another common fallacy is that acoustical insulation is necessary for the engine rooms of steel vessels. This is simply not so. Properly mounted engines are no more noisy in steel vessels than in boats of any other type; the amount of acoustical insulation necessary is a function primarily of the noise level to be tolerated by the owner rather than any inherent increase occasioned by steel itself. Of course, any steel bulkhead of plain sheet metal with no cross-bracing or stiffening might drum noisily, as might any other material, but the cure is not to spray the engine room with a lumpy, rough substance to limit noise and so spoil an otherwise neat and attractive part of the boat.

Before any finish or decorative interior work is done, the piping, wiring, engine controls, and other working systems should be installed. There are no specially unique instructions about this, except that all systems should be securely fastened and provision made for contraction and expansion either by suitable slack in lines, by loops or bends in piping, or the use of stuffing boxes where items pass through watertight bulkheads. Weld fittings for this purpose are manufactured for electric wiring. For piping, bulkhead stuffing boxes can be made easily by using short pipe nipples larger than the tubing involved and welded through the bulkhead, drilling the pipe caps just slightly larger than the outside diameter of the piping, inserting the lines, filling the space between the pipe and the nipple with shaft packing, and screwing up the caps (see Figure 12-8). This allows the pipes to slide in and out through the bulkhead as dimensional changes occur, but does not destroy their watertightness.

Where decorative woods, plyboards, panels, or other finish materials are to be installed, it will be necessary to fasten them to the hull framing by the use of firring strips, clips welded on, or similar means. Except in those cases where the decorative materials can be bolted directly to the metal, the use of wood firring strips is probably the most convenient method of making attachments. They can be curved or bent as desired, beveled and trimmed as necessary (see Figure 12-9). While they do require a great deal of drilling to be fixed permanently in place, they are receptive to nails, screws, bolts, and other fasteners.

Whenever possible, it is recommended that provision be made for easy removal of panels for inspection purposes. This, of course, will not be practical in some locations, but it is nice to be able to undo a few screws every few years and see that the hull is in good shape, that it is not collecting moisture or mildew. This is especially desirable in below-the-waterline locations where moisture might tend to collect if ventilation is restricted. Flooring, in particular, should be easily removable in generous sections to allow ready access to the bilges. While a steel boat will be as dry and as watertight as any boat can possibly be, some moisture is inevitably bound to find its way to the keel area, if only from occasional stuffing-box drip.

Also, it is highly desirable that, whenever practical, arrangement be made for ventilation behind decorative trim. Any small gap between the top and bottom of large panels or continuous woodwork will do a great deal toward promoting air circulation and maintaining a sweet-smelling boat. This applies equally to boats of any material — aluminum, fiberglass, or cement. Such gaps need not be at all unattractive and, in fact, with a little imagination, may even add to the decorative effect. Except where insulation is definitely desired and needed, every effort should be made to insure a free flow of air to every part of the boat. Boats, unlike houses, should not be sealed tight; they function under entirely different circumstances. A sealed clothes locker, which in a house can be tightly closed to keep out moths, on a boat can be a minor disaster.

Before deciding on full interior paneling, which might be expensive, some thought might be given to the fact that steel, frankly exposed and attractively painted and perhaps locally embellished with a little teak or mahongany trim, can be quite good looking, certainly more so than the rough finish of interior fiberglass or the seamed, ribbed, effect of wood. Steel is inherently smooth and receptive to almost any decorative paint finish. My own boat has a very minimum of paneling, only enough to supply the necessary compartments for storage of clothes and other necessities. Yet the total effect is pleasing and has the added advantage of providing the feeling of space. For those individuals, and they are many, for whom the cost of a boat is a major factor, this is a consideration. Trimming out the interior of a boat can be a costly business; in many cases, it need not be, with no sacrifice in either comfort or real aesthetic appeal.

An entire volume, or at least several long chapters, could be devoted here to interior decoration, to the installation of the innumerable devices and gadgets that the boating "public" has so come to love and believe necessary. Such a discussion would, really, be beyond the scope of this book and, in addition, a waste of good printer's ink. The subject has already been written to death in the various trade publications and in the literature of manufacturers with devices and materials to sell. The so-called "luxury trade" is not so likely to be concerned with the details and principles that form the subject of this dissertation, but rather with wall-to-wall carpeting, and whether the bathroom faucets are chrome or gold, and whether the lamps have pretty shades. This does not imply, or even suggest, that the steel boat should not, or cannot, be as luxurious as any other. But at the same time, it can also be as livable and as attractive, if not more so, than comparable boats of other materials, and with a lot less expense. Simplicity is very often a neglected feature in today's boating, at least in the yachting field, but it may, also, be an integral and important part of interior boat design.

Quite often I have been approached by people who are thinking of having boats built, and who are primarily concerned with such things as how wide the bunks should be, whether a shower or bathtub can be fitted into such and such a space, whether a shelf can be placed here to hold the television set, what about the bar and the open fireplace that would be nice on a chilly night? These amenities are, of course, very pleasant and certainly to be supplied if the owners wish. But they are only secondary to the real function of a boat. Sometimes these well-intentioned folk are quite taken aback when a plea is made for simplicity.

If the boat is to be used only for short junkets between marinas, fine, but if it is intended for any serious cruising, the importance of most of these appurtenances diminishes rapidly as one leaves the shore and the ever-present electric sockets of the United States. A surprising number of boats are launched each year well below their designed waterlines because they are so loaded with gadgetry that they are overweighted and are, also, as an inherent part of the same acquisitive tendency, much less spacious and comfortable than they could be. The happiest boat owners are usually those with the least to maintain and go wrong. The most attractive craft are those which are clean in line and uncomplicated both inside and out.

13 BOATBUILDING WITH ALUMINUM

by Thomas Colvin

The choice of materials in the construction of a vessel usually depends more on availability than on desire, except in highly industrialized countries or areas. It would be rather ridiculous to build a metal hull in the midst of a tropical forest, just as it would be more practical to construct with metal when living next door to a steel mill. So, forgive me, if it appears that my enthusiasm is not total in discussing the application and use of aluminum in the marine field. There *are* areas in which it is superbly suited and should be used to its fullest extent. There are other applications about which I am not overly enthusiastic, and I shall indicate these. However, I do not hold in disdain any material commonly used in the construction of a vessel. The primary consideration when deciding what material to use is the ultimate use of the vessel, and the application of one material or another must be compatible with that primary function.

My interest in aluminum has spanned two decades, and in this brief time the acceptance of the material in the marine industry has been due not so much to any improvement of alloying as much as it has been to the improved techniques in the fabrication, especially the welding, of the aluminum. The inert-gas-shielded welding procedures undoubtedly have been the greatest advancement in the assembling of aluminum and have led to a rapid development of that metal's application in the marine industry.

Background of Aluminum

Hans Oersted, professor of physics at the University of Copenhagen, Denmark, discovered aluminum in 1825. Apparently, his first product was a metallic aluminum. A couple of years later, a German scientist, Frederick Woehler, produced aluminum in the form of a gray powder.

By 1845 he was able to form particles of the powder into a solid. These particles were approximately the size of a pinhead. Frederick Woehler also discovered that aluminum was easy to shape and melt, and that it was stable in air. Aluminum sold for $545 per pound in 1852.

Henri Claire Deville, a French scientist, and Robert von Bunsen, a German professor, in separate discoveries in the year 1854 learned to isolate aluminum by using sodium instead of potassium, thus large chunks of aluminum could be formed where previously only small particles could be formed.

The greatest stride in aluminum was made in the year 1866, again by two men — Charles Martin Hall, an American, and Paul T. Heroult, a Frenchman — both the same age. Each man applied for and secured patents in his own country in the same year. Their basic discovery was that metallic aluminum could be produced by dissolving alumina in a molten cryolite at about 982° C, obtaining about 22 percent alumina, and then passing electric currents through the solution. As a result, in seven years' time, aluminum dropped in price from $11.33 per pound to 57¢ per pound. In 1900, aluminum was selling at 23¢ per pound; in 1942 at 14¢ per pound. Today, in 1972, it is approximately 60¢ per pound when purchased in minimum mill quantities in shapes and plates. The process invented by Hall and Heroult is called the electrolytic reduction process. Basically, this is the breaking down of alumina into aluminum and oxygen. The oxygen combines with carbon at the anode and passes off as carbon dioxide gas. Since cryolite melts at 982° C and the aluminum at about 650° C, the action is continuous.

About 20,000 kilowatt hours of electricity are required to produce a ton of aluminum. Approximately four tons of bauxite are required to make two tons of alumina, which results in one ton of metallic aluminum. Using this process, approximately 1,500 pounds of carbon electrodes are also consumed, so the making of aluminum requires more than just a small furnace in the backyard. Primary aluminum pig is the first molting, and becomes a primary aluminum ingot when it is fluxed and skimmed.

Sheets of aluminum are hot-rolled when their thickness exceeds 1/8" and cold-rolled when the thickness is below 1/8". Rods, bars, wires, and other shapes are drawn or extruded according to size. The weight of aluminum is about one-third that of copper, steel, or brass. Aluminum does not rust. The oxide that forms on the outer surface of aluminum, unlike rust in iron, protects the basic metal, whereas, in iron, the basic metal will rust continuously. Pure aluminum is rather soft and weak and has a very low yield strength of approximately 5,000 pounds.

Alloyed, some of the aluminums have a yield strength of 88,000 pounds. The common alloying material used to increase the strength of aluminum are such elements as manganese, magnesium, copper, and zinc. Basically, the alloys most used in the fabrication of hulls can be grouped into the 6000 (heat-treatable) series and the 5000 (non-heat-treatable) series.

Advantages and Disadvantages of Aluminum Construction

One of the primary advantages of aluminum is its light weight. It is readily available as a warehouse item, extremely easy to work with, requires very little maintenance, is clean, and can be formed, welded, riveted, or bolted. Aluminum construction can be utilized for many hull types that formerly were suitable only for wood construction. It is superior for the lining of ice chests, food containers, tanks, and fish holds, and is excellent for cryogenic work. The savings in weight when aluminum is used can result in an increased carrying capacity in a cargo vessel. Its use in superstructures lowers the center of gravity of a vessel. Its use in hull construction often results in the saving of fuel due to reduced displacement and the ability to plane (in the case of power hulls), when other material forms can not attain the lightness of construction due either to economic factors or to the nature of the material itself. It does not increase in weight from immersion. It is impervious to worms. Except for the bottom of the exposed hull, it does not require painting other than for cosmetic purposes. It is adaptable to many design innovations, and because of its light weight, methods of construction can be devised so that it can have outstanding structural integrity and strength.

Among the accomplishments of aluminum in the hull of a vessel is that a greater load-carrying capacity is available if the same design is used as that for wood or steel. If the difference is saved in the displacement of the hull, then this would result in greater speed using the same horsepower, which would result in the same fuel consumption; or, if the same speed is required, then a lower horsepower with less fuel consumption could be used; or, an increase in range with the same fuel capacity and the smaller engine would be possible. Also, using reduced draft for the same dead-weight tonnage is possible. Stability can increase because of the lower center of gravity of the aluminum hull. This is particularly important and noticeable in narrow hulls, such as canoes, sharpies, etc.

The advantage in designing and working with aluminum is that, while the variety of shapes are not available over the counter, it is possible to have dies made for the shapes most suited to the concept of the design with which one is working. The dies are rather inexpensive. They are good for a lifetime and are for the exclusive use of the originator. Therefore, many items that must be fabricated in other materials out of one or more pieces by machining, welding, or gluing, can be made in one piece in aluminum via extruding. Extruding is a very simple process, and the extrusions can be either hollow or solid.

Aluminum has a much better scrap value than steel. There is in practice, very little waste — in fact, it is extremely economical in this respect. In 20,000 pounds of purchased aluminum, a scrap loss of five percent would be high.

Welding of aluminum is extraordinarily fast. The welding speed is approximately three times that of steel, as is the cutting. Handling of aluminum, because of its lightness, either reduces labor or obviates the necessity for larger capacity lifting devices. So, in practice, if labor rates are high, the savings in labor by using aluminum very often completely offset the high cost of the material, with the end result that aluminum construction is either no costlier than steel or even cheaper.

The preparation of an aluminum hull for finishing is done by sanding rather than by grinding, which is also very rapid. It can be cut with hand tools, and any tool that is suitable for cutting wood is also suitable for cutting aluminum. In fact, an ordinary portable power saw with a carbide blade is the easiest way to cut the heavier material, such as plates and shapes. Lighter material can be cut and intricate cuts can be done with a saber saw or a bandsaw fitted with a metal-cutting blade with approximately 10 teeth per inch. Aluminum is very easily drilled, and compensates in some ways for the fact that repairs via welding are difficult to obtain throughout the world. A patch plate or a wood patch can be put on by drilling with a hand drill, and then by bolting or screwing the patch in place.

Aluminum can be used in many places where steel has not proven totally satisfactory. This is in areas that are affected by salt spray and heat, such as funnel casings where heat is in the vicinity of 180° to 200° C and where continually dry and wet conditions are experienced due to salt spray. It can also be used to great advantage in ventilators and ventilator trunks, since no corrosion is involved in the use of aluminum.

The disadvantages of aluminum are sometimes overlooked in the enthusiasm for total application of this material. Basically, they follow in order of severity. Throughout the world, the number of yards capable of repairing aluminum hulls are few. Actually, they are non-existent in 80 percent of the countries of the world. Even in the United States, there are only a few repair facilities on the Great Lakes, a half-dozen or so on the Atlantic Coast, probably no more than a dozen on the Gulf Coast, and a half-dozen or so on the West Coast. Many yards can build in aluminum but cannot repair, so any major work that must be done on aluminum almost automatically requires that the vessel be located in a highly industrialized country. Further requirements are that the compatible alloy for welding be available, and that the welding skills be available. Unlike wood, which can be repaired anywhere, or steel, which can be repaired almost anywhere, aluminum requires very sophisticated welding and construction techniques, and international compatibility of alloys for the most part does not exist. Hence, repair or extensive repair could become very costly.

Standard marine shapes in aluminum, i.e., Tees, flats, channels, angles, and eyes (I) are not available in the varieties that they are available in steel. Those that are available for small craft construction are totally unsuited for the task they have to perform. Although these shapes are adequate and are indeed designed specifically for large ship construction, the shapes and sizes do not aid the builder of small craft.

A significant disadvantage is the pricing structure of aluminum. Aluminum is priced on the assumption that 30,000 pounds of each item will be bought; this base price is set at x dollars per pound. Quantities of the same item over 30,000 are at the same price per pound. Quantities under the base incur an extra charge, which could amount to as much as three to five times x in very small quantities. On the other hand, steel prices are based on the total number of pounds purchased, regardless of the size or shape. For example, from the steel warehouse, one can buy 5,000 pounds of Tees, eyes, flat bars, angles, and channels of various sizes, 12,000 pounds of sheet and plate of various sizes to suit the requirement of minimum cutting, and 3,000 pounds of pipe. All of this adds up to 20,000 pounds or a base quantity with no extras incurred in the cost. This is not possible in aluminum. In wood, one purchases so many thousand feet of lumber, and it makes relatively little difference whether it is in 2″ x 4″, 1″ x 8″, 1″ x 10″, 4″ x 4″, etc., material, if it is all the same grade of lumber. Here there is no minimum order. But not so with aluminum. Aluminum is priced in such a way that, on a one-up basis for a small yard or an individual, the cost per pound of construction is extraordinarily high when compared with other materials. In practice, the average comes close to $1.00 per pound (1971 price). In yards building exclusively in aluminum, quantity purchasing is sufficient to offset the increase due to minimal needs of one size or another. The use of anything but the maximum size plate is not economical.

The cost of welding equipment, power requirements, and the high cost of welding have to be considered as disadvantages. Unlike steel welding, using a stick electrode is not an economical means of constructing with aluminum. It can be done, but it is too slow and too dirty to be generally feasible when there are other methods that are more eminently suited to the welding of this material.

A disadvantage as far as marine construction is concerned would be that aluminum is one of the best heat conductors; hence, sweating is more of a problem than in steel or wood. An additional cost in construction should be expected to compensate for this. Fire protection must be considered in some areas, as aluminum has a very low melting point — around 1100° F. Also, the metal is not compatible with many of the common fittings that are available to the marine industry; therefore, an increase in cost is required to overcome this inherent incompatibility. Consideration must be given at all times during construction to eliminate concentration of stress due to improper welding. Aluminum tears and is notch sensitive, so this is a design consideration. Even the hardest alloys can be easily scarred; therefore, care must be exercised to prevent gouging and scarring. Aluminum water-stains easily, and if the protective finish or bright finish as it is delivered from the mill is to be retained, proper storage of the material is a requirement.

In conclusion, if we lay the responsibility for the proper design of the structure on the designer, proper construction in the hands of the builder, the initial finishing and protection also on the doorstep of the builder, and the proper maintenance on the owner, the advantages in using aluminum as a medium of construction can more than offset the disadvantages involved.

Strength of Aluminum

To achieve the same strength as a steel hull, an aluminum hull will weigh approximately 50 percent that of steel. In extreme cases, it is of course possible to reduce the weight of aluminum even further down to about 35 or 38 percent that of steel. When extreme lightness is sought, it is usually at the expense of internal volume, which is rather self-defeating.

The strength of aluminum weldments for, say, 5083 plate is 44,000 pounds tensile strength with a yield of 31,000 pounds. The strength across the butt welds is 40,000 pounds tensile and a yield of 24,000 pounds. Therefore, tension members having equal strength would be 1 to 1.4, and the weight of aluminum versus steel would be .35 to .48.

For beams having equal bending strength, the cross-sectional area of aluminum versus steel would be 1 to 1.2, and the weight of the aluminum versus steel is .35 to .44. Plates having equal bending strength would be 1 to 1.2, and the weight of aluminum versus steel in this instance would be .35 to .41. So, utilizing aluminum, as it is possible to do, one can see that the increase in thickness in plate to make aluminum easier to work increases the strength of the aluminum to that of steel. Steel generally has a yield of 33,000 psi, except the Cor-ten steels, which have a yield strength of 55,000 psi.

Except in certain instances, it is of little importance for the builder to understand the mechanical differences of the design criteria between aluminum and steel other than that which has already been outlined. Generally speaking, it will suffice to say that greater thicknesses of plating are not the solution to greater strength. Once adequate strength has been achieved, to increase the strength of a certain portion of the hull to take severe loads can very easily be done by merely reinforcing the area to be worked rather than increasing either the plate or framing thickness, and this should be shown on the plans.

It is very seldom that a design prepared for one material is directly convertible to another material. Even in the case of steel, the hulls are usually not directly convertible to aluminum in that a great deal of consideration must be given at the time of designing to the amount of space that is required by the method of welding. The welding gun in aluminum construction is approximately 15″ in length and certain areas of the hull are inaccesible to it; therefore, the structure in these areas must be so thought-out that it is actually possible to do the construction. Even the best thought-out plans still require that the builder plan the sequence of construction in such a way that he has the maximum accessibility to perform the welding. While it is always best to think in the material that one is using, very often where a standard design is to be converted to aluminum, in preparing the construction plan, a builder can resort to some rules of thumb that will yield a hull comparable in strength and stiffness to steel. These formulas are in standard texts by Corlett, Muckle, or Jaegger. It will suffice to say that aluminum plating for unsheathed decks based on a steel design would be from about 1.1 to 1.25 times the thickness of steel; plating on deck houses, 1.1 to 1.5; the stiffeners would have a section modulus of 1.7 to 2.0; beams, girders, and stiffeners would have an inertia section of 2.0. Aluminum shell plating is nominally 1½ times thicker than steel.

Aluminum Alloys and their Workability

Aluminum alloys, aside from being broken down chemically into several hundred categories, are further broken down into heat-treatable and non-heat-treatable alloys. Basically, this means that those alloys that are non-heat-treatable do not depend on any heat treatment to achieve their mechanical properties and can be reheated without any appreciable drop in strength. Furthermore, they can be cold-worked with greater ease than any of the heat-treatable alloys. In fact, they cold-work easier or at least as easy as cold steel. Where heating is necessary, it must be a controlled heat, and 400° C is about maximum. The heat can be readily controlled by the use of temp sticks or a soft pine block. The temperature is correct when the color of the wax temp stick fades or when the pine block scorches after being rubbed on the surface of the aluminum.

The heat-treatable alloys are the most difficult to form, and conversely are the best members in many cases to use for longitudinals and other structures that are to be used for framing, inasmuch as they can be and often are of lighter dimensions than would be desirable in a non-heat-treatable alloy. The heat treating is done after extruding in large soaking pits under controlled temperatures. Quenching and aging take the aluminum from the annealed condition of zero temper to, in marine alloys at least, the T-6 temper, which is the greatest strength. As previously mentioned, heat-treatable alloys are rather difficult to form and do require localized heat to aid in severe forming. The heat should not be applied in one spot but spread over a rather large area. Exact control of heating can only be done in an electric furnace, which is beyond the capabilities of most small building yards or individuals.

An equally good method is to use acetylene oxygen with a large, soft flame rather than a hard, oxygen flame. Especially useful is a heating ring as opposed to the standard tip on the torch. With proper control in heating, flame bending of aluminum is just as easy to do as it is on steel. It must be remembered, however, that aluminum does not change color during heating as does steel, and therefore the unaided eye is totally ignorant of the true temperature of the surface.

When flanging or rolling, the tools must be brushed clean so that particles of steel are not embedded on the rolling plates, flanging, or the rolls of the forming tools, and in turn become embedded in the alloy, thereby causing corrosion. This is just one more case where extra care will pay dividends later.

Tools and Equipment Used in Aluminum Construction

With the exception of the welding machine, all other tools normally used in the boatyard are readily adaptable or directly usable on aluminum. This is perhaps one of the reasons why it is so easy when starting up a boatyard to go directly into aluminum construction. The bandsaw, sanders, electric drills, routers, etc., that are to be used in working the wooden portions of a hull can be used to work the aluminum portion of the hull either directly or by merely changing the cutting edge, such as on the bandsaw. A portable power saw, bench saw, or radial-arm saw already fitted with a carbide blade can be used on either wood or aluminum without changing the blade.

Needless to say, all tools used in the construction of a vessel should be of the heavy-duty type, rather than the home-workshop type, as the latter rarely have sufficient sustained power to be usable for any period of time without overheating or totally disintegrating. There are only a few specialized tools that need be purchased for the construction of aluminum vessels. Files — the toothing of a file for non-ferrous metals is coarser than those used for ferrous metals, but not as coarse as a wood rasp — are available in various sizes, both mill and bastards; and at least a half-dozen files varying from the smallest to the largest should be purchased. Sanding disks should be of a coarse grit — somewhere around 16 or 24. Stainless steel wire brushes are necessary for aluminum construction. Stick wax (Johnson No. 140) is required for lubrication; when cutting with a band saw or saber saw and in sanding, it is applied to the tool prior to, and at occasional intervals during, the cutting or sanding of the material in order to prevent clogging. A cleaning solution, which can be Tauol or Taulene, is also necessary for the cleaning of the material prior to welding and also for use as a de-greaser. High-speed drill bits when used for aluminum rather than steel are sharpened a little differently and have, in some instances, a different twist. If you will be working exclusively in aluminum, and you have to purchase drill bits anyway, get ones designed for aluminum rather than for steel; however, if the latter type is already on hand, these drill bits will work on aluminum and need not be modified.

It is in the area of welding that great care must be exercised in the selection of equipment. First of all, there must be adequate power. If available, three-phase (440 volt) is preferable and opens up a wider selection of welding machines. If the vessels to be built are small enough, single-phase can be used; however, because of high amperage requirements, a check with the local power company will determine if single-phase equipment can be used on their lines. Since the amperage limitation is usually less than 250 on the machine, building very small craft will pose no more problems than running an electric stove or dryer. This would give a 50 ampere or greater circuit breaker on the primary input line, and in some areas this is beyond the capacity of the line itself. I happen to live in an area where the power lines were originally set up to REA standards and are totally inadequate to handle large capacity welding machines. The cost of installing such lines is prohibitive; thus it is necessary to have a self-contained welder-generator. This can be either diesel or gasoline powered. It is a good solution for welding in aluminum, but it is certainly a noisy one.

A source of argon gas is a requirement. The more exotic mixtures such as helium, or helium and argon, are not necessary in constructing small craft. In fact, they are not really required at all in most marine applications of welding.

Also, if aluminum is to be bent on a bending slab, it is better to use flat palms on the hold-down dogs rather than the spiked palms. This will prevent any damage to the surface of the aluminum. Hammers for working aluminum should be rawhide faced to prevent abrasion, which can happen if steel hammers are used.

In general, the shearing, planing, rolling, and punching operations for aluminum are almost exactly the same as for steel. When working aluminum, the tools should be set with a slightly different gap differential than for steel. In rolling, there is a certain amount of springback in aluminum — in fact, much more so than in steel — so due allowance must be made for this. As mentioned, notching or cutting shapes can be done by any electric tool. Several routers are available for this type of work, and a common portable power saw with a carbide blade, two-speed saber saw, or a wood-working bandsaw with a metal-cutting blade are quite sufficient and provide a rapid means of working aluminum. Straight hand tools, such as a carpenter's saw, hacksaw, etc., can also be used to advantage in certain applications. It is well to remember that in cutting with a band saw, the guide rolls should be down very close to the work. The arm supporting these should be well lined-up and rigid.

Manual arc cutting of aluminum is possible and it can be done on thicknesses ranging from 1/8″ to 5″ with a gas tungsten arc. Such surfaces are fairly smooth and free of contamination. In small craft, however, there seems to be no reason that would justify the purchase of this type of equipment, though it is much faster than machine cutting of aluminum. For example, in 1/4″ plate, it is possible to cut manually up to 60 inches per minute. With automatic equipment, the rate of cutting is up to 300 inches per minute.

Some Design and Construction Considerations

Aluminum is an excellent substitute for either wood or steel. In its own right, it has so many advantages over any other form of construction that, when properly utilized, there is little reason not to build in this material. Aluminum lends itself best to light- and medium-displacement hulls. It is feasible in heavy-displacement hulls, usually when the savings in weight can be offset by increased fuel capacity, cargo-carrying capacity, or a combination of the two. It also permits greater fuel, water, or cargo capacity in a smaller hull form and lends itself to unusual hull forms for special purposes; however, to arbitrarily use it in very heavy displacement hulls is a waste of material and even poses some other problems that require solutions which are not always the best from either a design or handling standpoint. For example, aluminum is ideally adapted to a sharpie of any size from say 24 feet to 70 feet in length. In a smaller aluminum sharpie, perhaps only one or two frames or bulkheads would be required. These vessels would be lighter than would be possible in standard wood construction, and much lighter than would ever be possible in steel construction. The rigidity achieved without excessive weight would eliminate fiberglass altogether.

In the medium-displacement hulls, aluminum permits a refinement in lines and in weight distribution, resulting in a lower center of gravity due to an increased ballast/displacement ratio, in the case of sailing hulls. In power hulls, it permits an increase in engine weight or in fuel capacity, thereby increasing the range of the vessel under consideration.

In heavy-displacement sailing hulls, the amount of ballast becomes excessive in relation to the displacement of the hull, unless the hull is structurally grossly heavy. In an extreme case, it would be necessary to have a substantial portion of the ballast placed under the deck edge to reduce the stiffness of the hull.

Aluminum hull forms are not bound by any rigid design considerations. It is bound, as is all metal construction, by some economic considerations. Since aluminum can be readily sawed, the forming of frames in a round-bottom hull is of no particular problem; therefore, forming equipment, while opening up one design avenue, is not a requirement, inasmuch as frames can be fabricated from large sheets. Aluminum lends itself in all cases, economically as well as structurally, to longitudinal rather than

214

transverse framing. In the round-bottom hull form, this further simplifies the construction technique in utilizing bulkheads and partial bulkheads at random intervals. In V-bottom, multiple-chine, and flat-bottom hulls, the fabrication of aluminum framing is of no particular difficulty. It is less time consuming than wood or steel, in that aluminum frames do not require the gussets of wood and can be cut at three times the speed as those of steel.

The difficulty of round-bottom versus other hull forms is in the application of plating. Plating is usually taken off a model via the use of strips of paper, such as adding machine tape, to the nominal size of plate that will bend free of any distortion. Fortunately, the plating can be figured to lay either on a portion of a sphere, cone, or cylinder. From a model, the radiating lines can be determined which will then allow the designer to work out the sight edges of the plate. (A sight edge, for instance in lapped plates, is the plate edge that can be seen. The edge behind it is called the blind edge.) These in turn are re-established by the builder from what is called an expanded shell-plating drawing.

In yards that have three-roll benders, drop hammers, and other equipment for working aluminum, either cold or hot, round-bottom construction would not be as difficult as it would be in either an amateur backyard operation or in the small boatbuilding yard, which usually lacks any of the sophisticated equipment of the larger yards. In fact, many of the small boatbuilding yards throughout the world are nothing more than enlarged backyard operations, but unlike the amateur operation, there is a great deal of skilled know-how in the proper use of the equipment available. So it is quite possible to find two yards building the same hull, each in an entirely different sequence and manner.

The ratio of labor in metal construction to hull form is 1-2-3-5 for flat-bottom, V-bottom, multiple-chine, and round-bottom; i.e., round-bottom construction takes 5 times as much labor as flat-bottom. Generally speaking, unless the yard is quite well equipped, one would shy away from the labor involved in making the numerous joints in a round-bottom hull in favor of the application of large sheets over simple curves in the flat-bottom, V-bottom, and multiple-chine hull. This does bring up a further consideration, and that is whether or not to use conically developed surfaces in the design of the hull. Conically developed surfaces are used by many on the assumption that the plating is easier to apply and, therefore, there is a reduction in the cost of construction, so it is justified. This is often sacrificing hull shape to suit material. I think this is a wrong consideration and has application in only a few isolated instances. It is

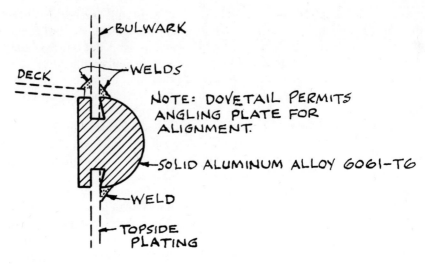

BULWARK

DECK

WELDS

NOTE: DOVETAIL PERMITS ANGLING PLATE FOR ALIGNMENT.

SOLID ALUMINUM ALLOY 6061-T6

WELD

TOPSIDE PLATING

13-1.   Gunwale for vessels over 35 feet.

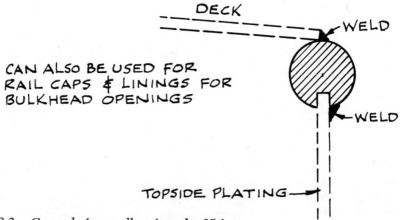

DECK

WELD

CAN ALSO BE USED FOR RAIL CAPS & LININGS FOR BULKHEAD OPENINGS

WELD

TOPSIDE PLATING

13-2.   Gunwale for small craft under 35 feet.

wrong to sacrifice seakeeping ability and shape of a hull to suit any material. About the only place that compound curves are involved is in the forebody plating of a V-bottom or multiple-chine hull, and this is usually not greater than one-fifth of the bottom length. All other sections are easy to plate and present no problems to any builder. Topside plating, unless some very fancy shapes are to be attempted, normally has no

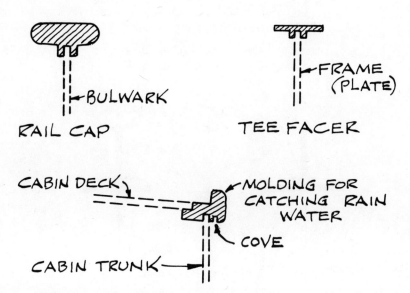

13-3. *Rail caps and moldings.*

reason to be conically developed. Ordinarily, in a spoon-bowed hull, the first few frames are convex, and if the hull is clipper-bowed, they are concave. The plate can usually be drawn in sufficiently without cutting to permit these plates to go on in one piece.

In the construction of an aluminum hull, after hull shape has been determined, the consideration of extrusions should be carefully thought out, for it is possible to devise a deck-edge extrusion that accepts not only the topside plating but makes a landing for the deck plate and a base for the bulwarks (see Figure 13-1). The rail cap can be extruded to accomplish a wide variety of shapes that will lend themselves to almost any design consideration that is necessary (see Figures 13-1 and 13-2).

Transverse frames can be fabricated from either plate or shapes. The use of deep floors suggests the use of plate and shapes only above the floor level. Topsides, however, are best formed with angles or flat bars. Angles have greater stability and make the lining-up of the hull much easier than if just flat bars are used. The longitudinals can be either of flat bars or T-bars. A flat bar is inherently weaker than a T-bar. When a flat bar is welded to the shell plating it becomes, in essence, a Tee. However, pressure applied externally to the hull will cause the flat bar to collapse as the upper, or inner, edge of the bar cannot expand as fast

217

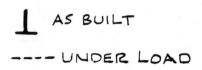

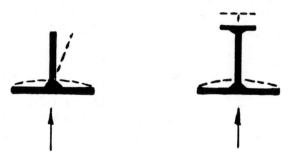

13-4. A flat bar and a tee bar welded to a plate.

as the lower edge. For example, under a severe grounding, it collapses and lays flat against the plate (see Figure 13-4). A T-bar, on the other hand, becomes an I-beam when welded, and it is very difficult to collapse the Tee. If the transverse supports are arranged at suitable intervals, the fracturing of a plate would probably come before the collapse of a T-bar.

The thickness of material to be used varies according to different designers and builders. Basically, there are two schools of thought. The first school is that it is better to have closely spaced frames and longitudinals, and to utilize the thinner material for a reduction in weight and the easier handling of materials. The other school says that it is better to use thicker plating, with its ease of welding, and use wider-spaced transverse and longitudinal framing, thus saving on labor. Both schools of thought are valid. My personal preference is to use a standardized plate thickness for all hulls — I like 1/4" material. To gain strength in larger hulls, I close up the longitudinal and transverse frame spaces, and, to reduce weight in the smaller hulls, I increase them.

In one-up building, the thinner material would permit a smaller welding machine and thus would have economic advantages; however, in a yard that would build not one but several aluminum hulls over a period of time, it is advantageous to standardize on a heavier plate, so that larger initial quantities could be ordered. In this way, the long-term

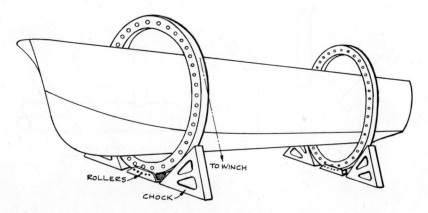

13-5. A revolving jig with a boat hull in place.

would effect a savings and permit the versatility of being able to build not only small but large hulls. The additional cost of purchasing heavier welding equipment would be justified in anticipating large as well as small vessel construction. The minimum thickness that can be worked readily with high-speed welding equipment is 3/16". If the welding machine is a pulse-arc type, then 1/8" is feasible, but there is a proportionately greater amount of distortion.

In construction, there are a number of things that must be predetermined. Whether to build the hull right side up or upside down is one decision that has to be made. Either method has its advantages and disadvantages. An advantage of building upside down is that the complete deck structure can be done first, allowing the frames to be set up on the deck beams, and the keel section hoisted into position after the hull is plated. Also, the keel and bottom sections are much easier to plumb upside down than the deck is in right-side-up construction. Right-side-up construction saves having to turn the boat over later; it permits the installation of machinery as the hull progresses; it also permits the initial starting and sometimes finishing of basic joinerwork before other sections of the hull are closed in. This can be done upside down, but it is not as convenient to do. Since there is an equal amount of welding inside as well as outside as far as the shell plating is concerned, it would make little difference one way or the other as one takes his choice of whether to overhead-weld the bottom shell upside down or to do the outside upside down.

The most economical way to build is with a revolving jig (see Figure 13-5). A hull so-built has all of the advantages of both methods of build-

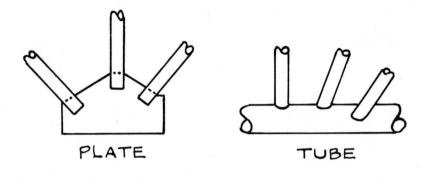

PLATE   TUBE

SPHERE

13-6.   Various ways to run a number of pipes into one point.

ing and a further advantage of being able to position all of the production welding to have the maximum speed and the resulting minimum distortion. It is very difficult to justify the cost of the rolls for only one hull, but the jig would more than pay for itself in that all welding could be done in the most advantageous position for the welder. It would totally eliminate all overhead welding; it would eliminate all vertical welding; and in more than one-up construction would reduce the cost of construction in the long run. An important factor when designing these rolls is to make them large enough to accommodate the largest vessel ever to be considered and yet small enough to take care of the smaller hulls.

In preparing any joint within the hull, great attention must be paid to the accessibility of the joint. Quite often, on properly prepared plans, there will be an indication of where these joints are to be located. They need not be precise except in certain instances. Generally speaking, the

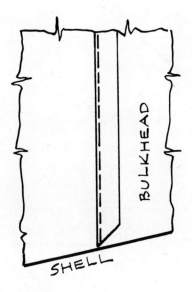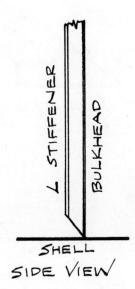

13-7. An L stiffener that has been sniped back to prevent a stress concentration.

joint should not be closer than 30 times the thickness of the material to any transverse frame, nor closer than 15 times the thickness of the material to any longitudinal frame (providing the longitudinal has not been designed and installed to accept the plating in the form of the backing bar of the butt weld).

There are several ways to run together numerous pipes or tubes into a conglomerate point. One is to have all of the smaller tubes enter into a tube of much larger diameter. Another is to have them end in a series of right angles or angled plates, or to have them enter into a sphere, the latter being the most pleasing in general effect and presenting the cleanest type of welding (see Figure 13-6). Needless to say, as in steel, the termination of all angles and channels must be sniped back at least to a 45° angle to prevent a stress concentration (see Figure 13-7). Trapezoidal stiffening is superior to straight-bar stiffening (see Figure 13-8).

Filler alloy can be selected by using tables furnished by the various aluminum companies, but the filler material should be chosen with a view towards corrosion resistance. Also to be determined are the cathodic properties of the base metal versus the filler metal, whether or not the finish will detract from the use of a particular filler metal versus another, whether the electrical potentials are similar, etc.

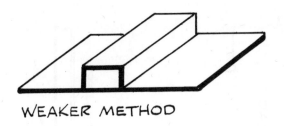

WEAKER METHOD

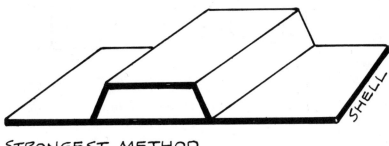

STRONGEST METHOD
OF STIFFENING

13-8.   Trapezoidal stiffening (bottom) and straight-bar stiffening (top).

Preparation of Aluminum for Welding

Aluminum must be correctly prepared if there is to be any success at all in welding. This includes making sure the weld is clean and there is a proper fit-up of the joint. Cleanliness of the weld zone cannot be stressed too highly. All moisture, oil film, grease, wax, condensates from fumes, thick oxide, and other foreign material on the edges of the metal must be removed or poor welds will be the result. These contaminants release hydrogen and other gases that become entrapped in the weld deposits, causing porosity, which, in turn, will affect the strength and ductility of the weld.

The melting point of aluminum oxide is about 2038°C, whereas the melting point of pure aluminum is 650°C. So you can see that unless the oxide is properly removed or broken up before or during welding, the temperature differential will allow the aluminum to melt long before the oxide film melts. This prevents the proper coalescence of the filler metal deposited and the base material. The entrapped oxide can cause a reduction in weld ductility and form metallurgical notches or cold laps.

De-greasing can be done with such solvents as Tauol or Taulene, and the surface merely needs to be wiped, sprayed, or dipped with this solvent. Steam cleaning could be used on small parts, but it is not practical on large hulls. Pencil identification marks that are on all aluminum sheets can be removed with acetone or alcohol. Cleaning and welding must be done in a well-ventilated room, as some of the gases caused during both operations could be harmful to the lungs. It is always best to do the clean-up prior to the fitting of the material and just prior to welding. Wire-brushing by hand with a stainless steel wire brush is sufficient to break up the oxide on an otherwise very clean joint. Mechanical cleaning of aluminum via power wire-brushing or grinding is not recommended. This is primarily because of the low melting point of aluminum. If extreme care is not exercised, there is the possibility that the surface of the material will be slightly melted, causing lapping in the weld. Special files are made for the rapid cleaning of sawn edges of aluminum and for general trimming up and fitting, and should be used in preference to any mechanical tool driven either by air or by electricity. Even the handling of the to-be-welded joint by hand or with dirty gloves will put sufficient oils or oxides in the weld zone to prevent good welding.

In aluminum welding, the arc travel speed controls the size of the bead. In welding uniform thicknesses, the angle of the electrode to the work should be equal on all sides. When welding in the horizontal position, it is better to point the gun slightly upward, allowing the weld material to flow down by gravity and even out. When welding a thick plate to a thin plate, the arc of the weld should be directed toward the heavier section. It is also helpful at times, when welding the thick and thin sections, to use a backhand angle to the gun rather than a forehand angle. In the root pass (first weld) of the joints on the heavier plates, it is desirable to have a shorter arc than it is on the subsequent passes that are to be made. Burn-backs can be caused by unsteady electrode feed wire or insufficient electrode feed wire, slippage of the driving rolls, bends or kinks in the electrode wire, improper or misaligned wire guides, or excessive clearance of the contact tube.

Insufficient cleaning action of the arc results in dirty welds and very poor wetting of the base metal. The primary cause of this difficulty is insufficient current, and often the incomplete oxide removal prior to welding or inadequate amounts of gas in the shielding will also cause dirty welds. Should this happen, the plate should be cleaned more thoroughly. If this still does not alleviate the problem, the welding current should be increased, and if this does not improve the situation, an increase in gas should be tried. It is wise not to do all three simultaneously, as then the welder is unable to determine which of the three items caused the malfunction, which may be habitual on the part of the welder.

Table 3 indicates the approximate amperage for welding aluminum from 3/16″ to 3/4″ in thickness, with the approximate speed and argon flow.

Usually, preheating of the aluminum is not a requirement, especially in the non-heat-treatable alloys. In cold weather, i.e., below 0°C, it is desirable to preheat the surface of the material in the weld area mainly to drive out any accumulated moisture. If the material is over 1/2″ in thickness, a short test run on scrap material will be sufficient to determine whether a preheat is desirable. The rise in temperature need not exceed 20°C.

Distortion is controlled by many factors, including the design of the structure, and how much of the structure is still free to move even slightly while it is being welded. The joints that have the greatest amount of contraction should be welded first. Needless to say, one would not weld up one side of the hull without doing the other side. Welding should progress in sequence from port to starboard, top to bottom. When more than one pass is to be made, such as in the butt joint of a heavy weldment, the passes should be alternated from side to

Table 3

THICKNESS	WIRE DIAMETER	POSITION	DC AMPS	ARC VOLTS	ARGON CFH (1)	WELD IN. PER MIN.	PASSES
3/16″	3/64″	FLAT HORIZ. & VERT. OVERHEAD	130-175 140-180 140-175	22 / 27	35 35 60	24-30 24-30 24-30	1 1 1-2
1/4″	3/64″	F H & V OH	175-200 165-190 180-200	25 / 29	40 45 50	24-30 25-35 25-35	1 2-3 2-3
3/8″	1/16″	F H & V OH	225-290 170-225 200-250	26 / 29	50 55 80	24-30 25-35 25-35	2 4 5
1/2″	3/32″ 1/16″	F H & V OH	240-330 190-240 225-240	26 / 31	50 60 80	16-24 12-20 18-20	2 3 8
3/4″	3/32″ 1/16″	F H & V OH	325-400 240-300 250-300	26 / 31	60 80 80	14-20 16-30 16-24	4 9 12

(1) CUBIC FEET PER HOUR

side. Once starting a weld pass on a heavy weldment butt joint, the pass should continue without stopping, if possible. In many instances, sub-assembly work can be done in rigid jigs, which will eliminate a great deal of distortion. In very heavy weldments of this nature, however, it would be wise to consider the possibility of stress-relieving, which can be done by oven-heating.

Weld defects are cracking, porosity, incomplete fusion, inadequate penetration, and inclusions, all of which can be prevented. Cracking is caused by wiring too small a bead in a highly stressed weldment, or using filler metal that is of insufficient strength. Cracks can also occur from craters formed at the beginning or end of a weldment. Cracking can be either in the heat-affected zone — i.e., approximately 1″ on either side of the weld — or in the weld metal itself. If it is in the weld metal itself, it is generally caused by cratering, which occurs when the weld itself forms a depression in the plate. Cracking in the heat-affected zone is found more often in the heat-treatable alloys than in the non-heat-treatable alloys, and it is caused by the molecular change in the granular boundaries of the material. It can normally be overcome by increasing the welding speed or changing the filler metal. If the latter is not possible, then at least the input of heat should be reduced. Cracking is not found too often in small craft construction, as there is a great deal of compatibility in the alloys normally used (the 60 and 50 series), so there are very few welding problems.

Some porosity in weldment is not objectionable, providing it is spread rather uniformly throughout the weldment. If it is clustered or gross, it can affect the weld joint, and the distribution of this type of porosity definitely determines whether or not it is an acceptable weldment. The major cause of porosity is hydrogen picked up during the welding process in the molten pool and released on solidification. Also causing porosity is the presence of foreign material, such as moisture, oil, grease, and oxides. There is generally very little porosity in the heat-affected zone, except in material such as castings. Improper voltage or arc length, variable arcs, or erratic wire feed also can cause porosity. Contaminated filler wire, either from the manufacturing or from handling in the shop, a leaking torch, contaminated shielding gas, or insufficient shielding gas are other contributing factors.

Incomplete fusion is caused primarily by incomplete cleaning and removal of oxide before welding, the improper back-chipping of the weldment prior to a subsequent pass, and also by improper voltage or amperage. Improper penetration comes from very few causes — pri-

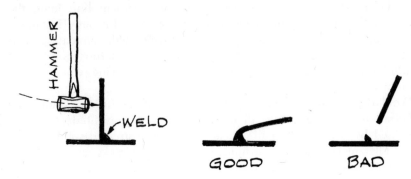

13-9. *Testing a T-Weld.*

marily improper joint design, too low a welding current, wrong size of filler metal, or excessive welding speed for the amount of current available.

Inclusions, which are foreign materials, can be of two types in aluminum alloys — metallic and non-metallic. In MIG welding (metal arc inert gas shield welding), inclusions can occur as a result of a burn-back and not nipping off enough clean metal, thus allowing the copper contaminated wire to be used in the weld zone. In TIG welding (tungsten inert gas shield welding), inclusions can be from tungsten and is caused by dipping the electrode in the molten pool. The improper use of wire brushes between passes can also cause inclusions. Non-metallic inclusions are primarily the result of poor cleaning of the base material or the inclusion of flux in the weld zone.

Welding of Aluminum
Aluminum welding is best done inside a building; however, if the vessel is to be constructed outside, there must be adequate protection for the welder by means of a suitable screen to keep wind and air currents from blowing away the shielding gas. This does not have to be too elaborate but it must be adequate. It is important to remember that in the welding of aluminum the ground must be proper. An improper ground will result in very poor welds in all instances, if any welding at all can be done. Those not familiar with the welding of aluminum should make several tests, which are easily done in the average workshop. One is to weld a T-weld, put it in a vise, and strike against the weld with a sledge hammer (see Figure 13-9). If the weld is proper, you will be able to flatten the plate over without breaking the weld. If it is done

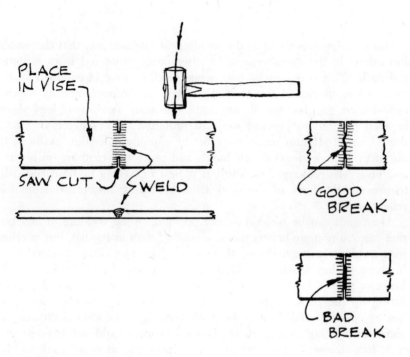

13-10. The nick-break test.

improperly, it will be possible to break the two joined plates apart without too much trouble. Visual inspection of the welds normally will indicate whether the weld is good. Undercutting usually indicates an improper weld, since the base of the weld will be free of the joined plate.

It is always well to remember that the voltage and amperage must be correct in order to have a good weld. The volts and amps to use vary according to whether you are making a flat, overhead, or vertical weld. They also vary according to the thickness of the material, joint preparation, and the correct amount of gas flow. The easiest test to make is the nick-break test (see Figure 13-10). Here again, all that is required is a vise. A test specimen about 2″ in width is placed in the vise after it has been sawn inward about 3/4″ from the ends. It is then struck with a hammer. A good weld will break, giving an indication of the amount of porosity in the weld itself. A bad break will look very irregular. Another test that is more elaborate is the guided-bend test. This can be accomplished with a hydraulic jack and a properly designed tool fixture. This test is not too difficult or expensive for the small boat builder.

Also to be remembered in the welding of aluminum is that the welder and others in the vicinity must be adequately protected from radiation and flash. This is especially true when work is done in confined spaces, such as the interior of the hull. The flash can be overcome by wearing well-shaded goggles, but in any case the arms, neck, and legs should be well covered to prevent sunburn radiation. The welder, of course, should never attempt to do any sort of aluminum welding without the use of protective gloves on his hands and protective clothing on his arms and body. In prolonged welding, it is best to wear a high-necked collar to prevent the back of the neck from becoming sunburned from flash reflection.

Aluminum can be welded in any position. Fillet welding in any position is not any more or less time-consuming than in the flat, but overhead butt-welding is much slower than vertical butt-welding. Distortion can be kept within reasonable limits relatively simply by positioning the butts in proper location to other structures, skip-welding, and properly fitting up the plates. The propagation of heat in aluminum welding is not as concentrated as it is in steel; therefore, the desirability of very short tacks is not as important. However, one should not attempt to do a 20-foot free weld, for example, and expect any success. Tack welds in aluminum must be of greater length — perhaps as much as 2″ in length — than in steel; whereas, the increment welds can be well over 10″ and up to 16″ in length before skipping.

Welding is done by forehand positioning the welding gun. This allows the argon to envelop the surface to be welded and has a tendency to blow the weld zone rather clean of minute amounts of moisture and to leave the area just completed absolutely clean without the necessity of wire-brushing. If perchance the welding must be accomplished the other way because of space limitations — i.e., the gun is advanced, but facing backwards — the smut from welding will be over the entire weld area and must be cleaned. There is some splatter from aluminum welding, and this splatter does not enter into the weld ahead of the welder, but with proper adjustment of arc length, it can be kept at a minimum and will not be at all detrimental to sound welds. Indeed, a properly adjusted welding gun with the correct argon flow and voltage and amperage controls will result in welds of X-ray quality, which is good quality, at least 90 percent of the time.

Most welding guns today have a self-adjusting arc, and a welding gun with this feature is by far the best type to use. Old equipment will have the non-adjusting arc, which can cause problems. A further refinement

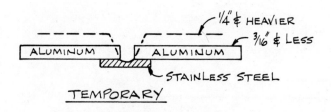

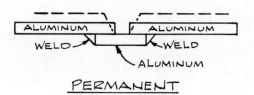

13-11. Using a back-up strip on a single-pass joint.

is a pulse-arc, which is also self-adjusting but at a constant flow of current. Pulse-arc equipment permits the welding of even thinner material than the recommended minimum of 3/16″. The length of the arc should be somewhere between 3/16″ and 5/16″. Too short an arc will cause porosity in the weld. The welding wire must be clean and dry and removed from the gun at the end of each work day. Air leaks in the equipment must be avoided, and dirt, moisture, and oil in the way of welds cannot be tolerated.

The cratering at the beginning and end of a weld can be eliminated by moving the gun back from the weld before extinguishing the arc at the end of the weld, and by starting about an inch ahead of the weld at the beginning. In multiple-pass welding, coincidence of starting and stopping must be avoided. A single-pass, downhand butt-weld can be made in plates up to about 3/8″ in thickness, but for anything heavier than this a multiple pass is advisable. The amount of heat induced in the plate is directly proportional to the size of the weld, which in turn is proportional to the fit-up of the plating itself. The more perfect the fit, the less distortion and the less shrinkage will occur in each of the welds to be made.

Without a back-up strip on a single-pass joint, it is difficult to control penetration of the filler material. Manual butt-welding requires a back-up bar. The choice merely becomes whether the back-up bar is to be temporary or permanent (see Figure 13-11). In certain structures, a tem-

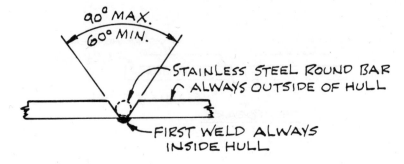

13-12. *Using a round bar when welding a single V-butt joint.*

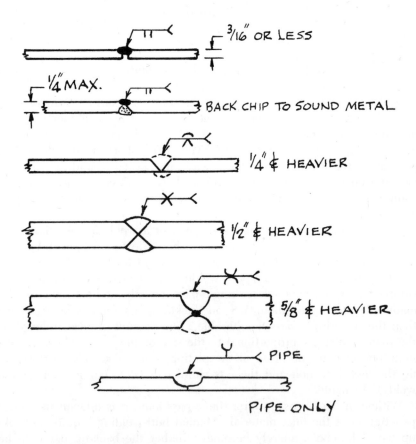

13-13. *Acceptable butt joints.*

porary bar of stainless steel would make a lighter and cleaner structure; however, in many instances, it is not objectionable to leave in the back-up bar. In such a case, the back-up bar should be of the same material as the plate being welded. Sometimes the structure of the hull can be so arranged in order that where Tees would normally be used throughout the longitudinal framing, an Eye of the same size as the Tee can be inserted, and the I-beam then becomes the back-up bar for the material. If this is to be done, it is strongly recommended that the builder adhere strictly to the practice of making all shell plating welds from the deck down to the keel, both inside and outside. The use of a back-up bar will require the making of two passes on the inside so that complete integrity of the joint is possible. When a back-up bar is not used, it is essential that the root of the weld on the opposite side be chipped out prior to making the final weld passes. This can be accomplished with either electrically or pneumatically driven tools.

In a single V-butt joint, it is best to weld the backside first. To accomplish this, a stainless steel round bar is fitted into the open Vee and clamped into position to keep it from moving during the entire backside weld sequence (see Figure 13-12). Once the sequence is completed, then the weld zone is chipped out to sound metal so that no problems, such as cracking or porosity, will be experienced in this joint. It is also well to remember that in the fitting up of the plates, uniformity of the joint is more important than the snugness of the joint. For example, in a square butt-joint, the two plates should never touch each other. A gap of about 1/8″ to 3/16″ can be tolerated in 3/16″ plate, and from 3/16″ to 1/4″ in 1/4″ plate. In using this type of joint, it will be necessary to make at least two and sometimes three passes. Such a joint should not be used in the way of fuel or water tanks or in areas that are to be airtight. It can be tolerated in certain portions of deck structures and bulkheads. In 3/16″ material, if the welding is positioned so that it is flat with a suitable back-up bar that is slightly grooved, a single pass can be made to suffice with a joint strength of about 80 percent. Figure 13-13 shows a series of butt joints that are acceptable in marine structures.

Quite often, doubler plates are desirable. Figure 13-14 shows the method of using doubler plates. It should be pointed out here that in some hull forms, lap-plating of the bow sections is more desirable than butt-jointing in these sections. Lap-straking of the forward plating results in a much easier fit-up and a better joint design than butt-welding. This is especially true in very deep V-sections where it is physically im-

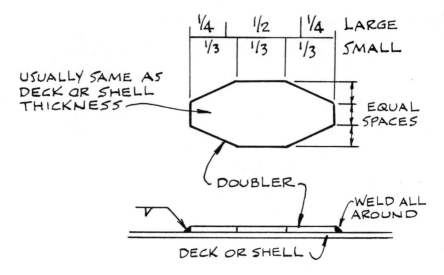

13-14.   Doubler plates.

possible to hold the welding gun at a proper angle to make the joint. Such joints will have between 90 percent and 100 percent efficiency and, in reality, are much stronger than an improperly done straight butt-joint. The lap-joint should never be less on the ends than 1-t (t being the thickness of the plate) as a starter, and should widen out so that the average for the entire length of the joint should be around 3-t. These joints are shown in figure 13-15.

Corrosion

There are several types of corrosion that affect all vessels, especially metal vessels. If left unattended and not recognized, they can lead to the deterioration or partial destruction and disintegration of the metals affected. Corrosion is an electro-chemical reaction. The electrical energy necessary for the reaction is from two sources — a galvanic cell, which occurs when two dissimilar metals are in electrical contact with one another, and the electrolytic cell, which is an external source of current that supplies the necessary energy for the reaction. The cause of corrosion can be further refined to corrosion due to scale, velocity, stray electrical currents, turbulent flow, salinity and thermal pollution, internal electrics, and straight galvanic action due to the mixing of metals.

In aluminum alloys, a careful selection of the various alloys to be combined is of primary importance. Generally speaking, the shell plating

232

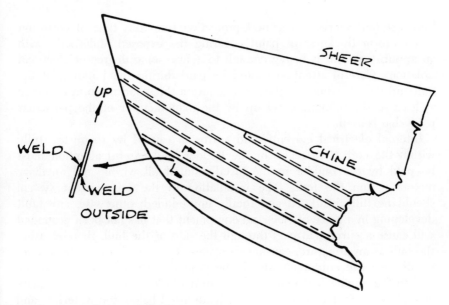

13-15.   Lap-plating of the bow section.

is of one alloy, with perhaps only a small portion of the keel in a dissimilar alloy. Careful selection must be made of the proper welding
alloy that is compatible corrosion-wise with the two metals to be joined.
There are tables furnished by the various aluminum companies that will
permit the builder to select the proper alloy. In any case, the underbody
of any vessel operating in sea water will, in all probability, be painted
with an anti-fouling type of paint, which will further isolate and minimize the mixing of any two alloys that are not totally compatible with
each other. I must emphasize, however, that such mixing should be
held to a minimum, as dependency on paint alone is not the solution
to the problem of corrosion.

As previously mentioned, aluminum will oxidize, and this in itself
forms a protective coating to the base metal. However, the scale that is
formed in the rolling of aluminum should, in most cases, be sandblasted
from the surface of the hull to permit the primer coats of paint to adhere
properly and also to eliminate the difference in electrical potential between the base metal and the scale that is formed.

It is beyond the scope of this book to go into detailed analysis of the
causes and cures for all of the types of corrosion that could occur.
Briefly, however, there is no cure for stray electrical currents caused

from external sources. The best protection from this type of corrosion is a uniform thickness of paint covering the exposed underbody with an application that is heavy enough to assure some degree of electrical isolation. Careful attention should be paid during the building of the hull and its subsequent outfitting to assure a thick and uniform coverage at least to the minimums set up by the manufacturer of the particular paint that is used.

Internal electrical currents, and corrosion caused by them, are fully within the corrective realm of the builder, and careful attention must be paid by the builder in the installation of all wiring and auxiliary motors within the hull. The installation of the DC current system should be fully insulated and totally ungrounded; otherwise, any fault developing in a piece of electrical equipment that has not been grounded will cause a current to pass through the skin of the hull, thereby using the hull as an armature, causing corrosion. In general, the metal frames of all electrical equipment should be grounded to the generator frame and to the engine bed plate via a neutral block. The engine bed plate should be grounded to a grounding plate fitted below the waterline and in an area that will be fully immersed at all times. The engine bed plate and the propeller shaft are very poor grounds in themselves. This is due primarily to the presence of oil and oil films, and a dependency on them will result in inadequate grounding, which could cause damage elsewhere in the system. The connections used in grounding should be the fully insulated type of conductor. Equipment is available on the market that requires a ground on one pole of the power connection. Such a ground would transform a fully insulated system into a grounded system, thus negating all of the prior attention taken to assure a fully insulated system. Rather than accept these items of electrical equipment, such as a radio-receiver, fathometer, etc., it would be better to choose a type from a different manufacturer that would allow an ungrounded system.

An excellent paper on coatings and corrosion was prepared by Mr. R. A. Hartley of the International Paint Company, entitled "Coatings and Corrosion." Another paper, entitled "Corrosion Resistance of Aluminum Alloys," is available from any one of the large aluminum manufacturing companies. It is recommended that anyone concerned with the technical aspects of corrosion and the chemical analyses of the various coatings and paints obtain this paper, as it, with its references and tables, is one of the best available.

Galvanic corrosion can be minimized by the proper gasketing and separation of dissimiliar metals using insulating materials of neoprene, micarta, ABS plastic, Thiokol, etc. For example, in the case of a propeller shaft and propeller, it would be best to insulate the shaft from the hull by using rubber bearings that have a hard plastic shell rather than bronze, which is normally used in a steel hull. The propeller shaft coupling should be insulated from the engine proper via the use of a high strength insulating coupling. Anodes on the exterior of the hull can be fastened directly to the propeller shaft and will take care of the dissimiliarity of metal between the propeller, propeller shaft, or hull envelope; however, if the underbody of the hull is properly painted, this will generally suffice. Sea cocks are normally of bronze and pose some insulation problems. A sea cock requires not only insulation from the hull itself, but also the intake portion of the sea cock should be further protected by a threaded insert of ABS plastic or Delrin with a flange, which also protects the raw edge of the opening. This, bedded in Thiokol, is a very effective insulating device that will give very little trouble throughout the life of the vessel. The flange of the sea cock can be through-bolted by drilling oversized holes and using nylon bolts that have been redrilled so that a smaller diameter stainless steel bolt can fit inside, thus assuring the strength of the steel with the insulating properties of the nylon. At best, the insulation of the various through-hull fittings to an aluminum boat is expensive and time-consuming. Every care and effort should be made to provide absolute protection and separation of dissimilar metals; otherwise, severe corrosion can and will result within a matter of a few weeks.

Since aluminum does not retain odors or vapors, it is safe to use it in drinking water tanks. In the proper alloys, aluminum is also safe to use for fuel tanks, there generally being no corrosion between the fuel and the aluminum. Construction of fuel tanks must be heavier gauge than would be used in steel, and careful attention must be paid to the integrity of the welds, as the speed of welding, especially in very small craft, is such that microscopic holes can be left. However, since aluminum is also a non-sparking material, it does present a safety factor that is not present when steel tanks are used for the carrying of fuel and gasoline. In the case of water tanks, some thought must be given to the eventual cleaning of these tanks. This is usually done by providing readily accessible handholes that are either bolted directly into the aluminum with stainless steel self-tapping bolts, or a flange type of arrangement where through-bolting is used. In any case, some water will cause bacteria build-up, which could result in accumulation of slime or other deposits within the tank that may require that the tank be cleaned.

Insulation

One minor disadvantage in the use of aluminum is the low melting point of aluminum alloys, a potential fire hazard. Internationally, the primary fire regulation to be concerned with is that proposed by the International Convention on Safety of Life at Sea. However, the most rigid fire regulations in the world are those of the United States Coast Guard, Safety of Life at Sea Requirements, Sub-Chapter 10. Vessels built to these regulations can be assured of passing the fire regulations of all other countries of the world.

Aluminum can be protected from fire by either the application of a suitable insulating material applied directly to the structure, which will not necessarily have a decorative appearance, or an overlay of asbestos board, fiberglass, or other liners, which can be given a painted or veneer finish, such as formica, micarta, or plywood paneling. The latter is the most economical way of solving the problem in the living quarters. Needless to say, it is not necessary to insulate the entire hull against fire. In the interest of safety, it would seem that as much as is practical would be the engine room and area of the galley, especially the cooking area. Recommended is to line the stove alcove and the area immediately overhead as well as the base with either galvanized iron or stainless steel, being sure that the corners are made in such a way as not to entrap liquids or grease that could propagate a fire into the interior recesses of any interior wood joiner work. The base under the stove may also be lined with fire retardant ceramic tiles, but in no case should the stove alcove ever be made of aluminum alloys, although this is frequently being done today. The installation of a sprinkler system is not practical on small vessels.

Finishing

On the exterior of the hull, there should be no direct connection of aluminum to wood without a proper sealer. The sealer can be either a bituminous compound, any of the butyl rubber compounds, or Thiokol. The reason for this is that certain of the hardwoods, such as oak, do have a slight corrosive effect on aluminum. Some of the tropical hardwoods fall in the same category. These, over a period of time, will cause corrosion. Another type of corrosion, known as the poultice effect of wood, is caused by the accumulation of salts from the water with alternate wetting and drying, which aids and abets the eventual rotting of the wood. Of course, under no circumstances should white lead be used for a bedding compound. Aluminum bolts and aluminum studs can be used to fasten wood to aluminum; however, the dowels should be bedded in either glue, zinc chromate, or zinc oxide paints rather than any compound containing lead, mercury, or copper.

If it is desirable to overlay the deck of an aluminum hull with wood, it would be better done in one of several ways. One is to eliminate the subdeck of aluminum, substituting a plywood subdeck which is laid over angle beams and bedded in a suitable bedding compound. Over this, a pine, fir, teak, or mahogany deck could be bedded or glued to the plywood and fastened from underneath between the beams. This would cause the least problems and would be the least expensive wood overlay type of deck structure. Another method is to overlay the aluminum subdeck with wood. This must be bedded in Thiokol or butyl compound for the reasons given above. The third bedding compound is a mastic overlay of which several are on the market. This type of overlay is not usually found in yacht construction, but does find some application in small passenger vessels and on certain commercial vessels. Such overlaying compounds should not contain magnesium chloride, which can cause corrosion of the aluminum substructure.

The entire exterior of an aluminum hull should be sandblasted to remove the mill scale, which is the bright shiny surface that is seen when the aluminum is in its natural state as purchased from the warehouse or mill. The sandblasting should be done at approximately 125 pounds pressure and 125 cubic feet of air per minute. The grade of sand used should be anywhere from fine — i.e., No. 1 — to a rather coarse grit, No. 3. This should be of a good dry grade of silica sand and the blasting should proceed smoothly and evenly. A long concentration at any one point will badly erode the aluminum plate and cause a reduction in section that could be harmful to the overall strength of the vessel. After sandblasting, the entire surface should be washed down with fresh water to remove any dust, but in no case should it be touched with bare hands or oily or greasy rags, clothes, or shoes.

From this point on, the builder has many options which he may exercise in the choice of final coatings. These coatings include oil-based paints, in which either linseed, fish, or tung oil or other oils are used, but remember that the use of pigments such as white lead or red lead could have harmful effects to any immersed portion of the hull. Oleoresinous paints are classified generally by short, medium, or long oil lengths. This is in reference to the amount of oil used with a fixed weight of resin. The short oil varnishes are more water resistant but have less durability than the long oil varnishes. Some of the oils used are linseed, tung, castor, or soybean. Many alkyd paints may also be used and are derivatives of alcohol and acid. Epoxy, either air-dried, catalyzed, or coal tar, and high-build coatings are normally used in the marine field. Polyurethanes fall into three general categories — oil-modified, moisture-cured, or two-component. Silicone paints include straight silicone resins and silicone-alkyd resins. These coatings are known as convertible coatings. Of the non-convertible coatings, the most popular are the vinyls. These are used quite frequently in all-metal construction and consist of an etch or wash primer containing phosphoric acid and a solvent. These are overcoated in turn with other vinyls that chemically bond and form a topcoat. Acrylics are technically very similar to vinyl coatings but have the ability to retain their gloss much longer, having better ultra-violet resistance. Rubber coatings are still another form of non-convertible coatings. Chlorinated rubber is the main type, although synthetic types have been developed and are extensively used. Bituminous coatings are also used but primarily in commercial vessels where the bitumin is dissolved in a solvent and is mixed with varnishes, Japan driers, and emulsions. They are an economical material to use but have very poor resistance to solvents and to heat. In small craft fitted with engines, gasoline and diesel oil are often a solvent to bituminous paint and therefore, this type should not be used in areas where oil can be found in concentrated forms. Grease coatings from either wax or petroleum products are often used where motion is minimal. For example, on a vessel to be stationery for a long period of time, the propeller could be coated with a heavy grease, thus retarding marine growth against the bronze itself. It is not very often used in small or large craft, but mainly on pilings, studs, and other structures that need a cheap coating that is not overly sensitive to the pre-treatment or surface preparation. Zinc-rich coatings, either the organic or inorganic type, are not required in aluminum construction.

Generally speaking, each boatyard will have its own favorite type of paint. Usually it will utilize by preference either the alkyds, the vinyls, or the epoxy system throughout. Each has its advantages and disadvantages, and each performs, upon proper application, satisfactory service and, based on longevity, one probably cannot be considered better than the other. The epoxy coatings have the advantage of very good adhesion and drying from the inside out. Most epoxy coatings used at the present time are the catalyzed type — i.e., a two-package unit. They are worked under optimum conditions of 70° to 90° F and should not be used below 60° F; they have a very short pot-life above 100° F. The epoxies can be further classified according to their end use. In the painting of the bottom of the hull, an epoxy primer must be used over the sandblasted surface. This can be overcoated with a coal-tar epoxy barrier coat and a coal-tar tributyl tin acetate anti-fouling paint for the final coat. With the coal-tar epoxies, and indeed most epoxies, there is an overcoat time based on temperature and humidity which must be strictly followed, otherwise subsequent paint applied will not adhere to the surface without re-sandblasting the hull. The coal-tar epoxies have very good water resistance, abrasion resistance, excellent adhesive qualities, and crude oil resistance; they are also inexpensive. Coatings can be anywhere from 8 to 10 or 11 mils dry film thickness in one coating; however, they are temperature sensitive. These bottom coatings cannot be used in contact with gasoline, naptha, and other white petroleums. Coal-tar epoxies are available in either black or dirty-brown color.

The topsides of an aluminum hull need not be painted other than for cosmetic reasons. They must, however, be sandblasted, and if left in this condition will have a mat-gray sort of finish that will darken with age. The pitting usually associated with aluminum that has the scale intact will not occur. A white powder will form on the surface after a period of time, but this is a self-protecting salt that is inherent in the aluminum itself. If epoxies are to be used, the metal must be overcoated with an epoxy primer. Then the use of any of the high-build epoxies would satisfy a film thickness required to maintain a selected or desired color.

The decks of an aluminum hull should be painted due to the absorption of heat in an unpainted surface which makes the living quarters, cargo hold, or engine room below very sensitive to the heat from the sun. In all cases, a white-painted deck absorbs the least amount of heat. Any additive color to the white, such as light gray, green, blue, orange, or tan will do nothing but increase the amount of heat retained in the deck structure. Again, epoxies may be used in this instance. The disadvantage of epoxies on the topsides and on the deck is found in the difficulty of repairing a marred finish. Without a doubt, the deck is best done in alkyd paints, which are easy to touch-up, present very few problems of incompatibility, and can be very thinly brightened up at annual or semi-annual periods to freshen the hull appearance. The topsides also present the same problem inasmuch as the epoxy can be applied in only rather heavy coats. Therefore, a vinyl or alkyd system would be much easier for maintenance.

If the underbody of the hull is to be coated with a vinyl system, a vinyl wash primer containing phosphoric acid must be used. This should then be overcoated with vinyl barrier coats of different colors so that the final mil thickness of the vinyls is not less than 6 mils and preferably between 9 and 10 mils. If the anti-fouling paint to be used contains copper, it is even more important to have the heavier sub-coatings for protection and prevention of the copper coming in contact with pinholes that may be inadvertently included in the sub-layers of paint. If, on the other hand, a vinyl organo-tin paint is to be used, then the danger of corrosion due to pinholes lessens and is almost non-existent. Under no circumstances should mercury bottom paint ever be used on an aluminum hull. While it is possible to apply some of the inorganic tin bottom paints directly to the aluminum, these in themselves do not have a high abrasion resistance, so inadvertent grounding or scratching of the hull surface would then expose other parts of the hull, which were dependent upon the paint system as a barrier coat to protect from corrosion, and possibly accelerate corrosion. Normally, the alkyd paints are not used on the underwater portion of an aluminum hull.

The interior of an aluminum hull need not be painted other than for cosmetic purposes. Since a large portion of the living area will be insulated for comfort, the overlaying material should receive the same painting system or varnishing as would be used in any other material normally used in hull construction. If the interior of an aluminum hull is to be painted, it must be thoroughly degreased and etched. This can be done chemically or via sandblasting, but in any case it must be done. It is more important to be assured of a greaseless, oil-free surface in aluminum than it is in steel. If only a wash-type degreaser is used, it would be wise to also consider power sanding of the area to be painted to assure a good tooth for the primer. Once adhesion of the primer is assured, then the subsequent overcoats present no more problem than they would in steel or wood construction. Paints containing red lead, white lead, etc. should be avoided. Latex-type paints can be used to an advantage on the interior as they are inexpensive, easy to wash, and very easy to overcoat at a later date.

Spars, Rigging, and Fittings for Aluminum Craft

Today, most aluminum spars are manufactured by sparmakers who have access to or own the required dies for extruding the various shapes that are used. The fittings are then manufactured by the sparmaker or sub-contracted to one of the many supply houses that stock standard tangs, spreaders, spreader fittings, tracks for the spinnaker poles, roller reefing gear, etc. These spars usually are anodized and are of relatively thin-wall construction. The type of extrusion or the manufacturer of the required extrusion is usually specified by the designer. However, it is well to note that in the spar conversion of some of the older vessels, especially those with gaff-rigs, it is quite possible to use aluminum pipe in lieu of solid wood. Here, the size of the pipe is denoted by the inside diameter nominal size. Thus a 5″ pipe would have an inside diameter of 5.047″ and an outside diameter of 5.563″, with a wall thickness of .258″ or slightly over 1/4″. Again, a rule of thumb is that if the vessel to be re-rigged has a 6″ solid wood spar, a 5″ aluminum Schedule 40 pipe would weigh approximately the same but would have about eight times the strength.

Extreme lightness is often carried to such lengths that by the time additional rigging is added, the savings in weight is at best quite nominal and the additional windage is phenomenal. Booms, gaffs, yards, and poles can be made of either standard pipe sections or of tubing. The difference between pipe and tubing is that pipe is measured by various scheduling such as Schedule 5, 10, 40, 80, and 120. A Schedule 5 pipe weighs 2.623 pounds per foot for 6″ diameter. The same diameter in Schedule 10 is 3.214 pounds; Schedule 40 is 6.556 pounds; and Schedule 80 is 9.884 pounds. Schedule 40 pipe is what is known as standard pipe; Schedule 80 is extra strong; and Schedule 120 is double extra strong. The best alloys to use for spars would be 6061 in the T-6 temper and, if anodized, a 6063 in the T-6 temper. The other alloys, while they are made in pipe, are not as resistant to corrosion in a sea atmosphere as is the 6061.

Tubing may have a wall thickness as little as 1/32″ on up. It is well to remember that a section that is too light is subject to buckling and must be investigated for buckling strength. Within certain limitations, there is no reason to strive for extreme lightness in booms, gaffs, or poles. It must be re-emphasized that thicknesses under 3/16″ are very difficult to weld unless TIG welding is available. Therefore, it will be almost mandatory to use mechanical joints in very thin wall sections.

On the heavier spars — Schedule 40 and up — it is possible to weld clips to the spars to act as shoulders for the shrouds or as a means of attaching halyard blocks. It is also possible to screw nickel-silver track directly to the aluminum spars. This application generally denotes a jib-headed sail plan; so, in this instance, the standard available extrusions have more to offer in the way of suitability of their use in sailing vessels than the aluminum pipe. It should be stressed that gaff-rigged boats could benefit more from the aluminum pipe than they could from any

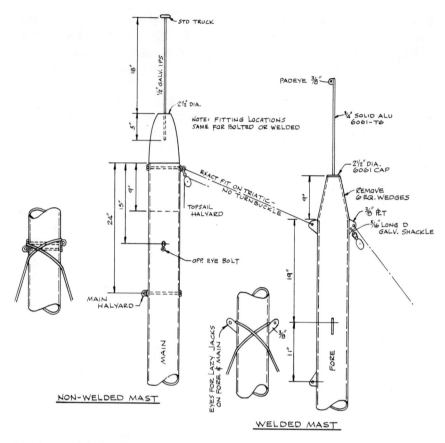

13-16. *Welded and non-welded masts.*

extrusion now used as spar material. The aluminum extrusions are usually available in lengths up to 44 feet on a 5″ or 6″ spar and up to 32 feet on an 8″ spar.

On a gaff-rigged vessel using regular Schedule 40 pipe, it is quite possible to utilize galvanized iron eye bolts through the mast, which form at one and the same time a shoulder for a passed-over shroud, as well as an eye to shackle blocks, such as those lazy jacks and, in square-rigged vessels, for lifts or braces. When these eye bolts are located in the fore-and-aft positions, they can be used for shackling halyard blocks. The top of the mast may be capped off with a plate welded to it or may be fitted with a block of wood turned on the lathe to form a taper (see

242

Figure 13-16). Normally the length of bury is roughly one to one-and-a-half diameters of the spar with a protrusion of two to three diameters of the spar, working in taper to one-half the spar diameter at the top. The same may be done by cutting a six-segment piece from the aluminum spar, annealing the section to be bent, and all of it pulled together into a cone and welded with the upper portion capped. A flag pole may then be welded into the aluminum spar. The truck can be either a plate of aluminum or a block attached by drilling. Aluminum should not be used for tangs or other fittings subject to loads from bending where the fastenings are in shear. In this instance, stainless steel or galvanized iron is much better. The latter does not have any inherent stress corrosion and would be a fitting choice for those vessels used in extensive ocean cruising.

Gaff jaws, gaff saddles, boom bales, etc. can be fabricated of aluminum. Cleats, bitts, bollards, lifeline stanchions, pinrails, pins, boarding ladders, gangways, binnacle stands, steering-gear bosses, deck boxes, anchor chocks, davits, and catheads may all be constructed of aluminum alloys either in plate, tube, bar, round stock, or extrusion. Aluminum should not be used where the surging of cables would be expected, as the alloys do not have sufficient resistance to wear to accommodate any type of cable for any life expectancy of the part in question, nor should it be used where chain or cable would surge over bitts.

Aluminum pipe makes excellent gallows frames. It can also be used throughout the hull for piping water, brine, and other liquids; however, the more modern practice of using either rigid plastic hose, plastic pipe, or plastic or fiberglass hose is much more economical, not only in cost but in time consumed in the installation. If pipe or tube is used and not anodized, it should then be treated much in the same manner as the hull; that is, painted or protected from the elements. Otherwise, some corrosion will occur.

Aluminum in deck structures can be fastened directly with galvanized iron bolts or stainless steel bolts. The economy of galvanized iron certainly outweighs any slight disadvantage that it may possess in regard to the coupling of the two materials together. Needless to say, it should be remembered that bronze fittings should not be bonded in any way to aluminum.

INDEX

Acetylene: how supplied. *See* Cutting torch.

Air intakes: for fuel and water tanks, 159; for engine rooms, 159-160; illustration of, 160-161.

Alignment: of engine beds, 189-191; of propeller shafts, 156-157; of shaft tubes; 157.

Aluminum: strength of, 17, 205, 209-210; relative cost, 25, 208-209; suitability for boat construction, 204; welding of, 204, 207-208, 210, 220, 222-224, 236-232; history of, 204-205; manufacture of, 205; weight of, 205-206; uses of, 206; advantages and disadvantages, 206-207, 209; finishing of, 207; repairing of, 207-208; shapes available, 208; sweating of, 209; design in, 210, 214-217; thickness of vs. steel, 210; alloys, 211; heat treatment of, 211; equipment for, 211-214; springback in, 213; extrusions, 217; framing of, 217-218; melting point of, 222; cleaning of, 223-225; preheating of, 224; distortion in, 224; defects in welding, 225; porosity in welding, 225; protection during welding, 226; corrosion of, 232-235; lap joints in, 231-232; interior finishing of, 236-237; spars and rigging, 240-241; gunwales, 216; rail caps and moldings, 217.

Angles: use of, 56; painting and cleaning of, 56; disorientation of in framing, 56-58.

Argon: in welding, 33, 213.

Ballast: in sailboat keels, 52; lead shot, 52; castings, 52; welding of cast ballast, 52-53.

Batteries: installation of, 198.

Beveling: for weld penetration, 80; of plating, 125.

Billets: fabrication of, 148-149.

Bitts: mooring, 147-148.

Bobstay fittings: fabrication of, 149.

Bowsprit gratings, 149.

Bulkheads: welding of, 60; watertight stuffing boxes for, 200-201.

Bulwarks: design of, 63-64; welding of, 123.

Cables: for welding, 34-35.

Carbon: effect in steel, 8.

Carbides: in stainless steels, 11.

Cast iron: keels, 53-54; welding of, 53-54.

Centerboards and wells: construction and design of, 62; cleaning of, 62; maintenance of, 62-63.

Chain plates: construction and design of, 64; fabrication, 149; illustration of, 64-65.

Chine bars: welding of, 120-121; erection of, 120, template for, 121.

Clementine: launching of, 188.

Cockpit drains: welding, 157.

Compartments: disadvantages, 59.

Compound curvatures: in steel boats, 22-23.

Compressed air units: 39-40.

Condensation: in steel boats, 21.

Construction drawings: effect of inadequate drawings, 50-51.

Cooling systems: types of, 158-159, 193-194; fabrication of, 158; keel coolers, 194.

Corrosion: in high tensile steels, 9; theory, 163-164; nature of, 163-165, 232; in dissimilar materials, 165: anodic and cathodic effects, 165; prevention of, 165-166; general rusting, 166-167; crevice, 167; in stainless steels, 167; pitting, 167-169; galvanic, 169, 185, 232, 234-235; stress-corrosion, 13; from stray electric currents, 185-186; of filler metal in aluminum welds, 221; in aluminum, 232-235.